Winning

by

Being Good

**The 15 Essential Pillars of Success:
a blueprint for thriving in the 21st century
for businesses, charities and social enterprises**

Sarah Brown

First published in 2025 by Fuzzy Flamingo
Copyright © Sarah Brown 2025

Sarah Brown has asserted her right to be identified as the author of this Work in accordance with the Copyright, Designs and Patents Act 1988.

ISBN: 978-1-0687637-1-7

Editing and design by Fuzzy Flamingo
www.fuzzyflamingo.co.uk

A catalogue for this book is available from the British Library.

Every effort has been made to obtain the necessary permissions with reference or copyright material, both illustrative and quoted. We apologise for any omissions in this respect and will be pleased to make the appropriate acknowledgements in any future edition.

Bulk discounts are available to use as promotions or for you to provide copies to everyone in your organisation.
For details email: sarah@inspire2aspire.co.uk

*To Bob my wonderful husband
who has suffered so many long cruises to allow me to write this.*

Contents

Foreword

Why this is not a book about traditional corporate social responsibility

"Businesses all over the world are already starting to show that doing good is good for business. It requires shifting from a narrow focus on short-term financial gains to a wider understanding of what it means to make profit. I'm talking about creating value for shareholders, employees, customers, the environment, and everyone affected by a business."

Richard Branson, *Screw Business as Usual*

I am a voracious reader and have read lots of inspirational books but never one that addresses the practical challenges facing businesses who want to be both ethical and financially successful. I am frustrated by the image of modern business given by programmes like *The Apprentice* suggesting that the pursuit of profit is what leads to success and is all that companies care about. The Covid-19 pandemic, which shut the world down in 2020, followed by the Ukraine and Israel-Gaza conflicts, reinforce the issues of complexity that all businesses face and why they need to think more broadly. It has highlighted any problems in companies and supply lines and also supercharged the move to online.

There are books about: corporate social responsibility (CSR), being green, leadership, treating staff well, marketing in the digital era, how artificial intelligence will have an impact on lives and, of course, thousands, if not millions, on making a profit; but none addressing all the needs of the twenty-first-century company that wants to act responsibly, be a success and needs help achieving it.

The goal of this book is to show that making profits is easier if you are *Good* across the whole of your business – not just in your corporate social responsibility department. This includes investing in your people, solving essential issues for your customers, working with the broader community and using fewer of the planet's resources. But it also includes creating a sustainable profit, being innovative and having a clear vision and values.

The book outlines the principles of the Responsible Organisation Charter© (ROC©). You can use the ROC© to monitor and manage your organisation as a whole as well as by area of activity. The goal is to help you achieve sustainable success. The framework of principles and tools can be applied across different types of organisations and different sectors. It is not prescriptive about what success looks like, but I have included case studies of how various organisations exemplify different elements. The framework has been developed based on my experience and the success that others have achieved. It should help you develop and refine your organisation, as self-help books help people develop themselves as individuals.

The limitations of CSR

> "For most companies, CSR does not go very deep. There are many interesting exceptions… but for most public companies, CSR is little more than a cosmetic treatment. The human face that CSR applies to capitalism goes on each morning, gets increasingly smeared by day and washes off at night."
>
> The Economist[1]

Most large companies have a CSR department and some set up charitable trusts and foundations, but being philanthropic is not enough to be a responsible organisation. Being responsible involves more than stand-alone initiatives like painting a charity building for a day. There's nothing wrong with corporate charity, but I believe a company needs to conduct its whole business so that benefits flow naturally to all the stakeholders, including employees, customers, business partners, the communities in which it operates, the wider world and, of course, shareholders.

> "The whole corporate social responsibility idea is trying to graft something onto the old profit maximisation model. What we need is a transformation (in) the way we think about business, what it's based on. People want businesses to do good in the world. It's that simple… We need a deeper, fundamental reform in the essence of business."
>
> John Mackey, CEO, Whole Foods

WINNING BY BEING GOOD

I share the Harvard Business School's view that corporate social responsibility "goes beyond philanthropy and compliance and addresses how companies manage their economic, social and environmental impacts, as well as their relationships in all key spheres of influence".

Some companies track their social impact as part of their annual report. However, this sort of CSR seems like a project that could end when a policy changes – it is not integral to how the company operates.

When I talk about *Winning by Being Good*, I am talking about how the business runs its everyday business. I believe that 'responsible' profits benefit the world and the organisation. You will attract investors, staff and customers who share your values.

But the ROC© includes other principles that are not directly related to ethics, but are critical for success; they need to be part of the principles of a winning organisation.

This book is based on my work and study. Over the last forty years, I have worked with: major corporates launching innovations; small start-ups, business and social enterprises seeking to change the world; charities wanting to continue improving the world in uncertain financial times; local and national government seeking to collaborate with all these sectors to more efficiently achieve their goals.

> *Being good is not an afterthought to be tacked on when you are successful: it is fundamental to your long-term success.*

The book includes examples from organisations including businesses, social enterprises, charities, councils, governments, sole traders or multinationals.

Non-business organisations have often been more successful than businesses in terms of long-term survival. Just think of universities such as Oxford and schools such as Eton, or charities like the RNLI; Almshouses started in the 900s and are still going. Part of the role of this book is to help learn the lessons of success from every sector.

The boundaries between the sectors are becoming ever more blurred; charities are trading for profits, businesses developing models based on social impact, public sector partnering with both private and charity sectors to achieve their goals.

Who should read this book?

"Never doubt that a small group of thoughtful committed citizens can change the world; indeed, it's the only thing that ever has."

Margaret Mead

I hope this book will inspire and help leaders, managers, entrepreneurs and anyone wanting to start an organisation to change the world for the better. It provides ideas and examples to help the reader assess the state of their organisation and start addressing how they can improve it holistically, creating balance and success as they seek to change the world. It also offers a comprehensive checklist for aspiring social entrepreneurs looking to kick-start a new venture.

It is for people who want to act responsibly as we face the uncertainties of the current world from pandemic to politics, war and changing technology. AI threatens mass unemployment. Political and social stress is already showing with the rise of the ultra-right and populist movements across many countries. Companies, governments and society at large (including educational and social care systems) will need to adapt to create an environment in which all can contribute and I hope this book can help by providing a sustainable business model.

The book is based on my learning from the best and worst of the different sectors I have worked with, and from the many business and psychology books I have read. It also reflects my natural systems thinking style and my desire to find practical solutions, which has prompted me to develop over 100 business tools over my career as a response to the issues of the organisations I am working with.

This book is for you if you want to avoid making errors similar to the UK government as it responded to Covid; for example, locking down without considering interconnected issues such as children's education, mental health or domestic violence and initially handling it like flu, so trying to solve the wrong problem.

At the centre of this book is the Responsible Organisation Charter© (ROC©). It is a simple diagnostic tool that creates a summary of the state of any type of organisation and can be used to identify areas of competitive advantage and potential threats. It summarises fifteen fundamental principles organised in five areas of focus for success in the twenty-first century – these make up the principles of *Being Good*.

It includes principles such as 'life changing', which are more generally thought of as the realm of the charitable sector. In my experience, using the questions and thought processes that the charity sector uses can also provide valuable insights for the business world. For example, charities are particularly good in terms of being mission-focused, cultivating staff that passionately share their values and attracting and keeping customers that loyally support them for years. Similarly, many charities can learn from how businesses use innovation and create a niche to stay financially viable.

The book includes how organisations have addressed issues based on the principles of the Responsible Organisation Charter©. The goal is to show that there are alternatives to just cutting costs and living by fear as you try to turn an organisation around.

> "... Business and charitable work can be complementary... while the fundamental goals of business success and venture philanthropy may differ (making money and growing your business and profits vs. raising money and assisting a non-profit cause), the ways in which these goals can be achieved remain the same: have a clear purpose, good management, a strong team, hard work and dedication."
>
> Rob Thielen, *Forbes*[2]

For companies, being *Good* has lots of benefits in terms of marketing, saving money, keeping and motivating staff, and feeling a sense of worth. Still, to date, there has not been any useful way to check how you are doing or how to manage responsibly on an ongoing basis. There are many excellent books on elements of being responsible, such as *Conscious Capitalism* by John Mackey and Raj Sisoda and *Becoming the Best* by Harry Kraemer Jr. But none link together the critical business principles like how being responsible can increase profits or deliver a market niche that provides a competitive advantage or offer collaboration opportunities with charities that can benefit both.

There have been books on why companies ought to be *Good* such as the Richard Branson book, *Screw Business As Usual* and books showing factors for success such as *Good to Great* by Jim Collins. But no book offering practical tools or a schematic to help companies keep on the straight and narrow – the equivalent of the Ten Commandments for business.

Naively, I assumed that there would be a workable model for businesses to use that would combine all these principles, but when I searched, I couldn't find it, so this book and the ROC© is my response.

The book provides insights on how to run any organisation in the twenty-first century, so it is successful, growing and changing the world, and fulfilling its purpose. It is not based on a single view of what is ethical, a preferred business model or what level of profits you should make. Instead, it is designed to help you develop the venture you want within the context of creating a better world. It also provides practical ideas and examples, so that you can turn the information about what makes a responsible organisation into action.

Introduction

"I'd like to ask everyone here – whether you're in business, government, or the non-profit world – to take on a project of creative capitalism… It doesn't have to be a new project; you could take an existing project and see where you might stretch the reach of market forces to help push things forward. When you award foreign aid, when you make charitable gifts, when you try to change the world – can you also find ways to put the power of market forces behind the effort to help the poor?"

Bill Gates[3]

My Perspective

Even at a young age, I didn't like to be limited to a single viewpoint. At school, I did arts and sciences, and at university opted for a mixed degree – politics, philosophy and economics (PPE) at Oxford.

I was always curious, but as with many, I was also strongly influenced by a great teacher, in my case Mrs Ferguson. She taught me history but more importantly stressed that there are always different perspectives. She told us to read both tabloid and broadsheet papers every day to understand how the same incident could be portrayed in totally different ways. She ordered us to question her and to realise that facts and truth depend on perspective. This book is a perspective and the examples, snapshots and, by the time you read it, the companies mentioned may have changed. When I started writing it, for example, no one would have doubted Boeing's commitment to safety.

I was always idealistic and wanted to change the world. Despite doing PPE at Oxford, I didn't find the world of the political parties appealing, so I got a job at Oxfam, but then found I couldn't afford to take it because the pay was so low.

So, by chance, I got a graduate traineeship at Advance, a laundry services company and a subsidiary of a conglomerate, BET. It was my first experience in the corporate world beyond some holiday work at an insurance company. I never stopped my questioning nature and desire to change the world even as I entered the business. This book, I hope, will be my legacy and become significant enough to help other people create responsible organisations that are both financially successful and change the world.

Early in my career, I learnt that companies giving people fulfilling work was world-changing.

I saw this first in Advance, which was incredibly well run and set a standard that I have rarely found in other companies. At the time, I didn't know how unusual it was.

Later, when I started to consult to charities, I realised how inspiring and motivational a vision could be but that, if used in isolation, it could also be an excuse for poor treatment, particularly of staff – the end justifying the means.

First as a manager and director, and then running my own consulting business, I have observed that, while the terms used may be different, the characteristics of success in charities, businesses, social enterprises and the public sector are the same. Each sector can learn from the others and gain from working with them, and one of my frustrations is that it doesn't happen enough; I hope this book will, in a little way, aid this process.

Sitting at the cusp of all these sectors is social enterprise, and I have been involved with setting up and supporting social enterprise development for over thirty years. Some were spin-outs from the public sector, others from charities wanting to generate more income and, more recently, many businesses that think that maybe they are more a social venture. Just as with the established organisational forms, there are good and bad examples.

I am less worried about the legal form or name of the organisation. The critical issue is creating a responsible organisation that has clarity about why it exists and how it will achieve its vision. So, whatever you are running or setting up, the principles in this book should apply and be relevant.

A Historical Perspective

"The real goal for an employer is to seek for others the best life of which they are capable."

Joseph Cadbury 1801-1889

Businesses and their leaders have been doing good for centuries, inspired sometimes by their beliefs and sometimes by enlightened self-interest. This has gone way beyond simple charitable donations to providing housing and benefits for staff and undertaking active roles in the local and wider community, such as setting up libraries and funding education. Many of the principles of the ROC© were first evident in these early companies.

The start of the first Industrial Revolution was as transformational as the Industrial Revolution we are now in (fourth, fifth or sixth, depending on what you read). The initial Industrial Revolution saw large numbers of the population moved from the country to the towns and cities to work in factories. In response, Quaker business owners saw their role as helping to create and support these new communities.

As business became more 'professional' in the twentieth century, there were initially books on management and strategy, and then academic courses such as MBAs and practical training on different business functions such as marketing. Unfortunately, the ethical view of the world and business began to be sidelined as this happened.

Various definitions of business exist that ignore the broader roles:

"The purpose of business is to create and keep customers."

Peter Drucker

"The sole purpose of business is to increase owner [shareholder] value."

Friedman, Sternberg

It was only in the 1990s that attempts began to fit CSR and environmentalism into a more robust management theory. The 'triple bottom line' was first described in 1994 by John Elkington, a sustainability consultant writing in *The Economist*.[4] It encapsulates the idea that a business's success should be assessed not only in terms of its financial profitability but also its impact on society and the environment. Since then, a range of companies have adopted this approach, from businesses wanting to improve their corporate image and cut costs to social enterprises motivated primarily by non-financial goals.

Sometimes it is called the 3Ps – people, planet and profit – and some companies include it in their annual reports; sometimes it is called 'sustainability' reporting.

"We believe the prosperity of business and society is inextricably linked."
Business in the Community

Investors and investment funds are also getting into the act with environmental, social and governance (ESG) criteria being used as a set of standards for a company's operations to help socially conscious investors find potential investments. Even Mark Carney, ex-governor of the Bank of England, believes capitalism has a role to play in addressing global environmental challenges and that "there will be great fortunes" for companies involved in helping tackle global warming.

If you build a culture that cares about its social and wider purpose then the 'triple bottom line' will be fulfilled automatically in everything you do, not just what you count.

The problem is how you track and report on all of this – it is very cumbersome and has become an industry in itself. The reporting has seemed to become the focus rather than running a business where you just do it – where it is integral, part of who you are.

The role of businesses is as relevant now as in the first Industrial Revolution, helping people to cope with the massive changes and challenges we face in every direction.

"It's up to us to use our platform to be a good citizen. Because not only is it a nice thing to do, it's a business imperative… If this wasn't good for business, we probably wouldn't do it."
Jeffrey Immelt, CEO, General Electric

It is critical for the future of the world that businesses begin to think beyond pure philanthropy because much of the operation of the world economy is dominated by the activities of multinational companies, which are bigger financially than many countries. *Forbes'* 2024 Global 2000 list valued Microsoft's market cap at approximately $3.1 trillion, surpassing the GDP of countries like the United Kingdom and India.[5] The impact companies have is far-reaching, and how they behave affects millions of people. For these companies, business is complex, particularly because they have to balance how and where they work across the world, dealing with multiple different cultures and perspectives.

They may feel they are large enough to set the agenda, but countries and consumers are trying to redress the balance; politicians are responding to public opinion and looking to enforce more responsible behaviour on the corporate world. I would argue that doing *Good* and being responsible before you are forced will make you more successful.

Current Business Challenges

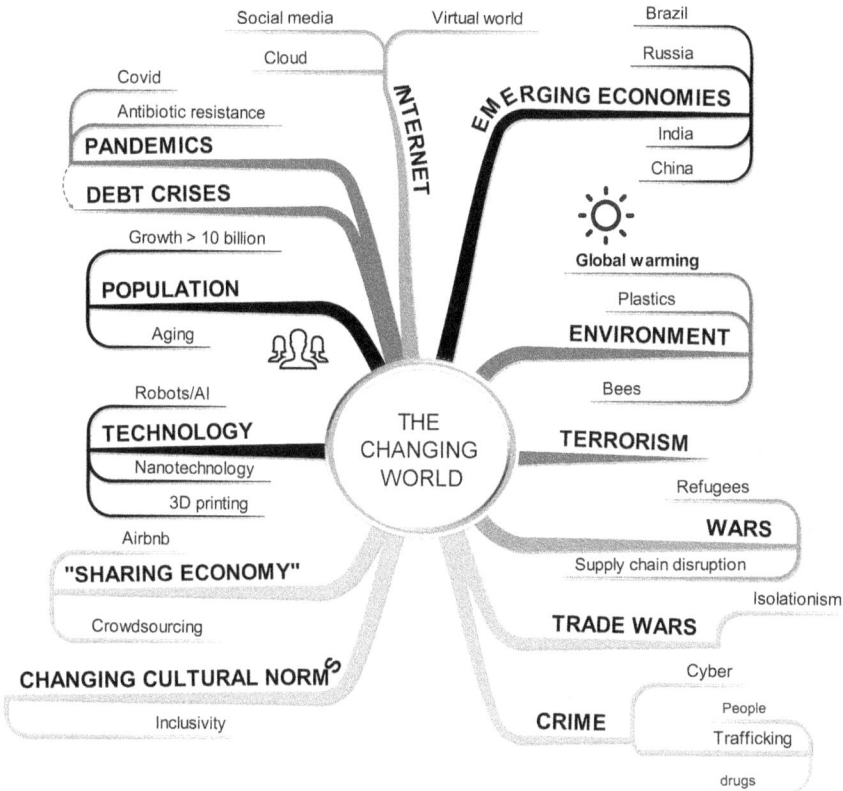

Figure 1: The changing world

As a leader, you face all the issues of the changing world mapped in Figure 1. There's also global competition, more and more innovation, pressure on margins, more legislation from governments, the need to recruit, motivate and retain great people if you are to grow and thrive, responses to hybrid working, etc, etc.

It is estimated that global knowledge is doubling every six-to-seven months – it took 1500 years for it to initially double from the invention of the wheel in approximately 3500 BC to 2000 BC and another 250 for it to double again.

> "The first Industrial Revolution used steam power to mechanise production. The second used electric power to create mass production. The third used electronics and information technology to automate production. Now a fourth Industrial Revolution is building on the third. It is characterised by a fusion of technologies that is blurring the lines between the physical, digital and biological spheres."
>
> Professor Klaus Schwab[6]

Many now believe that we are in the fourth Industrial Revolution, where physics, technology and biology collide. Then there are the new ways of operating, such as artificial intelligence, and digital platform businesses like Uber and Airbnb, who have no product and limited assets.

The World Economic Forum believes that there are four main impacts on business from the fourth Industrial Revolution: increasing customer expectations, the need for product enhancement, more collaborative innovation and new organisational forms.

In the business world, almost every day, business moves from the business pages of the papers to the news section because of a negative issue about the product itself or tax matters or how a company is treating its suppliers or staff or not addressing issues in social media. Robots taking jobs has become part of the political debate. Similarly, charities such as Oxfam have made the news because they have prioritised what they aim to achieve over how it is done, often at a cost to their staff and the communities they serve.

Capitalism, particularly in the guise of the banks, was judged as 'wicked' in the last financial downturn. The focus on money to the exclusion of broader societal needs has been generally condemned as unacceptable. Governments have been given a mandate by the electorate to legislate to make business 'better', from ensuring they pay tax to regulating how they reward their staff, package their goods or add sugar.

IBM research[7] in late 2023 showed 82% of European business leaders expected to or were using generative artificial intelligence (AI) "to ramp-up competitivity and grow" in 2024. "The pressure to adopt generative AI appears to be coming from all directions, with anticipation greatest among employees, board members and investors. This growing sense of urgency is being driven by a desire to improve efficiency by automating routine processes and freeing up employees to take on higher value work (45%), enhance the customer experience (43%) and improve sales (38%). In the boardroom, meanwhile, there's near unanimity; 95% of respondents agreed that generative AI has the power to help them make better decisions."

However, AI also increases the ethical issues and, while governments are considering policy, every organisation already has to work out what to do in practical terms and how to adjust their governance frameworks to address issues such as security, privacy and surveillance, and transparency, so everyone understands how and when it is used.

The report indicates that "AI deployment is transforming the concept of leadership – away from a focus on the bottom line towards a proactive role in managing the societal costs and benefits. Indeed, 96% of respondents who have implemented generative AI, or are planning on rolling it out, said they are already engaged in shaping new ethical and governance frameworks."

Sustainable long-term business

It's tough running a business today, and the statistics are that even big names such as Saab, Lehman Brothers, RBS or Kodak are having to close or seek help. Businesses are dying more quickly. In America, Professor Richard Foster from Yale University identified that the average life of a company listed in the S&P 500 index of leading US companies has decreased from sixty-seven years in the 1920s to fifteen years in the 2010s. Only seven of the original Forbes 100 companies exist from the original list in 1917.[8]

Not all businesses have a short life. In Japan, there are more than 20,000 companies that are more than a hundred years old and some over 1,000 years old. The earliest commercial company in the world is thought to be the hotel, Nissiyama Onsen Keiunkan, founded in 705AD. Even older is a traditional floral arranging organisation, Ikenobo Kadokaia, which has not always been commercial, but dates from 587 AD when it was founded in Kyoto.

The Japanese have studied what leads to long-term success and even have a word for long-living companies: *shinise*. Professor Makoto Kanda, who has studied *shinise* for decades, says that Japanese companies can survive for so long because they are small, mostly family-run and because they focus on a central belief or credo that is not tied solely to making a profit – *Winning by Being Good!*

In the UK, the Tercentenarian Club is for family-owned businesses that are over 300 years old. It has only about a dozen members ranging from Fortnum & Mason to a butcher established in 1515, hat maker, ribbon manufacturer, builder and a boatyard owner.

Businesses don't have to go on forever and often can lose their sparkle as they get older. Still, it can be a tragedy if a company dies too soon before it has fulfilled its potential, and so this book aims not only to help new organisations be more successful but also to help organisations thrive for longer.

The market has fundamentally changed as innovation has exponentially sped up. In order to survive, businesses have to innovate and adapt to the current commercial environment. For example, things that used to be charged for in the past are now often offered for free.

The smartphone, which has become the fastest-spreading technology in human history, is a classic example of this. What it now includes as 'free' features, such as videos, cameras and satellite navigation, would previously have been out of reach of most people, costing them thousands of pounds.

Mobiles highlight the fantastic change in terms of what has become standard and how short the mass-market life of a product can be. Niche users may still want to pay for video cameras and games consoles, but the occasional user is likely to be satisfied with the products available on their phone. How can you compete if your core business offering is now provided free as a part of another product or service?

Worldwide, economies and societies are under stress. Property prices in Shanghai increased fifty-fold in fifteen years with growing population and demand, and then have declined by more than 20% since peaking in mid-2022; young people struggle to find romantic partners in many countries and lots end up living with their parents well into adulthood because of the price of property and the changing nature of work. Trade wars, wars and terrorism, pandemics and refugees add to the turmoil of the planet in which businesses are trying to create a long-term future.

The court of social media

At the same time as an increase in interest in ethical business, technology has changed the dynamics of the marketplace and broader society. The internet means that people connect across the world, and anything anywhere can be instantly known and seen. Social media allows people to know and comment more on the brands they buy and the companies that run them. A study[9] found that nearly two-thirds of global consumers say they use social media to address or engage with companies around corporate social responsibility. Those percentages jump to 80–90% for consumers in countries like China, India and Brazil. According to the study, corporate citizenship has become the leading influencer of the public's view of a company's reputation.

The internet has created a new set of professional activists and watchdog bodies devoted to identifying and publicising corporate 'wrongdoing'. The net allows them to coordinate and share information that can be used to challenge claims that companies make about ethical and environmental standards.

Standards of behaviour

"Earnest concern for the common good is not a dangerous illusion; it is the cost of doing business in a connected society."

Scott Henderson, managing director, CauseShift

Several times in football, commercial sponsors have become involved in issues about either whether it is right for a club to employ a footballer convicted of rape or how, on a larger scale, FIFA operates. The media and individuals make judgements on the values of businesses and expect them to consider their impact on wider society.

If a business is judged to be unethical, it will struggle to succeed or even continue, but even being OK is not enough. 55% of consumers in research by Cone Communications said they would no longer use brands that they feel do not show socially responsible traits.

Research[10] indicates that over a fifth of consumers have boycotted a brand following a scandal or negative press. The "Inside the Mindset of a Brand Boycotter" report explores the nature of consumers that stop using a brand, and underlines how vital it is to appease their anger following adverse headlines. It shows that of those who stopped using a brand, over two-thirds still don't.

The attitudes of millennials, generation z and the rest

Many organisations are still run by baby boomers but the workforce mainly consists of millennials who reached young adulthood around the year 2000, and Generation Z consisting of those born in 1995 or later.

Many millennials[11] are values-driven idealists, with research indicating 61% of the millennial generation only want to work for organisations that do social good. Almost half deliberately seek out employers whose corporate responsibility behaviour reflects their values and 71% hope companies will take the lead on the social issues they find important.[12]

Millennials care deeply about having a job with a sense of purpose and working at companies that have a social conscience. Research[13] indicates that the third top consideration for millennials applying for a job is the company's involvement with causes, and more than 50% of millennials accept a position based upon a company's relationship with causes that they support.

Millennials give differently from other generations, doing so in a more integrated way. They[14] bring their passions to work and want to be inspired by the opportunities at their companies. "The idea isn't to be recognised for doing good; rather, the point is to be able to do good and make a tangible difference through the workplace."

Generation Z is more global in outlook, totally connected through social media, and making a meaningful contribution to the world is vital to them. They particularly care passionately about the environment, as Greta Thunberg (born January 2003) illustrates. Now known and followed worldwide, the Swedish environmental activist is credited with raising global awareness of the risks posed by climate change and with holding politicians to account for their lack of action on the climate crisis.

Whatever your age, studies[15] also show that more than 80% of corporate employees would strongly consider leaving an employer if they discovered that the business was using child labour in their supply chain. Two-thirds might leave if their employer was harming the environment and almost a third would consider leaving if their employer didn't donate to charity.

Expectations have been rising, and most recent studies show 70% of consumers expect businesses to actively address issues that are not directly related to their business.

All this illustrates how vital the ROC© principles now are, as I will discuss next.

Part 1

The Foundations

Chapter One

The Principles of Responsible Business

What makes a winning twenty-first century business

The financial and human benefits

John Mackey,[16] the CEO of Wholefoods, eloquently makes the financial case for companies having a higher purpose, showing that a basket of twenty-eight ethical businesses outperformed the S&P 500 over fifteen years by an amazing factor of 10.5.

The financial case is supported by Ethisphere[17] who, since 2007, has produced an annual list of the world's most ethical companies. They judge seven areas:

1. Corporate citizenship and responsibility
2. Corporate governance
3. Innovation leading to public well-being
4. Industry leadership
5. Executive leadership and tone from the top
6. Legal, regulatory and reputation track record
7. Internal systems and ethics or compliance programmes.

Collectively, the companies have outperformed the S&P 500 every year since it started by an average of 7.3% and have stronger brand reputations, higher customer loyalty and lower staff turnover.

The customer loyalty makes sense when you look at market research, as 87%[18] of consumers globally want a business to place at least equal weight on society's interests as compared to their company interests.

When, in the 1990s, Nike was found to be mistreating workers in its shoe manufacturing plants in Indonesia, it lost market share from a customer boycott. In contrast, its celebration of the thirtieth anniversary of the slogan

"Just Do It" with Colin Kaepernick, a controversial American football star, increased sales. Their customers have liked what they stand for.

In this brand-conscious era, people want to be associated with organisations that make them proud; this is true whether they are staff or customers or investors or even just neighbours wanting to feel proud of their connection. "I live near…", "I work for…" and "I've got…"

The supporting data for being good

Despite the image of business being obsessed with profit, a study by the Royal Bank of Scotland[19] suggests that one in five entrepreneurs want to commit themselves to social benefit, i.e. businesses focused on changing the world rather than profit. Two-thirds of the rest want to support social causes. The new competitive environment is going to include a lot more businesses using their social impact, the *Good* they do, as part of their offering.

I am approached weekly by people who have found our website and want advice on whether they should set up a business or a social enterprise, and the decision is not clear-cut. The boundaries are blurred. What would have traditionally been a business is now being run in a way that makes it more a social enterprise. I am also working with charities that are now focusing on where they can generate ongoing income to fund their charitable activities, so that they don't have to rely on donations and grants.

A review[20] of the mission statements of Fortune 500 businesses analysed how companies at the top differed from those at the bottom. In the top twenty companies, the mission statements placed more emphasis on non-financial issues than the lower down companies, and specifically mentioned social responsibility.

According to the Charities Aid Foundation(CAF) in 2019, British shoppers were increasingly defining themselves as ethical consumers. Spending on ethical products in the UK has more than quadrupled over the past twenty years with 29% of people stating that they had purchased an ethical product in the last year. However, this is somewhat undermined by the fact that almost 40% didn't know what made a product ethical. I am impressed by this honesty as I think it's not at all an easy call.

Increasingly evidence suggests that consumers want to be more actively engaged with brands that have an ethical reputation and help them be part of a common social good. CAF's UK Giving Report[21] – the UK's largest ongoing survey into donor behaviour – shows that people are becoming more selective when it comes to engaging with brands. Using YouGov data, it shows that over half of respondents (52%) think ethical reputation is important when choosing between brands. These results are reinforced by the fact that respondents also value the opportunity to recycle (77%) and want to buy from brands that help a customer understand their environmental footprint (62%). Less than half say it is important for brands to enable them to give to charity and just 40% said they saw importance in being offered a say in the charitable causes the brand supports.

There is real evidence of people's willingness to be ethical in their purchasing if there is an option. For example, a café in Monton in Manchester finds people are willing to buy an extra drink that can be donated to someone in need – a buy two get one offer.[22]

A Harvard research trial[23] found that sales increased 11% when a product was labelled: "These towels have been made under fair labour conditions, in a safe and healthy working environment, which is free of discrimination, and where management has committed to respecting the rights and dignity of workers". Interestingly, they then increased the price of the towels and sales increased further, resulting in a 62% gain in turnover.

Even in the less rarefied environment of eBay, where people are chasing a bargain, data shows vendors giving a percentage to charity make more sales at higher prices.

The financial case for treating staff well

"Releasing the potential of an engaged workforce holds the prospect of reducing costs associated with sickness, absence, employee turnover, production errors, accidents and inefficient processes. It also holds the prospect of improving productivity, customer satisfaction, customer retention and innovation."

UK Engage for Success Task Force Report

A fundamental principle of *Winning by Being Good* is how you treat your staff. In terms of managing staff well and involving them, businesses[24] with a highly engaged workforce have 3.9 times the earnings per share growth rate compared to their competitors in the same sector.

Marks & Spencer tracked sales in stores with staff who were more engaged and found that they delivered £62 million more in sales each year. Similarly, Sainsbury's found high engagement contributed up to 15% of a store's year-on-year growth.

Research,[25] however, indicates that only 10% of employees in the UK are "highly engaged", 14% are actively disengaged and almost three-quarters are not engaged. It was even worse during Covid but has slightly improved. I believe lack of engagement is one of the main reasons that UK productivity continues to lag behind other countries. Global rates of high engagement are 23%, and best organisations have 72% engagement.

Treating staff well has a radical effect on financial results. Being good at recruiting can double your profit margin and increase revenue by 350%, and managing staff well and providing excellent leadership development has a similar impact. Gallup calculates:

> "Low engagement costs the global economy $8.8 trillion dollars, or 9% of global GDP."[26]

All the principles of the ROC© have a role in an engaged workforce, which is fundamental to success, particularly in the current climate.

An introduction to the principles

The following are the operating principles that I have included in the Responsible Organisation Charter© and that I believe are fundamental to having a successful organisation. I will explain in the following chapters why I have chosen them and why I think they are important in creating a sustainable and prosperous organisation. In Part Two of the book, I will provide more detail about how they can be achieved, tracked and implemented, including examples.

Together, the principles of the Responsible Organisation Charter© create a balanced and integrated business designed to minimise your risks as you respond to the changing environment, innovate and grow.

The areas encompass the 'why' of your business, the 'how' you do it and the 'what' you do. They include the critical 5Ps of any organisation: people, products, process, promotion and profit. The fundamental starting point is to create a clear framework based on the 'why', which is a mix of the values that guide the organisation and the vision. Once these foundations are in place, then it is easy to develop the detail of how you operate within this framework.

"If you try and take a cat apart to see how it works, the first thing you have on your hands is a non-working cat."

Douglas Adams, author of
The Hitchhiker's Guide to the Galaxy

An organisation is a system and, like all systems, each area is essential, they are all interlinked and changing one part will have an impact on the others. However, an excellent place to start is with leadership.

The ROC© provides a concise and integrated way to regularly map how your business is doing and develop a guide for action.

Any type of organisation can assess how well they believe they are doing in each area with a maximum score of ten. The principles are grouped under five themes:

- Leadership
- Culture
- Relationships
- Product offering
- Financial success

You work to address the weaker areas and capitalise on stronger areas to provide a competitive advantage. It is a great tool to use with staff and managers to gather their perspectives and to help them understand all aspects of the organisation. Monitoring progress in each area and using it to identify opportunities and weaknesses gives a holistic company diagnostic.

Each principle is discussed in detail in Part Two; in Part One, there is a short introduction to each. As you read each introduction, start to score yourself on the ROC© Checker tool at the end of the section. You can download the tool from inspire2aspire.co.uk (see references).

Chapter Two

Leadership

There are many elements to leadership, but I believe that its primary role is to set the character, the values and the raison d'être of the business, i.e. its vision, so that everything else happens within clear guidelines. I fundamentally disagree with Peter Drucker on his view that "There is only one valid definition of business purpose: to create a customer." This is like saying that the fundamental purpose of a human being is to breathe. While it is true that breathing is critical to continued life, as it is true that customers are essential to continuing in a business, to breathe is not the reason I exist – I have a purpose beyond that. Similarly, economic success or profit could be compared to eating; it is essential for health but not a purpose. As a human, my brain/thoughts indicate my purpose; as a business, leadership starts the discussion on what is the purpose of the company.

The critical importance of leadership is illustrated by research[27] indicating that the 2008 financial crisis, which had an impact on the whole world and cost trillions in jobs, homes and lost productivity, could have been avoided with good leadership. The leadership issues identified included: a lack of transparency, integrity and respect; and irresponsibility to both shareholders and society. These issues contributed to the excessive leverage in financial markets and subsequent problems. The crisis also showed what can happen when behaviour becomes disconnected from values.

Similarly the critical role of leadership was highlighted during the Covid crisis at global, country and organisational levels. In western societies, leadership has often been linked to 'hard' traits around competition and strength. But the crisis illustrated the importance of softer qualities like empathy, adaptability and active listening in leadership style. But these are irrelevant if there is not a clear direction.

Fundamental principles of effective leadership

Behaviour driven by shared values	The vision and goals may change but the fundamental beliefs and ways the business act need to remain the same
Clear vision	An inspirational vision, which people can understand clearly and which motivates all stakeholders, even when the going gets tough
Action-focused	A culture of action set by the leader; too many large organisations create long business plans but take no action, so nothing is achieved

Behaviour driven by shared values

"It is no longer what you do that matters most and sets you apart from others, but how you do what you do. Sustainable advantage and enduring success – both for companies and the people who work for them – now lie in the realm of how, the new frontier of conduct."

Dov Seidman

Values set priorities and ways of acting. Even if you haven't identified clear values, your staff will guess at the values of the company because they need a framework for making decisions. The culture will develop informally leading to the classic: "This is the way we do things around here."

An extreme example of an organisation where the values being unclear led to disaster is the case of Barings Bank. The oldest merchant bank in London, Barings was started in 1762 by Sir Francis Baring but collapsed due to the exploits of one man, Nick Leeson, in 1995. He lost $1.3 billion, speculating primarily on futures contracts. Staff adhered to the value of "every man for himself" to attract the biggest bonuses, doing whatever it took to get them. So, in this environment, Leeson just reflected the corporate culture of following the money but unfortunately failed.

In Search of Excellence was written in 1982 and, even then, they were writing:

> "Clarifying the value system and breathing life into it are the greatest contributions a leader can make...
>
> Every excellent company we studied is clear on what it stands for and takes the process of value shaping seriously. In fact, we wonder whether it is possible to be an excellent company without clarity on values and without having the right sort of values."
>
> *In Search of Excellence* by Peters and Waterman

Behaviour is contagious, whether it be good or bad, so once good behaviour based on values becomes the norm, it will be adopted by new staff as the organisation grows.

> "Ethics is the new competitive environment."
>
> Peter Robinson, CEO, Mountain Equipment Co-op

But scarily, bad behaviour is just as contagious, as the whole 'partygate' scandal illustrates (the Channel 4 docudrama October 2023 brings it to life).

Scoring yourself on the ROC© Checker (end of Part 1)

Rate how well your values translate into how people work, the systems and the reward structure.

A score of ten would mean that your organisation brings your values to life. A low rating would indicate a lack of understanding or clarity about your values and what they mean in practice.

Clear Vision

> "The next wave of enduring great companies will be built not by technical or product visionaries but by social visionaries – those who see their company and how it operates as their ultimate creation and who invent entirely new ways of organising human effort and creativity."
>
> Jim Collins

Having a clear vision and goals is fundamental. If you do not know where you are going, how can you know when you have got there? A business without an inspirational vision will not flourish. Without a vision, there is nothing to inspire staff or customers or the other stakeholders or to differentiate the company in any meaningful way.

Business can learn a lot from charities in this area. Even the smallest charity set up by an individual is driven by a vision of how the world can be different. The vision inspires its supporters and keeps them going, even when times are tough. It also encourages volunteers who will be working for free.

Currently, for example, I am working with an individual who has a vision of better healthcare in his native African country; a vast idea for one man. Still, it has inspired senior people to support him even before we have written a plan.

A vision describes how the business will reach its fulfilment.

Vision without action is merely a dream. Action without vision just passes time. Vision with action can change the world.

If you read the financial pages, you might think the only reason companies exist is to make money. The talk is all of the profit, share price and return on investment. Economic theory talks about companies existing to provide products and services and to make life better, responding to market needs in developing their services.

Marketing and other management theories would argue businesses exist to satisfy and serve customers, and politicians often argue companies exist to create jobs.

"The future of profit is purpose… Profit with purpose is mindful, contributory and socially oriented."

Simon Mainwaring

I agree with the Simon Mainwaring quote above except I think success is measured by more than profit, though profit comes from a clear purpose. To be successful, businesses have to have customers, and have to have staff either directly or in collaboration, but this does not provide a purpose – the purpose sets what the business will do.

I have witnessed the extreme example of misunderstanding that business only exists to make money when working with charities that want to start generating income rather than relying on grants and donations. Too often, when I begin the process of identifying what they could do that they would charge for, the answer I get to the question "What would you do to make money?" is "Anything."

Unfortunately, I think many charities believe that business has no purpose other than to make money, so when they move into 'business', then they think that doing anything to make money is a strategy. This is absurd.

> "I think when you have big dreams you attract other big dreamers."
> Dr Robert H. Schuller

Three of the most significant modern companies have visions that are clear and simple:

- Amazon exists so that "people can find and discover anything they want to buy online."
- Facebook wants "to give people the power to share and make the world more open and connected."
- Google aims "to organise the world's information and make it universally accessible and useful."

No organisation can be successful without a vision of what success will look like, so that everyone knows where they are going. A clear vision also helps staff to decide if you are the right company for them and crucially encourages their engagement. You need people who are inspired and excited by your concept, so it needs to be communicated and shared. According to researchers,[28] "Effective visions expressed values that allow employees to identify with the organisation."

The vision of success is what helps people to keep going when it gets tough and its power is illustrated in charities, where people who are volunteers with no financial or legal commitment put in so much effort. Businesses can be equally inspirational, as examples later in this book show.

Scoring yourself on the ROC© Checker (end of Part 1)

Rate how well people in your organisation know and understand your vision.

A score of ten would mean that everyone knows and understands your vision, so that they can make informed decisions to take your organisation towards it. A low rating would indicate a lack of understanding or clarity about your vision or how people should act to create progress towards it.

Action-focused

Nothing happens if you don't take action. As a leader, you need to set a culture of action, create a sense of urgency.

A vision does not change the world until it is put into action.

However, action needs to be focused on achieving the vision and reflecting the values of the business – action for action's sake is not the basis for success.

Many visionaries have had people around them to make the action happen, and great leaders know that they can't do it all themselves. Bill Gates had a vision of a world where computers could help us reach our potential, but it was Paul Allen who built the company. Gates now has a vision of a world without malaria, but it is charities that are implementing it. Steve Jobs had the idea for Apple, but Steve Wozniak was the engineer who put it into action.

Walt Disney had the vision, but it was his brother Roy who had the business know-how. "If it hadn't been for my big brother, I'd have been in jail several times for cheques bouncing. I never knew what was in the bank. He kept me on the straight and narrow," said Walt Disney[29] in 1957.

The need for action is most clearly illustrated by the individuals who have ideas and then complain that someone else stole them and started a successful business – ideas are dreams unless they are turned into reality by taking action.

Right now, in the digital era, the need to act with a sense of urgency and respond to market needs is critical, and the leadership of a business must embody that responsiveness. If decisions take a long time and the company feels like it is stuck, then all the other principles of the ROC© are undermined.

Over-analysis is the enemy of action.

I used to write extended business plans for large organisations earlier in my career; now when I work with leaders, the focus is on mapping the future, if possible, on one large mind-map, which is one page to be put on every manager's wall.

> "When you're at the beginning, don't obsess about the middle, because the middle is going to look different once you get there. Just look for a strong beginning and a strong ending and get moving."
>
> *Switch: How to change things when change is hard*
> (Heath & Heath, 2010, p. 93)

Scoring yourself on the ROC© Checker (end of Part 1)

Rate how well people in your organisation are action-focused.

A score of ten would mean that everyone has a sense of urgency. The organisation has a sense of energy and purpose. A low score would indicate an organisation where there may be plenty of talk, but little action, and actions are not consistent.

Chapter Three

Culture

Successful twenty-first-century businesses need a culture that can support the other principles of the Responsible Organisation Charter©.

Fundamental principles of a good culture

Adaptable	It is a given that business needs to be able to change and adapt to world events; in fact, businesses have always had to adapt
Pioneer learning	To be adaptable you need to learn and be hungry to learn, keeping up to date and looking for ways to learn from other sectors, being a pioneer in trying new things and a culture where everyone is learning
Collaborative	No one can do it alone. Both within and beyond the business, collaborative organisations enjoy greater success; a culture of working together is critical

The first two are a response to the ever-increasing speed at which knowledge is growing and the third recognises that it is more efficient to share knowledge than to try to know everything yourself.

Adaptable

> "Within five years, if you're in the same business you are in now, you're going to be out of business... The best way to predict the future is to create it."
>
> Peter Drucker

If you are to achieve and implement all the other principles of the Responsible Organisation Charter©, everyone in the business must be adaptable. Change is a given in modern business and to respond, a company needs an adaptable culture. The speed of current change is unprecedented and universal, having an impact on every element of business and society. Adaptability will give a business huge competitive advantage and is critical for ongoing success. To be adaptable requires both a culture that allows it and structures that enable it to happen.

As Darwin identified, creatures that adapt, survive and thrive, and those that don't, become extinct. It was those that adapted rather than those that were the best.

Rigid organisations with rigid rules are like supertankers, finding it hard to change direction. Of course, adaptability only works if it is in a clear framework of values and a clear vision for success. Otherwise, it can become confused wandering, just following the latest potential opportunity or fashion.

The speed of change can make it challenging to decide when to adapt and when to wait to see if it is a temporary phenomenon. The critical issue is to be aware of what is happening so that you can at least consider adapting, and to have a culture that can cope with change because of its strength built on following the ROC© principles.

Scoring yourself on the ROC© Checker (end of Part 1)

Rate how adaptable your organisation and people are.

A score of ten would mean that you have systems and a culture of tracking the environment and adapting promptly when appropriate and change is implemented quickly. A low rating would indicate an organisation that is poor at adapting; for example, a late adopter of new technology and a lack of awareness of what is happening. It may also mean that, like many large organisations, implementing any change can be very slow and people are scared to try something new in case it goes wrong.

Pioneer Learning

> "Anyone who stops learning is old, whether at twenty or eighty. Anyone who keeps learning stays young."
>
> Henry Ford

I spent a long time thinking about what to call this section. I settled on Pioneer Learning, as to be successful, it is not enough to be a learning organisation; you need to be leading the learning and always seeking to get better.

The learning informs how you adapt and also how you run your business. The cliché now is that we are in the knowledge economy. Knowledge has become the key to success and the driver of change. A successful business needs to have a culture where everyone is learning and consequently getting better.

Pioneer learning is not just undertaking the training required to comply with mandatory legislation and industry regulations, such as health and safety. Nor does adding on soft skills such as leadership and team building make a business one that pioneers learning, though all these things are essential. It is more than formal training – it is a culture, learning from what happens in the business. It is also a culture that accepts that learning includes failing as well, so trying and failing is not penalised.

Generally, staff need to recognise and feel that learning is important in the business and that it is encouraged. Research indicates that people are more motivated in a culture that promotes and supports learning, as it helps people to develop their potential and it keeps them more employable. Learning together increases mutual understanding, improves team working and allows people to understand and appreciate other perspectives.

Learning should have a direct impact on profitability, service standards and innovation. Learning is inextricably linked to change and a learning culture will help a business to be adaptable, keep ahead of the competition and understand the changing needs of customers.

Scoring yourself on the ROC© Checker (end of Part 1)

Rate how much you encourage pioneer learning.

A score of ten would mean that you have people who want to learn, are learning in unexpected ways and from beyond your sector. A low rating would indicate an organisation that does little learning. It doesn't even learn from experience, discourages trying new things and does little or no training.

Collaborative

A collaborative culture is required both inside a successful business and with the outside world.

A company where each department and division fight to be top dog will waste resources and inevitably find it hard to learn from other parts of the organisation or to maximise the use of resources. People building kingdoms are not focusing on finding the most efficient ways to achieve results. Any collaboration will be undermined by people wanting to show what they have individually achieved to get further up the tree.

Collaborating in the wider world is one of the most effective ways to grow and increase your impact as an organisation. It can be particularly useful in the field of innovation, where the combining of different skills and products can lead to exciting new offerings.

Crowdsourcing is now used by many companies to create new products. There is a British Standard 1100 created for collaboration, and the desire to improve cooperation has led to the launch of numerous software packages to help people collaborate.

Scoring yourself on the ROC© Checker (end of Part 1)

Rate how collaborative your organisation and people are.

A score of ten would mean that you have systems and a culture of collaborating; collaboration is the norm and expected way to behave. A low rating would indicate an organisation that is poor at collaborating, both internally and externally. Symptoms are likely to be disputes and competition between departments and a lack of strong business relationships with other companies.

Chapter Four

Relationships

Even a business based on the internet is reliant on relationships for success. This section deals with all stakeholders, excluding customers. Relationships with customers are covered in detail by three parts of the Responsible Organisation Charter©: life changing, reliably consistent product offerings and an identifiable market niche.

Fundamental principles for Relationships

Treat staff well	It is a cliché but true that you are only as strong as your weakest link; often this is a staff member who is demotivated by your treatment or the culture and disengaged. Success is founded on creating the strongest engaged team possible
Treat suppliers fairly	No business is an island and you are bound to be reliant on suppliers – treating them badly makes you vulnerable and will ultimately affect your success
Good citizen	All organisations are part of the wider world and need to be good citizens. From paying fair taxes and being a good neighbour to showing care for people in need and rewarding investors

Treat staff well

> "We're in the business of building an organisation, an institution that we hope will be here fifty years from now. Paying good wages and keeping people working with you is very good business."
>
> Jim Sinegal, Costco

How you treat your staff is fundamental to your success. It is impossible to have a successful business in the long term if you mistreat your staff.

There is a direct link[30] between employee engagement and shareholder return; companies, where nine out of ten employees felt engaged, had earnings per share 147% higher than their competitors.

When jobs are scarce, it can be easy to recruit, and staff may stay despite poor conditions. However, the only way to provide exceptional service is to have a motivated and engaged team. That means that they need to be treated well and be in roles that play to their strengths. The cost of hiring the wrong person or managing staff so badly that they leave is high. It is calculated that the cost of recruitment is up to 2.5 times the annual salary cost of a role.

It is conservatively estimated[31] that the cost of staff turnover in the UK is £42bn a year. ACAS, the conciliation service, has also estimated[32] that bullying in the workplace alone costs the UK almost £18 billion annually due to the related absences, staff turnover and lost productivity.

For most people, the best thing that can happen to them is to enjoy fulfilling work. A business wins by being excellent in terms of the opportunities it provides for people to express their innate talents and passion.

Having been lucky enough to work in and with lots of businesses that provide fulfilling work and treat their staff well, I know how life changing that can be, for staff and their families. Fulfilling jobs are always better than a reliance on charity.

Scoring yourself on the ROC© Checker (end of Part 1)

Rate how well you treat your staff.

A score of ten would mean that you treat your staff wonderfully. The indicators of this would be low rates of staff turnover, high levels of staff engagement, initiative and productivity, strong teams and a culture that feels positive and welcoming. A low score would indicate an organisation that treats staff poorly with typical symptoms being high levels of staff turnover and absenteeism, low levels of engagement and productivity and a 'toxic' atmosphere.

Treat Suppliers Fairly

Often businesses don't view suppliers the same way they think of customers and employees. They treat them as if they should feel lucky just to get the orders. This poor treatment is very short-sighted and self-defeating, as a robust supply chain is critical to a business's ongoing success, as has become evident with Brexit and the pandemic. Key suppliers should be treated as partners with openness, payment on time and fair terms.

Treating suppliers as you would want to be treated and the way you treat your customers will help build valuable, trusting relationships. You will get an advantage over the many companies that still cling to traditional purchasing practices, squeezing suppliers hard and delaying payment as long as possible.

The closer you get to your suppliers, the stronger the relationship will be, because it will be based on trust and respect. The long-term benefits in terms of costs and word of mouth far outweigh any short-term gain from paying late. Late payments give the impression that your business is in trouble, both to suppliers and your staff, and waste everyone's time in chasing and answering calls. If you are a late payer and poor customer, you're likely to get a bad reputation and your credit rating may even suffer. The more you extend your creditor days, the more likely your credit rating will go down, and the more likely new suppliers will offer you unfavourable credit terms, even wanting cash in advance.

The UK government, in its information sheet on Treating Suppliers Fairly[33] even suggests that paying invoices on time is a "demonstration of corporate social responsibility."

Specific industries have noted reputations for maltreating suppliers. Research shows that all other things being equal, people will choose a fair trade product which is part of a fair supply chain above one that is not.

It takes time to build relationships, and businesses that treat their suppliers as a commodity do not get the benefits of a close relationship.

Treat your suppliers as secure, valued partners and you will get better pricing and terms, even if you are relatively small. They are also often best placed to identify ways for you to save money, but it is less likely they will help customers who have mistreated them. Similarly, you're likely to get better delivery deals and times, and if you then need a special favour as a good customer, your supplier is likely to make more effort to help.

Life is particularly complicated for businesses with overseas suppliers, where there may be issues of child labour or corruption, so trust in extended supply chains is even more critical.

Scoring yourself on the ROC© Checker (end of Part 1)

Rate how well you treat your suppliers.

A score of ten would mean that you treat them like trusted partners. You probably have long-term relationships and your suppliers are proactive in suggesting ways to help you in your business; they understand you and what you want to achieve. A low score would indicate the inadequate treatment of suppliers, with classic symptoms being late payments, driving down the price or even changing it after it has been agreed, little trust and regular changes in supplier because of problems.

Good Citizen

Being a good citizen is behaving well in all your relationships with stakeholders, i.e. anyone or any organisation that has a connection to you or you have an impact on, including your investors.

> *A good corporate citizen has financial, environmental and social responsibilities to the communities in which they live and operate.*

There are those, inside and outside the private sector, who believe that companies have a wider role to play in society. This broader role ranges from being a good neighbour and paying your taxes to supporting those in need with corporate giving, both financial and in kind.

For many people, giving to charity is a sign of a 'good' company. I believe it is only a part of *Being Good*; it is a crucial element and will help companies be more successful, but a good citizen is more than that. They also respond to the growing customer demand for socially responsible products and ways of working. They will allow time for volunteering and are active in supporting policy development relevant to their business. The direct impact of poverty and instability on global supply chains means that multinationals can no longer avoid being involved in the well-being of all the communities where they operate.

In the UK at a local level, The 2013 Public Services (Social Value) Act has linked the good that companies do in their community, environmentally, etc., to the tendering process. There is also legislation requiring larger companies to report on social and environmental issues.

However, long before this, there has been a long history of business involvement in the wider community. With the coming of the welfare state, businesses moved from direct support of the poor to developing relationships with charities.

There is a growing consensus that CSR has become a permanent part of the UK business agenda. Almost all the largest FTSE companies (with a market capitalisation of £6 billion or more) are among the top 300 corporate donors. They believe that *Being Good* provides benefits to shareholders beyond just increasing profit.

In the era of social media, failure to be a good citizen is a high-risk strategy for any business. While many gamble on the short memories of their customers, governments are also becoming more proactive in several areas around good citizenship, including addressing tax avoidance.

Scoring yourself on the ROC© Checker (end of Part 1)

Rate if your business is a good citizen.

A score of ten would mean you consider all your stakeholders and proactively find ways to be supportive. Classic examples are donations to charity, volunteering schemes for staff, involvement in industry bodies and relevant public bodies. A low score would indicate an organisation that is inward-looking and has a default position of no to requests from the outside.

Chapter Five

Product Offering

Your product offering is critical and what you provide will be dictated by what you want to achieve and how you want to do it. In the current climate, it is likely to be the section of the ROC© that changes most rapidly.

Whatever you are offering, these are the three critical factors for being *Good* and having a responsible organisation:

Fundamental principles for your product offering

Life changing	Successful products and services change people's lives, solve problems or fulfil dreams. You understand how you do it and track how successfully you are doing it
Reliably consistent	You need to be consistently good if you are to thrive in the world of social media, where anyone can tell millions how you let them down
Minimising environmental impact	This makes sense, not only because governments expect you to do it, but also because it will often save you money, attract customers and make you a good neighbour

Life changing

If you can identify how you change people's lives, you will have a powerful message for your marketing, your staff and everyone involved with you.

Any business can change lives, even if it is a local corner shop that calls an older person by their name and asks how they are when they come in for their paper. For that person, if you are their only human contact in the day, you are changing their life.

How you want to change lives has an impact on how you run your organisation. But changing lives is like dropping a stone in a pond, creating ripples that spread. For the relative of the older person living a long way away, knowing they have human contact makes them feel less worried. Social isolation is a significant part of mental illness and physical decline; maybe the person wouldn't even bother to walk to the shop if they didn't get the social contact and so would do no exercise. This simple hello and human connection means that healthcare costs reduce for this person; they can stay independent for longer and that part of the healthcare budget can be used to support others.

Life changing either means you address a problem for people, provide a new opportunity for them or help them fulfil a dream. If your product or service does none of these things, then you may be successful in the short term, but you cannot build long-term sustainable success.

Charities have always needed to be clear about how they change lives, their purpose, as this is part of gaining charitable status. However, now they have to quantify how they change lives because funders want to know the impact of what they have given.

The same discipline is also essential for a successful business. If you can quantify how you change lives, you can use it as part of your promotion, but also you can track how well you are doing it, make adaptations to improve what you offer and be able to identify if problems occur.

In the simple example of the older person and the corner shop, the shop owner can ask the customer if she is always treated well and welcomed when she comes to the shop. The feedback may identify some staff who don't reflect the shop's values of being welcoming and some who are doing something unusual that everyone should be doing. The shop can keep track of how often the customer visits as a quantitative measure. Additionally, they can collect contact details so that they can reach out to check if everything is okay if the customer hasn't visited as they usually do. Further to that, they could offer deliveries for people who can't carry much; they still come to the store to make contact and choose what they buy, plus maybe a small café area or just chairs would be excellent additions. The corner shop could encourage public health officials to compare health statistics for older people in their borough with a control area with no corner shop. This data could justify them getting planning permission to open a new corner shop in a residential area.

Everyone wants to make a difference.

In my experience, when a company understands how it changes lives, it inspires everyone in the company and always leads to greater success, as people strive to increase the impact they have.

Scoring yourself on the ROC© Checker (end of Part 1)

Do you change lives?

A score of ten would mean that you positively change lives in everything you do. This is hard to achieve, even for an organisation like a health provider; for example, is the waiting room a positive life-changing experience? You will know you change lives by feedback from customers and by objective measures, such as how fast you solve problems. A low score would indicate an organisation that is poor at understanding how it changes lives and probably that you aren't tracking what you need to know to understand if you change lives.

Reliably Consistent

Trust is the foundation of every successful relationship. Consistency is not enough, as that does not imply quality – people can expect you to fail consistently: "It was late again."

Consistency is the foundation of trust, and without trust, a business cannot function.

Reliable means meeting the expectations of customers, staff, suppliers, the community, government, shareholders or anyone else. The importance of reliability and its links to other parts of the ROC©, particularly values, is most dramatically illustrated by the case of the Boeing 737 Max. Boeing had been trusted to produce safe aircraft consistently, but it and the FAA did not respond promptly to reports from pilots on safety, and two major crashes occurred. The planes were grounded, resulted in Boeing losing about a $1 billion per month after the second crash. Then in April 2019, the shareholders submitted a class action for punitive damages, claiming that Boeing had defrauded them by "effectively {putting} profitability and growth ahead of airplane safety and honesty." A clear illustration of how sustainable profit, values and being reliably consistent are inextricably linked.

Particularly in the field of customer experience, being reliably consistent will make you more money and save you costs.

71% of business leaders believe that customer experience is the next corporate battleground[34] and four-fifths of US firms[35] would like to use customer experience as a form of differentiation.

I have written a lot of this book on various cruises and some cruise lines struggle with reliable consistency. Some staff are great, some poor, some ships have good food based on the chef, some poor (within the same cruise line) and so on, from entertainment to facilities and what is provided. The only reason we choose an inconsistent cruise line is if they are offering an exciting itinerary, but it has to be at a reasonable price. However, competing on price leads to a downward spiral for them as they reduce revenue and the service and consistency is put under even more pressure.

Reliable consistency is not just about what you offer the customer but also about how you operate, particularly in terms of compliance with legislation and with safety requirements. Failure to be reliably consistent is particularly mission-critical when talking about safety – one inconsistency can cost lives.

Scoring yourself on the ROC© Checker (end of Part 1)

Rate how reliably consistent you are.
A score of ten would mean total consistency. No mistakes, no complaints, consistent responses at all times. A low rating would indicate an inconsistent organisation. How customers are treated depends on who they talk to or the time of day; there are many complaints and returned items as a result of faults; customers don't trust you to deliver and keep checking.

Minimising Environmental Impact

Sustainable development has been written about and supported by thousands who are much smarter and more knowledgeable than I am. Within the context of the successful twenty-first century business, minimising environmental impact is crucial. It can reduce costs or liabilities for tax, it is part of being a good citizen and, as part of your values, will help attract and retain Millennials and Generation Z as customers and staff.

The pressure to care about the environment first arose in the 1960s and 1970s as concerns grew over the depletion of resources and increased pollution. Regulations have steadily increased. The UN Global Compact aims to encourage businesses across the world to adopt sustainable and socially responsible policies.

It is not always straightforward. But being conscious of the impact of a business in environmental terms is now a given, certainly in the developed world. Being associated, for example, with pollution, even in another country, can have an impact on a business and its image. Long-term success can only be achieved if it is produced in an environmentally friendly way.

Any business, service or manufacturing, needs to be aware of its environmental impact.

Scoring yourself on the ROC© Checker (end of Part 1)

Rate whether you are minimising your environmental impact.

A score of ten would mean that you have systems and a culture of thinking about the environment and are constantly striving to minimise your impact and that of everyone you work with. If you manufacture products, you minimise packaging and encourage reuse. A low score would indicate an organisation that doesn't think about the environment. Symptoms are leaving equipment like computers on all the time, not using environmentally friendly vehicles and not recycling or reusing where possible.

Chapter Six

Financial Success

"My goal was never to just create a company. A lot of people misinterpret that, as if I don't care about revenue or profit or any of those things. But what not being just a company means to me is not being just that – building something that actually makes a really big change in the world."

Mark Zuckerberg

Finally, we come to what many businesses consider first. If it were ever right that being financially successful was enough, it certainly isn't right for business today.

It is not my intention to explore the issues of whether profit is a good thing. I would highlight that one of the most successful companies of the modern era, Amazon, the biggest online retailer in the world with a market valuation of over $1 trillion and in the top forty of most valuable brands, has taken a long time to make consistent profits.

Amazon has spent most of its time as a public company reporting losses or negligible profits, with founder Jeff Bezos consistently stating he would rather reinvest sales revenue into the company to set up a better, more profitable future.

Not chasing quick profits seems to have paid off, as Amazon had an estimated net income of $4.5bn in quarter three of 2023, making it one of Wall Street's most profitable companies.

Unlike the Amazon example, most businesses need to make money more quickly. The basis of this book is that financial success is not enough, but it is essential. You cannot deliver the other principles of the Responsible Organisation Charter© without economic success. For example, how can you treat staff and suppliers well if you cannot afford to?

For today's business, sustainable financial success can only be achieved if three principles come together:

Fundamental principles for financial success

An identifiable market niche	A means of differentiating the business so that it can establish a strong market position
Innovative growth	Innovations that will keep you ahead in a niche or help you identify new niches to help growth, as an existing niche becomes less attractive. NB: growth is not just about selling more, it can be in reputation, knowledge, relationships and impact
Sustainable profit	Ongoing profit, which is secure because it is not overreliant on a few customers, a declining or vulnerable market or a single product

An Identifiable Market Niche

To have ongoing financial success, you need to have a strong market position. This means a clear niche or market proposition. By this, I do not necessarily imply a specific customer segment; it could be an area of expertise or way of working.

It has always been useful to have a niche. Still, in the digital era and the global market, businesses are now competing with millions of others and competition can be extremely fierce.

In the past, before the internet and cheap travel, a business could have a natural niche because of its location and what it offered, which there might only be a few others supplying locally. Now the first step when people are considering purchasing most things, be it personally or professionally, is to look on the internet, so being local is now rarely enough.

Beyond this, having a niche will also make you more money. A niche makes it easier and cheaper to market your business. You are less likely to be affected by competition, you have reduced price sensitivity as the 'expert' or 'specialist product or service' and consequently can increase profits.

Scoring yourself on the ROC© Checker (end of Part 1)

Rate how strong your market niche is.

A score of ten would mean a well-defined niche, which people understand, that allows you to stand out from the crowd. You are not troubled by competition because you are perceived as different. A low score would indicate an organisation that is all things to all people and has no recognisable niche. Symptoms are few referrals because people don't know what you offer that is special and, generally, you can't describe why you are different when asked. You suffer from competition based on price.

Innovative Growth

A winning business is also a growing business. Even if it is not growing in financial terms, it needs to be building across other factors, be it knowledge, reputation or relationships, and it needs to be innovating.

> "We're entering an age of acceleration… Because of the explosive power of exponential growth, the twenty-first century will be equivalent to 20,000 years of progress at today's rate of progress; organizations have to be able to redefine themselves at a faster and faster pace."
>
> Ray Kurzweil

While not everyone agrees with the futurist Ray Kurzweil, no one can disagree that technology is progressing faster and faster. By most estimates, there has been as much technological change in the last 250 years as there was in the preceding 250,000 years.

Add computers into the mix and you get 'Moore's law' – so named after the Intel co-founder Gordon Moore, who postulated it in 1965. Moore's law is a prediction that the number of transistors on a chip doubles every two years, making computers faster and cheaper. Many predicted this would be a short-term law and could not continue for long. Yet, nearly fifty years later, it is ongoing. Smartphones provide more data than a computer would have ten years ago, and the rate of change is now spreading into many other fields, such as biology. AI is the latest example of rapid innovation.

The increase in knowledge is leading to innovation not only in terms of totally new ideas but more often as a result of combining old ideas in new ways. Dyson developed his cleaner after visiting a wood merchant and seeing how they controlled dust. It wasn't a simple journey to his end product and other people had patented similar cyclone-based products, but no one had spent the time to keep on testing and refining it to make it work.

The impact of the changes in transport, communications and computing has radically transformed business over the last fifty years. You can talk and do business with anyone wherever you are, including the beach, and you can generally then get a product to someone within a day wherever they are. Some feel the 2020 pandemic radically changed business in three months.

With the ever-increasing speed of change, innovation has become critical for long-term sustainability. For example, estimates are that in four years, 70% of what we will buy will be new, i.e. not currently available. If you are not innovative, then it is hard to see how you will grow or even keep your existing market share or position.

"Every organisation needs one core competence: innovation."

Peter Drucker

However, it is not just technology that is changing. The world order in terms of power is undergoing fundamental shifts that will have an impact on everyone. The population and environment are changing radically as pressure on natural resources grows and the population ages.

Innovation is critical to financial success, as it allows a business to respond and capitalise on the changing world. It links strongly to other aspects of the ROC©, particularly collaboration and learning.

"Innovative firms are twice as profitable (on average) than other firms."

Managing Innovation by J Tidd and J Bessant

Innovation and growth are linked; you can be growing without innovating but that growth is not likely to be secure in the longer term, and you may just be creating a riskier scenario. For example, many retailers grew by expanding their outlets but are now regretting this as more and more consumers move to purchase on the internet and high streets decline. Conversely, innovating without growing is not generally a financially sustainable model, even though it may be essential to maintain market share.

Scoring yourself on the ROC© Checker (end of Part 1)

Rate how you rank in terms of innovative growth.

A score of ten would mean that you have systems and a culture of tracking how much of your growth comes from innovation and it is a significant amount. A low score would indicate an organisation that probably doesn't even know what part of its growth comes from innovation and has little innovation anyway. NB: innovation does not have to be a new product or service, it could be adapting how you offer existing products and services, leading to growth, e.g. letting people rent instead of buy.

Sustainable Profit

> "Long-term profits are maximised by not making them the primary goal."
>
> John Mackey, founder and CEO, Whole Foods

When I talk about sustainable profit, I am not referring to sustainable in terms of the environment but rather to the need to be able to consistently make a profit over the long term, so that the business is sustainable over time.

Sustainable profit is significant because it funds every other aspect of the Responsible Organisation Charter©, allowing you to pay suppliers fairly, compensate staff, support your community, develop new products and provide an excellent service to customers. Losing money and closing down does not help anyone, whatever their sector, as the high-profile closure of Kids Company in 2015 in the charity sector showed. Their financial failure left many children with no support and raised questions about how public funds had been spent.

Often people who are ethical find charging higher prices uncomfortable because they are not focused on money and do not want to be seen as greedy. While it is a function of being *Good* not to overcharge, having high enough prices and profits to enable you to be *Good* is essential and is not unethical.

After all, the earnings of people like Cadbury and Gates have changed the world for the good.

Similarly, being a *Good* company also involves effectively managing costs to ensure sustainable profitability.

Scoring yourself on the ROC© Checker (end of Part 1)

Rate how you perform in terms of sustainable profit.

A score of ten would mean that you are not reliant on a single large customer; in fact, no customer accounts for more than 15% of your profits. You are likely to have at least some regular income rather than just one-off sales and a good return on the money invested in overheads, equipment and stock. Your cost of getting a customer is much lower than the lifetime value of your customers. A low score would indicate the reverse of all the above: high overheads; low rates of stock turnover, if appropriate; high cost of acquiring customers and low lifetime value; a few large customers who dominate where you get your profits.

Chapter Seven

Where Are You Now?

When you are completing the ROC©, it is useful to think about how you instinctively score yourself for each principle before you consider it in detail, so make sure you have completed the Responsible Organisation Charter© Checker below before going on to section two.

Each principle you score out of ten, with ten being you are totally happy about how you apply this principle, it is a real strength and could not be better; eight or nine mean it is working well but could still be improved.

A score of one would mean it was not in place at all; ratings between four to seven indicate it could be better, you are doing it, but it does not give you a competitive advantage.

	Poor			Average			Excellent		
	1	2	3	4	5	6	7	8	9
Leadership									
Behaviour driven by shared values									
Clear vision									
Action-focused									
Culture									
Adapatable									
Pioneer learning									
Collaborative									

	Poor			Average			Excellent		
	1	**2**	**3**	**4**	**5**	**6**	**7**	**8**	**9**
Relationships									
Treat staff well									
Treat suppliers fairly									
Good citizen									
Product offering									
Life-changing									
Reliably consistent									
Minimising environmental impact									
Financial success									
An identifiable market niche									
Innovative growth									
Sustainable profit									

Beginning to build your ROC©

Now you have scored yourself on the ROC© Checker, you will know where you are starting from. The goal of this book is to help you build a powerful Responsible Organisation Charter© for your company.

So, as you read Part 2, you may want to focus first on the chapters about the areas where you are weakest, so that you can start to implement some changes.

After reading the book and having had a chance to implement some of the examples and ideas, you can rescore yourself on the audit to see what has changed and how you have improved.

A word of warning! Your scores may have gone down because when you read about what others are doing, your aspirations have grown, and you recognise you have further to travel than you thought. Your ROC© is a living thing and so will change and grow with your business, but hopefully, you will find it is useful.

Getting others' perspective

Before you start reading Part 2, you might also like to get others to score your business on the ROC© and ask for their feedback and perspectives. Their comments may highlight some issues that you may come across as you consider each of the segments of the ROC© in more detail.

Throughout Part 2, there are ROC© challenges that are designed to make you think and challenge where you are in terms of each of the principles.

Part 2
Putting It into Practice

Chapter Eight

Leadership

Creating a business that will succeed without you

"Great leadership is authentic leadership. Authenticity is not a characteristic; it is who you are. It means knowing who you are and what your purpose is. Your True North is what you believe at the deepest level, what truly defines you – your beliefs, your values, your passions and the principles you live by."

Bill George, former CEO of Medtronic

The role of leadership in a responsible organisation is to create an ethos that will outlast the leader and does not rely on the leader to exist. It starts with a compelling purpose that everyone understands, clear values and expectations of behaviour and a focus on achieving things to reach the vision and exemplify the values – taking action. If when a leader leaves everything falls over, then however charismatic they have been, they have not been a great leader.

"In the face of turbulence and change, culture and values become the major source of continuity and coherence, of renewal and sustainability. Leaders must be institution-builders who imbue the organisation with meaning that inspires today and endures tomorrow. They must find an underlying purpose and a strong set of values that serve as a basis for longer-term decisions even in the midst of volatility. They must find the common purpose and universal values that unite highly diverse people while still permitting individual identities to be expressed and enhanced. Indeed, emphasising purpose and values helps leaders support and facilitate self-organising networks that can respond quickly to change because they share an understanding of the right thing to do."

Rosabeth Moss Kanter, Harvard Business School

Being a great leader is an ongoing project. This is not specifically a book about leadership, so I would recommend *Becoming the Best* by Harry M Jansen Kraemer if you want a book about leadership that aligns with the concepts in this book. It recognises that being a great leader is work in progress.

Leadership is so critical because no mission, either commercial or philanthropic, can be achieved without other people or without using the attributes of a great leader to keep you focused, on track and moving ahead. As companies mature, they require leaders and managers with different skill sets, so it is sensible to ask if you have the right leadership in place.

In *Great by Choice* by Collins and Hansen, there is much evidence that leadership based on self-serving ego and flamboyancy is less effective. A leadership style that shows concern for those you lead, learning from others and detailed preparation, discipline and hard work to achieve a long-term goal has more success.

Leadership is about relationships

Research[36] shows that the more generous we are, the more influence and respect we get, which has an impact on how we should act as a leader. Willer explains: "The findings suggest that anyone who acts only in his or her narrow self-interest will be shunned, disrespected, even hated. But those who behave generously with others are held in high self-esteem by their peers and thus rise in status."

Often when times are difficult in an organisation, leaders can ignore their staff because they are so focused on the problems. They become inward-looking and pass by everyone without seeing them.

Remember: staff can be a valuable source of great ideas, but if you ignore your team, it can lead to problems. When people are unsure about what's going on, they tend to imagine the worst and rumours can cause panic. This can lead to employees seeking new jobs or feeling stressed, having an impact on their work. Ironically, if you focus too much on the problem and stop communicating or if your staff think you're hiding things, it can make the problem worse.

Focusing on the core issues

A good leader recognises what is essential and focuses on the core issues.

An excellent example of leading staff and working on the core issues occurred in 2008 when Starbucks faced problems, was closing stores and making people redundant. Starbucks' issues coincided with Howard Schultz, who had led the company to success, returning as its leader.

He focused on reconnecting the company to its purpose:

"From the very beginning we always believed that the only way we could exceed the expectations of our customers was to exceed the expectations of our people. So given the external pressures, the cataclysmic financial crisis, it was time to return to the intimacy of communicating directly with our people, galvanising our organisation against a core purpose and asking our people to understand what was at stake."

Howard Schultz, Starbucks

Schultz's leadership focusing on the purpose and the staff turned the company around so that net profits increased by 300% and the share price rose from $7 to over $50 in three years.

In some senses, this is a success story, but as a leader, Schultz had initially failed because he hadn't embedded the purpose into the organisation strongly enough that it survived when he left the first time.

Great leaders will influence every part of the Responsible Organisation Charter©, so they need a range of skills and the ability to recruit the people who can complement their skills and fill any gaps.

Leadership is about thinking about the future while also focusing on the present, and that is why it can be so challenging. There is no single type of best leader; Churchill was seen as a great war leader but then lost the election in 1945 to lead Britain in peacetime. Boris Johnson led the Tories to election success but struggled as a leader during Covid.

It is not always the great leaders that history remembers or praises, as great leadership is about ensuring the detail is right and creating the environment for others to succeed. It may include inspiration, but there are other ways, not just the persuasive speeches that Churchill used to such effect. A quiet leader who has an inspirational purpose can be just as effective providing an environment where people are empowered and able to achieve that purpose.

"Victory awaits him who has everything in order – luck, people call it. Defeat is certain for him who has neglected to take the necessary precautions in time; this is called bad luck."

Roald Amundsen, *The South Pole*

A Case Study: Two differing styles of leadership

A story – the race to the South Pole

In 1911, Amundsen and Scott both led famous expeditions to the South Pole – one to disaster, the other success. In *Great by Choice* (Collins and Hansen, 2011), the differences in style of leadership are outlined and used to illustrate the differences in leaders of successful businesses and also those who fail.

Superficially, Amundsen and Scott were similar; both had led successful expeditions in cold climates before and were only four years apart in age, at thirty-nine and forty-three respectively. However, Amundsen was continually seeking to grow, improve and be prepared for the unexpected. He spent time in his twenties obtaining a sailing master's certificate, experimenting with eating raw dolphin in case he ever needed to eat it to survive and living with the Inuits to learn how they managed in sub-zero conditions.

As well as observing how they used dog sleighs, he also learnt that they didn't rush, so that they avoided sweating. Sweat turns to ice in the cold. From his time with them, he decided to use dog sleighs and capitalise on the dogs being carnivores, by killing the weaker ones to feed the others as the journey progressed. He also adopted Eskimo clothing – loose and protective, designed to minimise sweat.

In contrast, Scott didn't build on others' knowledge and experience. He chose to use ponies for the expedition because he had used them before. Their weight made them sink in the snow and they struggled in the extreme cold. Ponies don't eat meat, so couldn't be used to feed the others if they died, and they all died very early into the expedition. He also used unproven motor sledges, the engines of which broke within the first few days. He chose them because they could carry more weight and he wanted to be innovative. Consequently, for most of the journey, Scott's men had to pull the sledges themselves, using up their calories and physical strength.

Both had storage depots, but Scott had only stored one tonne of supplies for seventeen men compared to Amundsen, who had three tonnes for his team of five. Amundsen also carried enough extra supplies so that if they missed a single depot, they would still have enough left over to go another 100 miles. In contrast, Scott carried very few spare supplies so that missing any depot would be disastrous and, of course, he had also not allowed for the extra calories needed for the manual labour of towing the sledges.

To find the primary storage depots, Amundsen used twenty black pennants spread out around, so he could more easily find his supplies if he got off course because of bad weather. Scott used a single flag for his storage depots and left no markings on the path, so if he got lost, there was little chance of finding the depot. Similarly, Scott had a single thermometer for vital altitude measurements and got angry when it broke. In contrast, Amundsen had four thermometers to cover for accidents.

When things started to go wrong for Scott, he blamed bad luck, particularly the weather. They both left about the same time. Amundsen reached the South Pole on the 15th of December and was back at his base camp in good shape as planned on the 25th of January. Scott was much slower because his men had to haul the sledges, and only reached the Pole on the 17th of January, over a month later than Amundsen. He was then starting his return as the weather began to get worse. He and his final two companions died in March just ten miles short of his supply depot.

YOUR ROC© CHALLENGE

Are you Scott or Amundsen when you run your company?

How much are you trusting to chance and blaming lousy luck, market changes or other factors?

As the Scott and Amundsen story illustrates, a good leader is as prepared as they can be for the unknown and takes responsibility rather than blaming luck.

Scott focused on the goal, like many companies are focused on profit, but success involves many principles, as the Responsible Organisation Charter© illustrates. Your business needs to be ready to cope with change and the unexpected.

An organisation that is being responsible has to have good leadership. Leaders are often the visible face of the business. The strong personality of the owner or leader, such as Musk or Trump, can become synonymous with the corporate identity. This can limit the organisation as the focus is on the individual rather than the needs of the company.

How the leadership behaves in all the critical relationships of the business will set the tone – if the leaders do not act responsibly, then the company cannot be responsible. For example, if you are rude, judgemental or dismissive, then the business will do less well than if you are good at building relationships.

> "Great leaders have discipline, creativity and "productive paranoia" and underlying "is a motivating force: passion and ambition for a cause or company larger than themselves. They have egos, but their egos are channelled into their companies and their purposes, not personal aggrandisement."
>
> Jim Collins and Morten T Hansen, *Great by Choice*

In the Responsible Organisation Charter©, leadership has an impact on each area, e.g. consistency, but generally the practical responsibility for implementing the other areas is likely to be done by others. However, it is essential that good leaders lead by example in terms of culture by innovating and showing it is OK to fail; by learning and being adaptable.

> "As long as we keep purpose in focus in both our organisational and private lives, we are able to wander through the realms of chaos, make decisions about what actions will be consistent with our purpose and emerge with a discernible pattern or shape to our lives."
>
> Margaret Wheatley

The central role of leaders is to be involved in the critical tasks of setting the direction, the vision, the way the organisation works, its values and building relationships with crucial outsiders and collaborations.

Edwin Locke, in his book *The Prime Movers*, identifies the core mental traits of great business leaders like Steve Jobs, Sam Walton, Jack Welch, Bill Gates and Walt Disney. While lots of things contribute to their success, the critical trait he identifies that they all shared was a vision.

> "It's the ability to see ahead that truly set each of these men apart."
>
> Edwin Locke, *The Prime Movers*

Research[37] indicates that the top three leadership qualities are the ability to:

1. Motivate staff   35%
2. Work well across cultures   34%
3. Facilitate change   32%

The least essential qualities were technical expertise (11%) and "bringing in the numbers" (10%).

Leadership is essential and it has three critical roles that we will address in the next three chapters:

- creating a business where behaviour is driven by shared values,
- setting a vision, which inspires
- creating a culture where people take action.

Chapter Nine

Shared Values

Guiding Principles for Everyone's Behaviour

"In reality, all organisations are values-driven. The critical issue is whether these values are conscious, shared and lived, or remain unconscious and undiscussed. When values are not defined, the culture of the organisation is subject to the vagaries of the personality of the leader. When the leader changes, the values will change accordingly."

Values-Driven Organisation, Richard Barrett

A leader's role is to create clarity about how the values of your organisation translate into actions. These values need to be understood and shared by everyone, so that when you are not with a member of staff, which is most of the time, they are still applied.

The values of an organisation set the rules by which it lives and define the culture.

However good the vision or strategy, everything starts with the values that drive the behaviour in the company, which is why it is the first principle I am discussing.

As Peter Drucker says, "Culture eats strategy for breakfast."

If everyone lives by the same rules and the same values, then people trust each other. If there are no shared values, then it will lead to anarchy and generally people will not feel part of a coherent whole.

Shared positive values allow people to feel pride in the organisation that they work for.

"We as a team are our values. We use them daily as a touchstone to help inform every decision we make."

Jack Clark, rugby coach, University of California[38]

Values that are *Good* for an organisation can be split into four different themes:

- Improving the quality of what people receive from you and how they can live their lives – changing the world for your customers.
- Doing something in a more responsible or better way that, for example, is kinder to the environment, involves people in need or encourages others to act more responsibly – changing the wider world.
- Ensuring sustainable profit that can be used for social or environmental causes or to employ more people – creating business success so that the company has the resources to continue changing the world.
- How the business works in terms of culture, staff involvement (particularly decision making), rewards and recognition – ensuring how you change the world empowers and fulfils your people so that you enrich their lives.

Usually, a business has values across the four different themes.

Having values does not stop you making money or focusing on profit; it just defines how you do it and helps other people understand the real corporate you.

A company with no clear values will not be successful.

If there are no agreed values, or the values say one thing and people do another, then staff will use their judgement as to what they should do. People will act inconsistently, and there can be a feeling of a lack of fairness, disputes and confusion, both within the staff and from customers who just won't know what to expect.

> "A funny thing happened when we actually communicated (our purpose) to our employees. We found that suddenly employees were a lot more passionate about the company, a lot more engaged and, when customers called, they could sense the personality at the other end of the phone wasn't there just for a paycheque."
>
> Tony Hsieh, CEO, Zappos

Values need to be easy to understand and to translate into behaviour standards that are consistently upheld. For example, a company might have a value of being 'international' because it wants to sell worldwide. However, the 'international' value is meaningless if:

- the staff can only speak English;
- there are no foreign papers in reception for visitors;
- the website only focuses on the UK;
- all the staff are British;
- the accounts staff can't cope with currency and local tax queries.

Despite many businesses including 'international' in their mission statements or values, their actions may not reflect a global perspective. In reality, the organisation will not truly embody 'international' as a value despite what it claims.

The need for values to be more than words is backed up by research[39] that indicates that just publishing your values does not improve financial performance. However, where the values translate into a strong culture recognised by the staff, there was an improved organisational performance and higher levels of customer satisfaction.

Interestingly the research also found that privately-owned companies tended to have higher levels of integrity and values than publicly quoted companies. Could this be because the pressure to perform each quarter for the market analysts overwhelms the values?

"You can never repeat the past, but you can be inspired by it."
Charles Morgan, Morgan Motor Company[40]

Values generally are timeless. For example, Morgan's values are about creating fun in driving and they have been in place for over 100 years, but this has not stopped them reinventing their business for every generation.

"Brands with purpose and brands with meaning."
Keith Weed, Chief Marketing Officer, Unilever

Values need to address all the different levels of a company's needs as expressed in the Responsible Organisation Charter©, and these need to translate into clear behaviour standards. They also need to be integral to the brand you are creating in terms of your marketing.

"Nothing seems more obvious to me than that a product or service only becomes a brand when it is imbued with profound values that translate into fact… Everybody appreciates being treated decently. Everybody wants excellence and value. Everyone likes to have fun and to feel part of something bigger than themselves."

Sir Richard Branson

Any value that is a noun needs to translate into a verb to become a behaviour so that it is clear how to act.

The classic and most common example of this is the value 'quality'. How often do you hear a company talk about their 'high-quality service' but what verbs bring this to life? Is it rushing to respond, is it being caring, is it being focused on detail, is it being attentive to individual needs? These would all lead to quality service but are entirely different.

Ranking values

The ranking of your values has an impact on all your decisions based on them. Suppose people believe the top value is making money at any cost, as they appeared to in Barings Bank or Volkswagen. In that case, the values of risk management, quality, environmentalism and honesty look to be subordinate and less important. Managers and staff will be tempted to do what they think is most valued – make money at any cost.

We use a method to rank values, so the priority is clear. The top value is what is core to your business. In *Good Profit*,[41] Koch talks about reducing the number of accidents by changing the priority from production to safety so that employees felt empowered to stop operations if necessary, rather than trying to keep going to maintain production.

It is not possible to be prescriptive about every situation, so, like the Ten Commandments, a business's values need to set overarching principles that help answer issues as they arise in the company.

The following are some examples of ethical value-led questions that indicate the complexity of decision making and how important it is to rank your values:

How much do we consult with the local community about decisions that will affect lots of people outside the company but will reduce our environmental impact?
- A wind turbine may be useful in reducing carbon footprint, but the noise

and its size may have an impact on the local community – planning rules may allow it, but does it fit your values? Which is more important, the local community or the wider world?

Is a manager's responsibility first to their staff or to their customers?
- I went on holiday and, when I returned, my staff were distraught, as a valued customer had sworn and been rude to them because we could not supply a parking space for a meeting in central London. The management, in my absence, had not supported the staff and had apologised to the customer. What would and should happen at your company?

What is more important, a fault-free service or meeting a deadline?
- When I was advising a PR consultancy, I worked with the board on values. The directors all thought meeting a deadline was the top value, the MD thought never sending anything out with an error the most important. In a perfect world, neither happen, but when the courier is waiting for the document and it has a spelling mistake, who does the receptionist lie to, the directors or the board? What can the customers' trust, do they have to check everything carefully for errors or worry about it being late?

These are all more complex than just talking about integrity, innovation or quality – these are the reality of how they work in your company.

YOUR ROC© CHALLENGE

Can you and your staff rank your values and explain what each means in terms of behaviour? Do you have an exact value equation: "We believe in x, which means that we always y."

What values?

"Let us suppose that we were asked for one all-purpose bit of advice for management, one truth that we were able to distil from the excellent company's research. We might be tempted to reply: 'figure out your value system. Decide what your company stands for. What does your enterprise do that gives everyone most pride?'"

In Search of Excellence, Peters and Waterman

There is not a single definitive set of *Good* values. They will vary and will be affected by the vision and mission, the state of the company, the industry sector and even the national culture. Some values are now generally regarded as universal and expected, such as equal treatment for all with no discrimination, health and safety at work, including no sexual harassment.

When these fundamental values are violated, then staff will react, as has been shown by walkouts at Google citing a 'toxic culture' involving harassment and inequity.

Values need to include a mix of impact and performance. It is all very well having a desire to save the world, but if there are no values or behaviours to drive performance, we may all be dead before you achieve it.

While there needs to be a mix of values that include performance standards, i.e. how we do things, generally the top value focuses on purpose or ethics, why we do things. Consequently, there needs to be a significant purpose; for example, the performance value of winning as a top value is likely to result in behaviour that does not fit within the mission.

A global example is Volkswagen, who may have had ethical performance values and had spent years talking about caring about the environment. Still, somewhere within the organisation, people believed that the most important value was business success, even if this meant lying to regulators. The Volkswagen emissions scandal first came to light in 2015, when it was revealed that VW had been using software to cheat on emissions tests. The software, known as a 'defeat device', was designed to turn on emission controls when the vehicle was being tested, but to turn them off when the vehicle was being driven on the road. As a result, the vehicles emitted significantly higher levels of pollutants during normal driving conditions than they did during emissions testing. The revelation of the emissions scandal was a major shock to the public and the automotive industry. It was a significant blow to Volkswagen's reputation, which had previously been built on a foundation of innovation and quality.

The scandal had significant financial consequences for the company, with its stock price plummeting and its reputation among investors and customers taking a major hit. By 2017, the scandal has cost the company twenty-five billion euros in fines, settlements and remediation. VW admitted in 2015 to equipping about eleven million cars worldwide with devices to fool the testing equipment.

It didn't stop there, investigations also uncovered evidence of other unethical practices, including the use of false statements and documents to mislead regulators and consumers.

The scandal had a negative impact on the company's sales and profits, the stock price plummeted, and the company faced significant financial challenges. The investigations into Volkswagen revealed a culture of secrecy and cover-up within the company, which contributed to the severity of the scandal.

Even in the not-for-profit sector, values can come under pressure when they are not ranked in order of importance.

For example, I was working with a fair trade social enterprise and charity, which had recruited someone from the commercial sector to improve their financial performance. To do this, they had manipulated one of their values on salary scales and given the individual a brief to consider anything to improve performance. Staff became confused and assumed that making money was the priority, so to improve cashflow started to pay suppliers late. For a fair trade organisation, this was a disaster, as there was a lack of consistency in following values and a failure to rank values so that fair trade was top. It also illustrates how a lack of clarity about how values can translate into behaviour can lead to values that have no meaning. To the accounts staff, late payment of suppliers in the UK was not linked to the mission of fair trade promoted with developing countries.

Values do not have to be boring. Iceland, the frozen food firm, has a value of fun, which translates into staff who are happy, fun names for food, decorated stores and staff who are glad to chat with customers. Southwest Airlines include fun as well, but in a more defined way. Under its section for staff "Me – How I Show Up", it has a heading 'humility', including "Don't take yourself too seriously."[42] Their values are reinforced with things such as a staff member of the month on the website. That their values worked was evidenced by the ongoing awards, including consistently[43] receiving the lowest ratio of complaints per passengers boarded of all major US carriers that have been reporting statistics to the Department of Transportation (DOT) from September 1987 to the end of the 2010s. However, even they struggled in the aftermath of Covid when flying recommenced, and they couldn't cope, upsetting both staff and customers. Values and their ranking need to adjust to changes in circumstances.

Do your values work?

"Tribes form horizontally. Change happens from person to person, rarely from the top down. Organizations establish a culture, the way we do things around here, as much from the craftsmen on the shop floor as from what the CEO does in her office."

Seth Godin

While values should not be restricted to a narrow definition of business ethics, your values and behaviour standards must cover ethical areas.

A useful way to create values and behaviours is to discuss how you should respond to different ethical dilemmas. Here are some examples:

In operating the business, what should you do when you are asked to or tempted to:

1. cut corners
2. reduce quality where no one sees
3. lie about a problem
4. pay a bribe as it is the custom of the country?

In dealing with customers, what is the priority:

1. solve any problems as fast as possible
2. solve any problems as cheaply as possible
3. ensure the customer is happy?

A member of staff needs to know that the leadership will support them if they refuse to act on the orders of their manager or supervisor because they believe they are being asked to perform in a way which doesn't fit with the business's values and behaviour standards.

It is also essential to understand what your staff may hold as values and what they want to happen in the world, particularly if you are reviewing and updating your values. If you impose a new value which people feel uncomfortable with, it can have significant consequences. Excellent staff may leave; it may be ignored or followed with little enthusiasm.

Generally, an optimum number of values is four or five so that everyone knows them and can easily remember them.

Varying values

The types of values a company has will vary depending on the kinds of activity and the issues staff are addressing. Similarly, in a time of change or crisis, there may be some different values that are applied, or the ranking may need to change, as is suggested by the Southwest Airlines example above.

For instance, a company seeking to move to profitability might rank highly a value about minimising costs, which in normal times is less important.

It is interesting how employees see things. Research[44] indicates that across ten countries and twenty-one business sectors, two-thirds of employees rank employee recognition as the most desired value they would like in the company they work for. In my experience, this is particularly true in companies with many quite low-skilled or repetitive jobs where there is not much scope for creativity or fulfilment.

Thinking in terms of Maslow's hierarchy of needs, these staff are looking for recognition and security in terms of reasonable levels of pay, thanks and appreciation for a job well done, and awards for excelling so that they can feel pride. Additionally, they may be looking for opportunities to learn and progress. I have worked with teams where morale was transformed by merely increasing the awareness of the need to say thank you and to praise a job that has been well done.

Knowledge workers undertaking more complex roles tend to look for values that will allow them to use their skills, grow, learn and give their life a purpose. But they also like and need recognition.

However, some values are universal, such as the desire for fairness and the inspiration of doing work that changes the world. If a business has a value of valuing everyone's contribution, then everyone can feel part of achieving a higher purpose. Poorer people who appear to need to focus lower down Maslow's hierarchy on food and shelter do not have less humanity or desire to change the world, they may just rank their critical values differently.

When you are developing values, it needs always to be a balance of the organisational needs and the needs of the staff. *The Values-Driven Organisation* by Richard Barrett outlines these issues very well.

The more the values of your staff and your company align, the stronger the organisation will be. As many charities show, staff who passionately support your cause will go way beyond the call of duty. Indeed, charities attract volunteers who work for nothing because they believe in what the charity is doing. If you publicise your values and vision, as charities do, then you are more likely to get staff applying who share those values.

Whatever you do as a company, you can have inspirational values. For example, any company can have a value to help staff fulfil themselves. Their job role in the company may be quite 'structured', but you can include helping people to achieve their values by, for example, giving them time to volunteer for causes they support or time to pursue their interests or areas of growth.

How clear values and purpose lead to staff engagement

In 2009, Capital One, the global credit card company, had only 26% of their staff who were considered to be fully engaged, and almost a third felt disengaged. Within three years, by creating a compelling purpose and clear shared values, they had shifted to 83% fully engaged and only 2% disengaged.

> "I truly believe that Capital One lives and breathes its values and that there is a shared, common vision to Make Lives Better. This is not just a slogan that's stuck on a wall for people to occasionally read but is enforced through everything we do."
>
> Employee comment

In 2023, Capital One was fifteenth in the Fortune 100 Best Companies to Work For®, included in the list for the twelfth consecutive year. They now head their 'About Us' page on their website with words that reflect their values and how they implement them, including the spaces that they work in:

> "Capital One is on a mission to help our customers succeed by bringing ingenuity, simplicity and humanity to banking. We were founded on the belief that the banking industry would be revolutionized by information and technology, beginning with credit cards.
>
> Founder-led by Chairman and Chief Executive Officer Richard Fairbank, we believe that innovation is powered by perspective and that teamwork and respect for each other lead to superior results. Across the company, we're building customer experiences that are real time and intelligent. We measure our efforts by the success our customers enjoy and the advocacy they exhibit.

We're enabling great talent with great spaces. Our award-winning office designs promote creativity and collaboration. In 2018, we opened our new headquarters in McLean, Virginia, where engineers, designers, and data scientists work side by side to imagine the next great chapter of Capital One."[45]

Capital One illustrates how a culture can be changed in a few years when everyone understands the vision and values. In their case, they aim to 'Make Lives Better'. The case study below shows how clearly ranked values that empower staff members to take initiative can have a massive impact.

A Case Study: How clear values can give competitive advantage

A story – how FedEx got started

Many years ago, I went to a marketing course in Orange County with Jay Abrahams and one of the speakers had been a senior manager in Federal Express in the early days.

He told the tale of how it had been set up so that the founder could have an airline to run. All the depots, planes and staff were in place but few customers. The founder Fred Smith famously even went to Las Vegas one week to gamble on blackjack to win the wages.

Late one Friday, the phone rang at a depot and the only person there was the receptionist. The caller was a bride waiting for her wedding dress, which hadn't been delivered. The receptionist didn't hesitate: the company value was "absolutely positively overnight", so she located the dress, chartered a plane and got it there for the wedding the next day. Fred Smith, the founder of the company, demanded that his workers "treat every package as if it were the last package FedEx will ever handle". Not only was there the clear value 'absolutely positively overnight' but Fred Smith had translated it into this very clear behaviour.

On Monday, the man relating the story explained his reaction of shock at finding out what she had done. He asked what she had been thinking. "Well," she said, "I know we guarantee 'absolutely positively overnight', so I was delivering, and besides, we're going bust anyway."

Not surprisingly, the FedEx story was the talk of the wedding reception. At that wedding was someone who worked for a large photo processing company with a need for lots of overnight deliveries – they became a critical early large client of FedEx and, as they say, the rest is history.

YOUR ROC© CHALLENGE

What outrageous act would your staff feel they could do to uphold your top value?

I wanted to check some facts as I was writing up the FedEx story, so I ended up on their corporate website and couldn't resist downloading their current mission.

Your values should be so clear that anyone in the company will instinctively know what behaviour will make them a hero and what will make them a villain without them having to check with a manager or corporate guidelines.

I am not sure that a receptionist would now have the courage to charter a plane based on what is written below which does not translate into any single powerful message or behaviour standard, unlike other bits of the website that are inspirational.

FEDEX[46] Mission
Connect people and possibilities around the world

Here are a couple of examples of values that companies use to guide their behaviour:
- The century-old Novo Nordisk specifies that any decision must be "financially, socially and environmentally responsible." In 2023's second quarter, Novo's sales climbed 30% to 107.7 billion Danish kroner (about $15.9 billion), the highest quarterly growth in the last twenty years. All their production is now powered by renewable energy.
- Johnson & Johnson, the multinational conglomerate, has a seventy-year-old statement that the company must "support good works and charities and bear our fair share of taxes."

Translating values into behaviours

> "Great customer service has to come from the inside out. You cannot mandate it. You can't threaten, reward, or coerce people to care. You can only awaken the desire and then give them the permission and encouragement to make it come alive in their work."
>
> Barbara Glanz

The purpose of values is that they provide the principles that everyone in the organisation use between themselves and with the outside world.

There may be two or three behaviour statements for each value, which may reflect the different roles people play or areas of the organisation. The behaviour statements should clarify what the value means in action, so people know how to behave. They also provide a way to measure if people are living the values. It is useful to get staff involved in developing what the values mean in action in their role or department, talking through scenarios and typical issues.

It is also useful to use the values and behaviour standards in your recruitment process, to understand if candidates are compatible with how you will need them to behave. If consistency is a value, for example, and a candidate likes to take short cuts, then there is an issue about compatibility.

Reinforce your values and behaviours by having systems and rewards that reflect them. For example, Timpsons has a strong emphasis on customer service and trusting their staff. They give each frontline member of staff the power to spend up to £500 sorting any individual customer problem – a convincing behaviour standard and reinforcement of the customer service value. They have only two rules in their shop: put the money in the till and look the part. Staff can decide discounts, opening hours and what stock to order. New starters are told 'Please ignore all memos and do what you think is right'.

Volvo IT[47] has a full-time culture manager and culture ambassadors, who add this role to their full-time staff role, to promote the behaviours agreed and improve alignment with vision and values. They act as role models for the culture and ethics. The Volvo Group culture is defined by a set of five carefully chosen values,[48] which include customer success, trust, passion, change and performance.

Avoid cliché values that every organisation tends to have, such as quality and teamwork. Without definition, they can be meaningless. Quality should be a given and quality alone is not remarkable. I can remember working with a computer company that was excited when they achieved a British Standard quality award and wanted to publicise it until I explained that this would suggest that previously they hadn't been offering a high-quality product!

The more that suppliers, customers and collaborators share your values, the easier it will be for everyone's behaviour to align. Again, this is exemplified by some charities where donors share the values of the charity they support and actively help the charity achieve their mission.

In the UK, the BBC came under the spotlight initially for its role with Jimmy Saville and the sex and child abuse scandals, and then when the behaviour of Jeremy Clarkson came under scrutiny. More recently, the scrutiny has been about inequalities in how they pay people, particularly the wide variations between presenters on the same programme, which happened to coincide with whether they are male or female.

The BBC values when I first started writing this book several years ago were:

- Trust is the foundation of the BBC: we are independent, impartial and honest.
- Audiences are at the heart of everything we do.
- We take pride in delivering quality and value for money.
- Creativity is the lifeblood of our organisation.
- We respect each other and celebrate our diversity so that everyone can give their best.
- We are one BBC: great things happen when we work together.

However, interestingly, these have now been updated[49] with kindness and inclusivity added to the respect value and collaboration, learning and growing together to the one BBC and a new accountable value (see italics for changes):

- We **RESPECT** each other – *we're kind, and we champion inclusivity.*
- *We are **ACCOUNTABLE** and deliver work of the highest quality.*
- We are **ONE BBC** – *we collaborate, learn and grow together.*

I assume these changes came partly from the issues the organisation has been addressing.

With a value of 'respect', how could they have acted differently with

Clarkson when he hit a fellow member of staff and stayed loyal to the value? Respecting people does not mean condoning someone hitting a colleague. Values and behaviour standards only have meaning if there are no exceptions. If it is OK for one person to hit another if they are a star and generate lots of money, then every corporate statement about how people should treat each other becomes meaningless. I suppose updating the value of 'respect' to include kindness makes it totally clear that hitting a fellow member of staff is wrong, just in case people were confused! However, as I was doing the final edit before publication, *Strictly Come Dancing* hit the news suggesting kindness is still not a behaviour embedded into the BBC culture.

If values are not followed then the unwritten culture becomes the one that people believe in. For example, if you achieve results or are a 'celebrity', you're OK whatever you do, the words are just words. One has to assume that in the time of Jimmy Saville that is what people believed, whether it was true or not, and so the dreadful acts happened. However, the same people who were so appalled by that did not all support the departure of Jeremy Clarkson. Being *Good* is not always easy, but if you have a robust framework of values and agreed behaviours, it should seem fair and understandable.

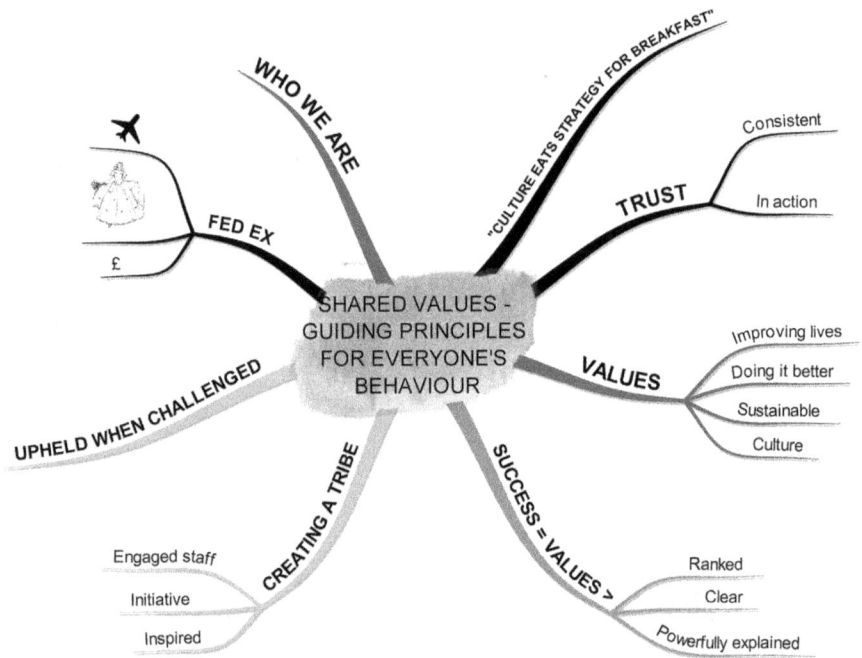

Figure 2: Shared Values – guiding principles for everyone's behaviour

Scoring yourself on the ROC©

Rate how well people in your organisation understand and implement your values.

A score of ten would mean that everyone would respond in the same way to a challenge or issue, reflecting how the organisation believes it should act. A low score would indicate a lack of understanding or clarity about your values or how they translate, and would mean that the response to a challenge or issue would depend on who was addressing it in the organisation.

Chapter Ten

A Clear Vision

An Inspirational Future

"To extend our love and care beyond our narrow self-interest is antithetical to neither our human nature nor our financial success. Rather, it leads to the further fulfilment of both. Why do we not encourage this in our theories of business and economics? Why do we restrict our theories to such a pessimistic and crabby view of human nature? What are we afraid of?"

John Mackey, founder and CEO, Whole Foods

Southwest Airlines was a classic example of the power of a strong vision supported by a robust set of values that translate into a culture.

"Our Purpose: Connect people to what's important in their lives through friendly, reliable, low-cost air travel.
Our Vision: To become the world's most loved, most flown and most profitable airline."

Southwest Airlines website

Its founder Herb Kelleher wanted to democratise air travel. When he started the airline, fewer than half of Americans used planes; now over 80% do. He recognised it was important for the staff to be "involved in a cause instead of just a business." The model resulted in the most profitable US airline, with forty-five years (to 2017) of unbroken profit, an unprecedented achievement in the domestic airline industry. Even during the recession, their commitment to staff and customers meant they neither laid off staff nor cut routes.

Despite their strong culture, they continue to look for ways to stand out from the crowd and fulfil their vision of making it possible for everyone to fly. Consequently, they decided to move to free luggage; 'bags fly free', despite the loss of $500 million in baggage fees. Analysts were extremely doubtful, but after the policy change, they increased market share by $1 billion, some of which is likely to be from the policy. Even in 2020, as Covid struck, it managed the lowest consumer complaint rate at 2.64 per 100,000 passengers. But, post-pandemic, the company has struggled with staff shortages and has been investigated after a service meltdown that led to nearly 17,000 cancelled flights in December 2022. This illustrates the need to be constantly working on how to achieve your vision as the world changes.

> "Whatever you do, you need a reason to exist… know what you stand for."
>
> Wayne Hemingway, Red or Dead[50]

Ignore your vision and things can quickly go wrong.

A Case Study: What happens when you stop following your vision and mission[51]

A story – how Kodak lost its way

Kodak started as the Eastman Dry Plate Company, based on the invention of George Eastman. He realised how inconvenient the wet-plate technology was for taking photos when he wanted to take a camera on holiday.

Soon after, in 1884, Eastman invented roll film, even though the camera that could use it only came four years later! Over time, Eastman came to define the purpose of Kodak as wanting to make photography "as convenient as a pencil".

For a century, Kodak innovated and developed its technology, leading the way, so that by 1996 it had 140,000 employees and a market worth of $28 billion. In the USA, they had 90% of the film market and 85% of the camera market. It appeared to have become more sophisticated in its understanding of its purpose – it was about recording memories – the 'Kodak Moment'.

Their research was still leading the way in innovation, and in 1975, Steven Sasson, working for Kodak's Apparatus Division research laboratory, created the world's first digital still camera and digital recording device. It weighed 8.5lbs and had a resolution of only 0.01 megapixel. It could only take thirty black and white images – a number chosen to fit with the size of Kodak films – and the photos were stored on a cassette tape. It also took twenty-three seconds to shoot and save a single picture. Clearly, it had a long way to go, but Kodak was leading the field and could have potentially dominated.

However, unfortunately for Kodak, they didn't capitalise on the innovation. Firstly, they thought it would be a long time before a practical digital camera would exist, ignoring Moore's law of exponential growth, and secondly, they lost sight of what their purpose was. Whether it was to be as simple as the pencil or to capture memories, both could be achieved with digital cameras. Still, they could only see that most of their profit came from processing films, so developing digital photography would be like a turkey promoting Christmas.

They didn't want to compete with themselves, but unfortunately, others did. As a result, Kodak started to struggle in the nineties, stopped being profitable in 2007 and filed for bankruptcy in January 2012.

YOUR ROC© CHALLENGE

Is your vision clear enough to guide your strategy?

A conflict of vision or the loss of vision is the root cause of the failure of many companies.

> "A business must have a vision specific enough to guide its strategies, decision making, allocation of resources and the roles, responsibilities and expectations of all employees. Each vision also needs to be aspirational in order to expand the thinking of leaders and employees throughout the organisation."
>
> Charles G Koch

Sometimes, a vision can be world-changing – some of the big companies' ones are well-known like the Microsoft vision:

> "A computer on every desk and in every home."
> Bill Gates, Microsoft chairman and chief executive officer, 1980

Hard to imagine, but when Bill Gates came up with that vision, he wasn't at all sure he could achieve it, as this quote makes clear:

> "We had dreams about the impact it could have… It's been amazing to see so much of that dream become a reality and touch so many lives. I never imagined what an incredible and important company would spring from those original ideas."
>
> Bill Gates, 2008

This vision is curious because Microsoft doesn't even make computers, just the software that drives about 90% of them. It all grew from an obsession with computers and how they could change the world.

> "Achieving 65% of the impossible is better than 100% of the ordinary. Setting impossible goals and achieving part of them sets you on a completely different path than the safe route."
>
> Dan Dodge, Google

Sometimes, a vision is less profound – just to offer a better or cheaper service – but it stills needs to be inspirational and stretching. Thinking big will increase your success. As Jeff Bezos from Amazon illustrates, he always thinks big.

The clearer and simpler you can be about why you exist, the more likely you are to have an attractive, compelling and consistent corporate culture.

However, if your vision and goals are just numbers, finances and market share, they will not inspire – they will not have emotional pull for most people. Worse, the vision and goals will undermine any values you claim to have beyond making money.

Inspirational vision is an area where many businesses can learn from charities because even the smallest charity is required to tell the Charity Commission why it exists. Most founders set up their charities because they have a driving passion to right a wrong or address a need.

In contrast, often, businesses are set up because someone needs to earn money or doesn't want to work for someone else. The problem then is that the goal of making money does not create an attractive or consistent culture or a successful business. It is not inspirational to staff or customers, nor does it set a direction.

Existing to make a profit is rather like saying the point of your life is to eat. You need to eat and you need a profit, but there should be more to life than that. Your vision is your why.

A clear vision helps to identify the structure and company ethos that is needed. It generally is going to be a vision for at least ten years in the future and might be thirty or more.

In the charity sector, money is a means to an end, not an end in itself. While charities must know how to generate revenue and control costs, their goal is to fulfil the organisation's mission.

An example is microfinance non-profit Kiva, which arranges business loans for entrepreneurs in developing countries, and has as its mission "to connect people through lending to alleviate poverty." Their vision is:

> "We envision a world where all people – even in the most remote areas of the globe – hold the power to create opportunity for themselves and others.
>
> We believe providing safe, affordable access to capital to those in need helps people create better lives for themselves and their families."

It has attracted more than two million lenders and loaned $1.68 billion to almost 1.7 million people since 2005.[52]

Despite the generally held view that business is about money, particularly for publicly quoted companies, most visions and mission statements of successful and profitable companies do not focus on finances.

In my experience, despite the apparent gulf between the charity and business sector, they both have the same issues. Charities need to generate revenue to fulfil their mission, and a successful business's mission must recognise the world at large and have an inspirational vision to inspire its stakeholders if it is to be successful in the twenty-first century.

> "When you have a powerful, long-term vision for something, even against all odds and adversity, you will continue to make progress and people will want to get on board. Why? Because everybody wants to be a part of something great."
>
> Robin Crow

WINNING BY BEING GOOD

A Case Study: How a game of Monopoly changed a town

A story – one man's dream achieved with ROC© principles

Russell Lilley didn't like school and he made it clear, so he left at fifteen. He could be top of the class, but he didn't like the way the teachers treated the pupils. For the head, the feeling was mutual and he predicted Russell would 'end up in jail'. Russell was based near Christchurch in New Zealand in a growing town called Rolleston.

A clear vision

He worked in a tile factory, became an apprentice carpenter and then, at seventeen, he was playing a game of Monopoly with three mates when he thought, 'Why can't I make my life like this?' His vision and goal had been born, and it wasn't to fulfil the 'go to jail, do not pass go' prediction of his headteacher.

Initially, he bought land, planted potatoes and gradually earnt enough to start buying property, just like in Monopoly. By twenty-three, he had done sufficiently well to have the confidence to go out on his own. It wasn't easy as a young man to get finance, but he had his vision and knew what he wanted to achieve. He also knew that he wanted to enjoy the game. On reaching sixty-five, he thinks he may have finally passed go, as he now gets a regular pension!

Adaptable

As the opportunities to fill his Monopoly board have arisen, Russell has been flexible, starting companies as needed and taking advantage of opportunities. When he moved to Rolleston, initially he built houses, then he realised the town required shops as it grew, so he developed two shopping centres. Then, as in Monopoly, you need to have a hotel, so he bought one, as well as building a motel. The hotel, which included a bar, wasn't successful, so he renamed it the Rolly Inn and coined the marketing phrase 'jobs on' based on what pilots say when taking off. This catchphrase caught on and has been promoted worldwide, with his personalised number plate even being stolen and taken to the States where it has developed as a cult for race car drivers. He welcomed army personnel from the local camp and, after initial problems, they became the bar's most prominent supporters, building a Rolly Inn on bases overseas as a tribute to the bar.

When the earthquake in Christchurch happened, he created a business providing transportable homes. "Everything I look at I see an opportunity." He learnt from his parents to 'always look and listen' and to 'learn from your mistakes', so he adapts and grows.

Treat staff well

Russell is really proud that he can offer young people jobs and support those that others may see as 'bad lots'. He feels that young people should be given a chance and not be written off because they make the silly mistakes that the young can make. He will look beyond the lack of exams to the skills and attitudes.

He argued for a lad who was convicted of drink driving, saying he would oversee him if he wasn't sent to jail so that his life would not be ruined.

He knows you need the right people around you: "Who you employ makes you a successful person." He also grows and develops staff, with someone who started as an apprentice, for example, now running Russell Lilly Construction.

He rewards and motivates critical staff by giving them a share of the businesses that they are working in, thus encouraging them to be entrepreneurial.

Good citizen

Russell's values put the community at the top, followed by family, plus always telling the truth, loyalty and trust.

Everything he has done addresses community needs, including poor people. The town needed infrastructure, such as sewers, so with other key people, he helped develop a vision for the town, which included developing an industrial quarter to create jobs. He has funded the local rugby team and their clubhouse. He also was, for many years, part of the volunteer firefighter service.

As he has developed his personal Monopoly board, he has helped the community to grow from 1,200 to 12,000 people and it is estimated by 2040 it will be a city of 50,000.

Rolleston Square is now the retail and community heart of Rolleston and the Selwyn District is the fastest growing district in New Zealand.

Retailers in the centre sell an outstanding range of fashion, giftware, flowers and bakery goods, while onsite hospitality outlets include cafés, restaurants and fast food outlets. You can pick up a bargain at The Warehouse, drop off your dry-cleaning, buy a house and do your banking – a medical centre, chemist, hair salon and barber shop complete the full range of services available.

His simple vision of replicating Monopoly has created successful businesses and changed lives and the community.

YOUR ROC© CHALLENGE

What story explains your vision?

Setting a vision

"I think many people assume, wrongly, that a company exists simply to make money. While this is an important result of a company's existence, we have to go deeper and find the real reasons for our being."

David Packard, Hewlett Packard

Your vision is your big goal, your primary purpose why your business exists. Many companies had a purpose when they started, but over time the product, service and market changed, and the mission and vision have become blurred.

Strong visions are simple and compelling.

YOUR ROC© CHALLENGE

Is your vision a single person's or shared? Will it change when the leader changes?

Having a vision that fits with *Winning by being Good* means thinking beyond an idea of a multi-million-pound business to the raison d'être, your why.

Just having a monetary vision is totally lacking in inspiration – how do you motivate staff by saying we want to create a big business! You don't. It provides no direction or help in making decisions.

Your vision needs to give you a purpose and a way of working, an area of activity, a focus. It needs to be attractive to both staff and customers, and it needs to be shared.

> "The driving thrust of our company, from the day it was founded, was renewal. So, we've never had to discover the need for change."
> Robert Galvin, chairman, Motorola

Over time, your vision may change and grow; the vision for the USA has moved from getting a man on the moon to getting a man to Mars.

Amundsen originally had a vision of being the first person to the North Pole. He'd raised money to go to the North Pole, assembled his team based on that, had done all his planning based on it, and then heard the news that the North Pole had been reached. So, he changed his plans to be the first person to the South Pole, only telling his team after they left port.

If you need to create or revitalise your vision, here are some useful questions to use in a creative session:

What would you do if you had no limits?

- Resources: What would you do if your business had access to unlimited money and resources?
- Powers: What would you do if there were no legal constraints?
- Invention: What would you invent if you could make it profitably and successfully?
- Life changing: What would you do that would most change the lives of your customers for the better?

Another route to use is a technique I have used frequently as a consultant, which allows you to involve lots of people in creating the vision.

The technique involves imagining you have won an award. Imagine it is five years in the future and you have won a prize. What is that award for? It can be imaginary. Example awards might be:

- Best national, regional or local provider of [decide your service].
- The best type of organisation, e.g. charity, social enterprise, small business, big business.
- Fastest growth.
- Most positive impact on [the environment; improving people's lives; wider society].

Make it vivid and alive by picturing the article in the paper, or hearing the radio interview. Picture picking up the trophy. Then imagine describing the steps you took to achieve your vision. How did you get there, what did you do to get the award – strategy and details? What core competencies did you need in the organisation to achieve this success?

The vision of a company is often created by its founder. However, involving the staff or leadership team in creating a vision can be very powerful but also more complicated. This process can lead to a real creative breakthrough, or it can result in setting low, achievable goals that are not visionary. In that case, coaching may be needed to develop a more inspirational vision.

Your vision needs to be written in powerful and inspirational language to express your powerful ideas.

A Case Study: How a charity changed direction

A story – how a dream can get bigger

I worked with an Asian women's refuge that wanted to revitalise its vision. They wanted to involve all the staff and other people, so I ran a Creative Think Tank strategic session. Their initial vision of secure accommodation for abused women had been achieved. They were now thinking about moving on, but why, and for what impact?

As part of the event, I ran the award creative thinking session, breaking the attendees into groups. I don't remember the other presentations because of the overwhelming power of one group's vision. They stood up and explained that their award was for the Spice Girls! We all sat up and wondered what a pop group had to do with a refuge. They then explained that giving shelter was only the start; they wanted to help women create a new life by teaching them how to run businesses and grow the spices that are needed in Asian cooking, so that they could launch a successful company, 'The Spice Girls'. The room came alive, as people visualised a refuge with space for business training, running a business and growing herbs and spices. The vision was inspirational, simple and powerful, and took the organisation forward.

"Keep away from people who try to belittle your ambitions. Small people always do that, but the really great make you feel that you too can become great."

Mark Twain

Translating your vision into reality through your mission

If your vision is where you are going, your cause – your mission – is how you will get there.

Generally, a mission statement defines the area of an organisation's expertise and often the target market(s). It has an essential role in keeping a business focused on what is core to it and is also a guide to how a company will operate with its key stakeholders, particularly employees, and links strongly to the values. It should also be inspirational.

Questions are a powerful way to develop your mission and how it should relate to your vision and values. To create inspirational answers about how you should operate, ask questions like these:

- What stories would you like to hear about your company?
- What inspiring tales would you like your staff to tell you and others about your company?
- What would make you proud of your company?
- Who should be your different stakeholders, and what do you want to achieve for them?
- How do you want to change the world?

Merck, the pharmaceutical company, uses its mission statement to outline how it works to be *Good*:[53]

"To provide society with superior products and services – innovations and solutions that satisfy customers' needs and improve the quality of life – to provide employees with meaningful work and advancement opportunities and investors with a superior rate of return."

A Case Study: How a vision can change vision[54]

A story – how LensCrafters sees clearly

LensCrafters is an American optician with a passion for eyes and helping people across the world to have better sight.

WINNING BY BEING GOOD

They explain how they will do it. The mission includes some goals/measurables for: "creating customers for life by delivering legendary customer service, developing and energising associates and leaders in the world's best workplace, crafting perfect-quality eyewear in about an hour and delivering superior overall value to meet each customer's individual needs... helping the world to see by... being conveniently available to people everywhere, ensuring people think of us as the first choice for eye care, serving more people in our markets than all other optical retailers do combined and giving the gift of sight to those who have the least and need us the most."

The mission translates into a charitable programme that works in twenty-five developing countries around the world, collecting and recycling old glasses in collaboration with Lions Club International, as well as providing new glasses and eye tests to people in need in the States.

Its goal is to provide the gift of sight to millions of people around the world. Its staff volunteer and go out to local nursing homes, homeless shelters and inner-city schools to reach those who cannot afford eye care. The staff talk movingly about the joy of seeing a small child smile when they see correctly for the first time, or a man being able to see clearly enough to be able to apply for jobs.

Their mission translates into stories that get told and celebrated around the organisation, such as the time someone broke their glasses as they left for a two-week holiday from San Francisco. More in hope than certainty, they rang LensCrafters from the plane and told them what had happened. When they stepped off the plane in New York, a LensCrafters member of staff met the plane with a replacement pair of glasses – helping the world see better in reality.

Another story was of a premature baby with severe sight problems and a poor prognosis for which the company specially made some glasses so it could see its parents clearly before it died.

YOUR ROC© CHALLENGE

What stories do people share in your organisation?

A mission should be timeless, unlike the vision, which can change. In a winning company, the company mission links to each employee's purpose.

When this happens, people find fulfilment, work with passion and the corporate culture is consistent and robust.

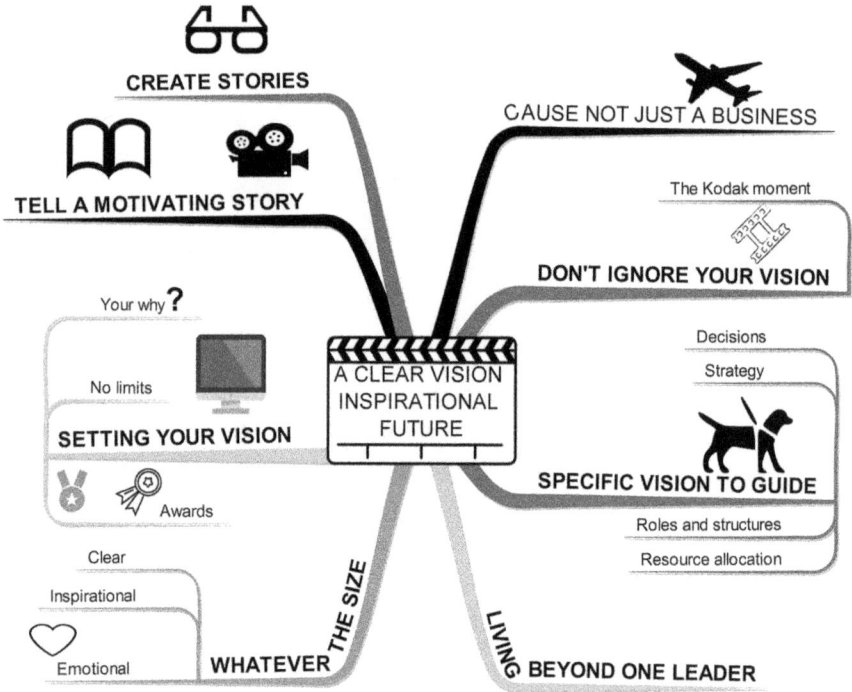

Figure 3: A Clear Vision – inspirational future

Scoring yourself on the ROC©

Rate how well people in your organisation understand and implement your vision.

A score of ten would mean that everyone understands your vision and uses it to guide their decision making and actions. A low rating would indicate a lack of understanding or clarity about your vision with immediate issues guiding decision making rather than the bigger picture.

Chapter Eleven

Action-focused

Creating a sense of urgency

"We are now faced with the fact that tomorrow is today. We are confronted with the fierce urgency of now. In this unfolding conundrum of life and history, there 'is' such a thing as being too late. This is no time for apathy or complacency. This is a time for vigorous and positive action."

Martin Luther King, Jr

Unfortunately, I have met too many people who have planned and developed their vision and values and planned some more but never felt they are ready enough to take action. This chapter is action-focused and designed to help you take action.

Even people who are action-focused can struggle at times to take action. Some people know they need to take steps to move them towards their vision, but the idea can seem so far away that they don't take any action.

Some think, 'let's get a full and perfect plan in place before we act'. Others are active but unfocused, just reacting, so they have no exact destination.

It is critical to get started and get everyone in the business into the habit of taking actions to take you towards your longer-term vision and your short-term goals. You'll never have complete information and a perfect plan, so don't wait until they exist.

However, this is not about blindly taking action. You may need to correct your course on the journey to your vision, your destination, just as an aircraft is continually making adjustments. A plane takes off, even though the pilot knows he will not be following the perfect route. If he never took off, he would never get there. The same is true of a vision and plans – they are just a flight plan until you take off, until you take action.

"The secret to getting ahead is getting started. The secret to getting started is breaking your complex, overwhelming tasks into small, manageable tasks, and then starting on the first."

Mark Twain

Committing to all the principles of the Responsible Organisation Charter© and putting in place systems to achieve them will inevitably take you towards your vision, but it is a daunting challenge.

You don't have to solve everything immediately; focus on the most critical issues and get started. Often inaction can be caused by too many things to do, the confusion about where to start.

Research[55] in organisations seeking to change indicates setting goals is not enough to generate the action that creates change.

Over 85% of all organisations set goals, but the organisations that achieved the most successful change were more likely to set behavioural goals; 89% versus just a third in the least successful organisations.

An organisational goal might be to improve stock turn by 50%, the behavioural goal might be that project teams would meet once a week and each side would include at least one representative of every functional area. The behavioural target feels doable and is less vague than the big goal.

These are tactical goals, strategies towards the big goal, which are much easier to achieve and thus much more likely to be put into action.

When I work with companies on change management, I always look for the quick wins that are also very obvious, so people can feel that change is possible. It could be as simple as a change of uniform, which I helped one organisation put in place to support a much more significant culture shift.

Other proven ways to change behaviour and create the action-focused culture you want is to systematise the actions needed. It is easier to take action in unfamiliar areas or in a different way if you have clear guidelines.

For example, to reduce the avoidable deaths in hospitals, a checklist of simple, critical tasks to be undertaken was introduced. Just by following this simple system of a checklist, they radically reduced the number of deaths and prompted the right actions to be taken.

Similarly, for meetings, have a simple template that includes action-focused prompts for before, during and after the session:
1. What is the goal of the meeting?
2. Any reading or actions required in preparation for the meeting.

3. Timing of the session: start and finish.
4. Key activities agreed at the meeting.
5. Ongoing issues. NB: not everything can be acted on immediately but shouldn't be lost.

When you focus on taking action, instead of the big goal, you can get a sense of achievement and improve at the same time. The critical issue with *Winning by Being Good* is that 'goodness' needs to become habitual. That happens by doing *Good* things repeatedly, rather than just saying it is your goal. The repetition and actions are the vital things.

> "Now here, you see, it takes all the running you can do to keep in the same place. If you want to get somewhere else, you must run at least twice as fast as that."
>
> The Red Queen to Alice
> *Alice's Adventures in Wonderland*, Lewis Carroll

Setting goals is about predicting the future. Sometimes it will work, but we can't always predict the future, as the 2020s have shown. What we can do is take action towards our goals, see what is working, adjust our behaviour and encourage everyone involved in our businesses to do the same.

Have small, exact goals, which can be acted upon. A sizeable general goal can terrify people into inactivity, taking them too far into the future. The secret is to get people moving and then to provide immediate feedback, so that you can work out how to do it better.

Delay giving them feedback and it isn't meaningful. Consequently, annual appraisals must be part of far more regular feedback.

I play bridge, the card game, and if I get immediate feedback after playing a hand, I can remember why I did what I did, learn from it and even practice by putting the learning into action over the next hands. Wait even to the end of the evening when I have played twenty-eight hands and the feedback will be much less useful. Additionally, I can't immediately put it into action; tell me days or weeks later and the feedback and translation will be much harder and potentially meaningless.

The skill is also in getting the right people to undertake the actions. They must find them stimulating, not too hard and not too easy, and they must also preferably use their unique abilities.

It is essential to understand why there may be a culture of not taking action. Failure to act might be because people don't know what to do and the culture doesn't encourage them to ask or show initiative. Alternatively, it might be a fear of failure because people have seen the consequences of failing and it has put them off.

You can encourage action by creating a group ethos, 'We're the type of people who...' or show the impact their lack of action has on other people.

Leaders and managers in business[56] need to develop a focus on actions that will create solutions rather than dwelling on problems.

YOUR ROC© CHALLENGE

How much of your time focuses on solving problems rather than scaling successes?

You must encourage focused action, which needs to achieve results, not just doing something for the sake of doing anything – the classic reorganising the deckchairs on the sinking ship.

The most depressing example I have come across of meaningless action was in a social enterprise run by a local council. It involved people with learning disabilities making greetings cards. It operated in an industrial unit with little natural light and no outside views. They diligently worked, making the cards, which were then piled in the corner. The pile just got higher and higher, until it reached the ceiling. It was demotivating, depressing and patronising. This project was not a social enterprise; it was just filling time.

The social enterprise is an extreme example, but in your organisation, do you keep people at work when there is no useful work to be done? Either explicitly or implicitly, are you merely encouraging a culture of 'working long hours is good' or 'presenteeism'?

Are you destroying your culture of action focus by being impressed by the long hours some people put in?

YOUR ROC© CHALLENGE

Do people have a sense of urgency? Is your business a place where it feels like things get done, or does it feel stuck?

Unfortunately, you undermine a culture of being action-focused if you have a culture of 'presenteeism'. Are people more respected for being at work a long time even if they are not achieving much or don't have much to do?

Action-focused could also be described as being achievement-focused, as just being at work is not enough; you want everyone to be achieving, as this will create a buzz and positive feeling.

Measuring the movement towards achieving a goal is a good way of tracking activity and showing that action is essential, but only if it delivers results. Tracking results will identify when milestones are achieved, and then you can celebrate. There is nothing worse than working hard and getting no feedback or acknowledgement of your progress.

Emotion, not just statistics

If everything seems OK, people can get stuck doing what they have always done. Taking action is obvious when you are in a crisis, as you know you have to act; when you are drowning, you start to swim. But when a business is in a steady-state, creating a sense of urgency can be more difficult.

Creating a focus on action usually means finding an emotional trigger. Charities find this easier because generally they are involved with activities that naturally have an emotional pull. Businesses, particularly the parts which are not customer facing, have to be more creative to create an emotional impact that generates action, as the case study below illustrates.

A Case Study: Generating action in purchasing[57]

A story – how to shift behaviour

If you want to create a step-change in a large company, you need to think differently. Jon Stegner worked for a large manufacturer that he believed could save money in its purchasing. Rather than just a couple of per cent, he thought that the company could save $1 billion over the next five years if it took action.

To achieve this would require senior management support. With limited resources, just having one intern, he searched for an example that would galvanise people into action.

He focused on gloves. He got his intern to identify all the types of gloves used across the company's factories and then tracked back to establish the price paid for each.

The intern established that the factories bought 424 different gloves from all sorts of suppliers (though some the same style), negotiating assorted pricing deals. The same pair of gloves bought for $5 in one place cost $17 elsewhere.

At this point, Stegner could have created a slideshow or Excel spreadsheet, but instead, he got his intern to buy all 424 different types of gloves and put a price tag on each. He then put all the gloves on the boardroom table and invited the division presidents to come to visit the 'glove shrine'. Stegner describes the scene:

> "What they saw was a large, expensive table, normally clean or with a few papers, now stacked high with gloves. Each of our executives stared at this display for a minute. Then each said something like, 'We really buy all these different kinds of gloves?' Well, as a matter of fact, we do. 'Really?' Yes, really. Then they walked around the table... They could see the prices. They looked at two gloves that seemed exactly alike, yet one was marked $3.22 and the other $10.55. It's a rare event when these people don't have anything to say. But that day, they just stood with their mouths gaping."

The gloves exhibit travelled the country to various factories and everyone realised that it was mad. People took action and the company saved much money, just from the work and imagination of two people to prompt the change.

It seems unlikely that a report on glove purchasing would have had the same impact and would probably have been filed or seen as atypical, if considered at all.

YOUR ROC© CHALLENGE

How could you bring to life the need to take action in your organisation?

Humans run businesses and are not always logical, so even though there are many reasons to do something, sometimes it needs an emotional jolt to push people into action.

Data can prompt a simple, incremental change, but a significant change that will have a considerable impact needs to be reinforced by emotional understanding, as well as data. People need to understand how bad the problem is emotionally or see how good the solution looks to prompt the significant action required.

Measurement

"Action without study is fatal. Study without action is futile."

Mary Beard[58]

Generally, what gets measured is what gets done. If something is important enough to measure, then people will take it as important to the organisation. Measurements should be of things that are essential in achieving the organisation's purpose and values, and also in tracking how the organisation is performing on the Responsible Organisation Charter©.

There are four types of measurement:

- Activity: Measurements of actions and inputs, e.g. calls, meetings, machinery, workforce diversity and makeup.
- Outputs: Measurements of what you produce, how efficiently, at what quality, etc.
- Outcomes: Measurements that will relate to results and goals, such as turnover, profit, customer retention, market share, staff turnover and also how you change the world, i.e. impact.
- Organisational: Generally more qualitative measurements, these track cultural issues like values and mission alignment, staff engagement, well-being, learning culture, collaboration; many of the principles of the Responsible Organisation Charter©.

Before trying to implement the Responsible Organisation Charter©, it is useful to benchmark where you are by taking baseline measurements. It would be best if you also decided what you might track for each element of the Responsible Organisation Charter©. What you track needs to be relevant to your organisation.

"Not everything that counts can be counted, and not everything that can be counted counts."

Einstein[59]

As Koch comments in his book *Good Profit*, you need to take care that you measure things that will lead to profitable action, not just something that is simple to calculate.

> "The most valuable measures keep us on track in advancing our vision by enabling us to identify opportunities and problems, and by stimulating innovations."
>
> Koch[60]

Example measures/benchmarks

It is best if you are action-focused in each of the principles of the Responsible Organisation Charter©.

Measures to track action and results for each principle of the Responsible Organisation Charter© will depend on the organisation, but here are some examples to help you get started:

Behaviour driven by shared values
Put measures in place relevant to each behaviour and link these to staff appraisals and performance targets. Track the actions staff take to live the values and reward outstanding examples. Measure staff engagement and how much they believe values are being implemented consistently.

Use mystery shopping and customer surveys to see if your values are translating into actions, which are visible to the outside world.

Clear vision
Track actions taken to raise awareness/understanding of the vision among critical internal and external stakeholders, including mentions in staff newsletters, training, blogs, use in ads and videos, etc.

Action-focused
Track behaviour and goals performance against targets and speed of response.

An Identifiable Market Niche
Track actions to create and maintain a niche and raise awareness/understanding of it within critical internal and external stakeholders.

Innovative Growth

Measure percentage of turnover from products/services less than three years old.

Track the number of test products and the percentage launched.

Review the systems and processes that encourage innovation and the actions that result.

Sustainable Profit

Agree on the critical criteria such as the percentage from one customer or product and then the actions to be taken to achieve these criteria.

Adaptable

Track actions that indicate the company is adaptable, using staff appraisals, performance targets and stakeholder satisfaction surveys.

Pioneer Learning

Track the percentage of staff undertaking training and learning. Use staff appraisals and performance targets to track the percentage of success/failure in any trial of new activities. Target people to try something new.

Collaborative

Track the number of joint working projects across departments and the number of external collaborations, plus the levels and areas of cooperation.

Treat staff well

Agree on what constitutes treating staff well and track actions taken to achieve these goals. Use staff appraisals and performance targets to monitor success – benchmark success by following your ranking in 'good employer' surveys and assessing levels of staff engagement.

Treat suppliers fairly

Agree what constitutes treating suppliers fairly and track actions taken to achieve these goals, such as the speed of payment.

Survey suppliers to monitor success and the longevity of relationships.

Good citizen

Agree what constitutes being a good citizen for the company, such as the percentage of turnover/profit donated to charity/community; levels of volunteering; numbers of collaborations. Agree who and where this applies and survey critical stakeholders to identify success.

Life changing

Identify how you change lives and what actions are needed to achieve this. Track the impact by using data, such as numbers of fans and advocates; customer surveys; and impact measurement.

Reliably consistent

Take actions to ensure consistency – track complaints and critical measures of performance, such as the speed of response.

Minimising Environmental Impact

Identify and encourage actions to minimise your direct environmental footprint and your broader impact through your supply chain.

A Case Study: creating profit from clear, simple actions

A story – getting the railway running using some ROC© principles

In 1995, Brazil privatised its railways and the 'southern line' started being run by a company called America Latina Logistica (ALL)[61] in 1997. The infrastructure was in a deplorable state, with 50% of the network's bridges needing repair and 20% almost in a state of collapse. The technology was old fashioned; across the country, there were still twenty steam trains in operation. In 1998, the company had a net loss of 80 million Brazilian reals (BRL).

Action-focused

A new MD came in, along with some new personnel, but generally, there was chaos. Early on, a mid-level manager had begged for five million BRL to repair a single bridge, but the company simply couldn't afford it. Four clear rules were put in place to govern the company's investments and guide prompt action:

- Rule 1: Money would be invested only in projects that would allow ALL to earn more revenue in the short term (sustainable profit – spend only to make money).

- Rule 2: The best solution to any problem was the one that would cost the least money upfront – even if it would cost more in the long term and was a lower-quality solution (they didn't have the money for anything else).
- Rule 3: Choose options that would fix a problem quickly rather than slower options that would provide superior long-term fixes (action-focused – move quickly).
- Rule 4: Reusing or recycling existing materials was better than acquiring new materials (minimising environmental impact – reuse where possible).

Other things were also crucial in the business, but by providing a clear focus on what required action, people could get going and be confident they were doing the right things.

Minimising environmental impact
While ALL's competitors negotiated for new locomotives, ALL's engineers worked around the clock repairing theirs and found a way to boost their fuel capacity, so that they could operate for longer without refuelling, reducing downtime and allowing more routes per engine. Instead of spending US$400 per tonne on new metal rails, the engineers ripped up tracks at abandoned stations and installed them on active routes so that the trains could go faster.

Sustainable profit
The simple strategy based on the four rules for effective investment meant that, within three years, the loss had changed to a profit of twenty-four million BRL.

YOUR ROC© CHALLENGE

Do you have clear rules to help people identify the best action to take?

The case study above illustrates how valuable it can be to have some simple rules to help people understand what actions they should take. These rules must work with your values and will change over time as internal and external circumstances alter.

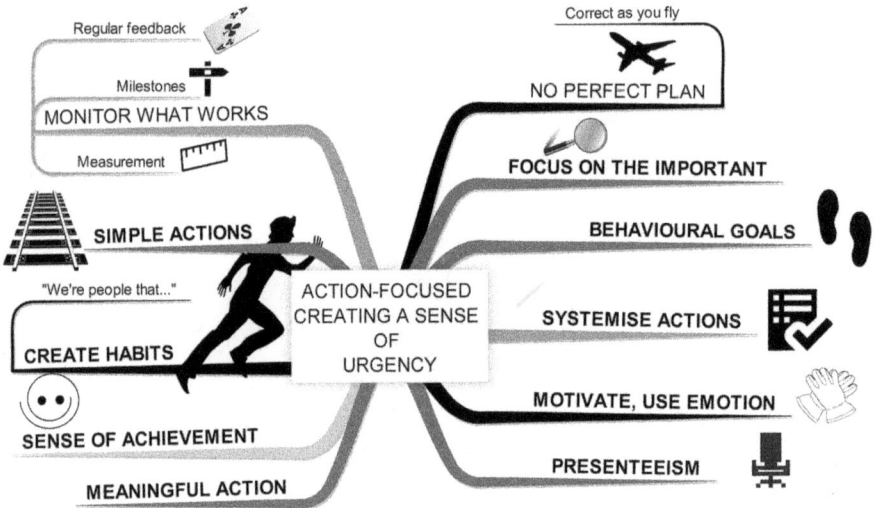

Figure 4: Action-focused – creating a sense of urgency

Scoring yourself on the ROC©

Rate how action-focused people are.

A score of ten would mean that everyone has a sense of urgency, takes action, tracks results and adjusts activity as required. A low rating would indicate much talk, maybe much planning, but no action, or action which has no focus and doesn't reflect your vision or values.

Chapter Twelve

Culture

How we do things round here

"We measure everything at work except what counts. Numbers are comforting – income, expenditure, productivity, engagement, staff turnover – and create an illusion of control. But when we're confronted by spectacular success or failure, everyone from the CEO to the janitor points in the same direction: the culture... The paradox of organisational culture lies in the fact that while it makes a big difference, it is comprised of small actions, habits and choices. The accumulation of these behaviours – coming from everywhere, from the top and the bottom of the hierarchy, from inside and outside of the company itself – creates an organisation's culture."

Margaret Heffernan, *Beyond Measure*

The culture of a company is like a person's personality, and similarly, it will be part of the reason you like or dislike the company.

In a sense, every part of the Responsible Organisation Charter© contributes to culture, particularly the values, which is why it is critical that the organisation's values drive behaviour. The most significant element of culture is how things are done in an organisation. If the culture is not right, you will put at risk all the other aspects of the ROC©. The fundamental principles of culture I believe are: being adaptable – which the Coronavirus pandemic has highlighted as critical for survival – pioneer learning and being collaborative. To paraphrase John Donne:

No business is an island.

Culture is built up over time and reinforced by the stories/legends of the company. This is the sort of company we are; this is the sort of people we are; this is how we do things here. And this is why changing culture can be so hard. As with an individual, it becomes a belief that can be hard to change. People look for evidence that confirms their opinion and ignore anything that doesn't fit.

If an organisation has a history of being very hierarchical, then a move to a more free-thinking culture will not just happen because the CEO says so. Look at the story in the Pioneer Learning chapter (Chapter 14) about Gary Kaplan in the health sector to see how this works in practice. For example, if you rely on a hierarchy, then you are not likely to be very adaptable. You are likely to recruit individuals who align with that culture. Those who are more independent and value autonomy may either adapt to the culture or, more probably, leave. Like any change, people can find it scary, and this is particularly so with culture that has an impact on how you act. People can get very defensive about being asked to change how they behave.

Culture is much more than just words; it is the logo, the dress, the buildings and their layout, the way people act, what is measured, what is praised and rewarded, what is ignored and, most importantly, how people interact.

Your culture includes things like politics, cliques, power struggles and the impact of the culture of the nationalities involved; some countries have more deferential citizens, some more independent, for example. Within a multinational organisation, the divisions in different countries may have different cultures.

Optimising your corporate culture will have an impact on all aspects of your organisation and its success, including:

- Staff engagement
- Recruitment
- Induction
- Customer satisfaction
- Innovation
- Staff morale

The ROC© focuses on three fundamental principles of culture: adaptability, learning and collaboration. These should all be supported by a robust set of values and vision. The principles are all linked by being critical to business success in the current fast-changing environment.

The following parable explores the theme of culture and the impact the principles can have on a business, even if you are using the same business model.

A parable for our time: The burger sellers

Once upon a time, there were four people who had all been franchisees of a very successful burger business. Each decided that they would go out on their own, but they would follow the successful business model they had learnt in the franchise. They were friends and agreed to keep in touch and planned a big get-together to celebrate their first year in business as independents.

Andy managed to get a great spot in the financial district of a city. He had chosen the site after doing extensive research, seeking to learn everything that he could. Not only had Andy looked for the perfect building, which would be easy to convert and cost-effective to run, but he had also stood on the street tracking how many people went past, even noting if they had been to a shop to get their lunch or breakfast. Andy identified burger joints in other financial centres and rang them up to ask them how their business was doing and what tips they could give him. Some information he had to ignore because it didn't fit the business model, like the demand for vegan burgers that some of them had identified and the need to open from 6am to catch those coming into work early.

He talked to people already running businesses in the area to get their ideas and support. He knew from his franchise days that leaflets and offers could work well, and he agreed with several businesses that they would collaborate, promoting each other with joint offers. He wasn't successful with the big gym in the area because they weren't happy that he had enough healthy options on the menu. He would have like to collaborate with them as so many people used it, but he knew that the business model and food options from the franchise he had come from worked well and he wasn't going to change a winning formula.

Once he had opened, Andy was meticulous about tracking his results. He knew which of the businesses he collaborated with generated the most business for him and built on this to do even more with them, starting to run joint events. However, Andy had to refuse when one company wanted him to do some outside catering for an event. It just didn't fit with the business model. Unfortunately, that ended the relationship, as they found another partner. With others, he didn't seem to get much, and he didn't waste his time or money on them. His staff knew he was always keen to find new organisations to collaborate with and would give him suggestions that he would then research to learn if they made sense. One referral was a large charity where they did a very successful collaboration of a joint promotion, which got them donations and him new customers.

Pete was different from Andy and just wanted to get on with it. He found a site quickly and signed the lease. He didn't know much about the area or the business potential, but he knew the model for running the burger joint was proven and the sooner he started, the more money he would make. It looked a pretty good site on a busy road, even though there was limited car parking on the site. He hadn't noticed any on-road parking restrictions and, because he had done no research, didn't realise that a new residents' parking scheme was about to be put in place, which would mean people couldn't stop. When he got into the building, he also found out why it was so cheap; he hadn't bothered with a full survey, and there were a lot of structural problems.

Once he got started, he approached the businesses near him. He also had a big gym close by, and in chatting with them, he realised he could collaborate with them as they had no café but did have a big car park and lots of users. He offered to provide a special healthy menu for them with items even named after the gym that people could order, and he would deliver to the gym, or they could pick up from his site. It meant adapting the business model a bit and the menu. Still, it was a great collaboration that generated lots of repeat and profitable business, particularly the salads and vegan burgers. Pete did get frustrated because he changed the salads each week, and he couldn't work out why some were so much more popular than others. He wanted variety, so he wouldn't just change one ingredient but the whole thing, and sometimes there was lots of waste, though Pete had got a relationship with a local food bank and he donated the food waste to them. The collaboration with them made him feel good, and he knew his staff and customers also appreciated his support of the local charity.

Chloe was as careful as Andy in doing her research before she opened and found an excellent lively town centre with lots of other successful cafés and restaurants. She tracked the footfall, researched the best location and even checked failure rates of businesses in the area. By the time Chloe opened, she was confident she had got the perfect site because of her research. She didn't talk to any of the local businesses, as she didn't want her plans to get out.

From day one, she tracked every element of the business, and when the company didn't seem to be doing as well as she'd liked, she researched why some other companies locally seemed to be successful. She identified some dishes they sold as specialities and adapted her menu to add them. She charged slightly less to attract away their customers. She was approached by some of the local businesses and charities and schools to work together, but that wasn't her style, she wanted to stay focused on creating a successful business. But the culture of the local area was very collaborative, and when the locals heard, they stopped coming, which had a severe impact on her turnover. She also found that her best staff were leaving because they didn't like working for a business that their family and friends thought was unethical.

Maria, the final ex-franchisee, realised that her success would involve using the business model she had learnt as a foundation but adapting to circumstances. She was keen to become part of a local community where she could run a business that would make a difference. She used her contacts, including those on social media, to get ideas of opportunities about where she could start her business, and she learnt of a catering business that had closed due to retirement and was ideal for her new venture. She still did her due diligence, researching the area and standing in the street to observe footfall at different times of the day. She also canvassed the local businesses nearby to get their input and to lay the foundations for future collaborations. Once she had started, it became clear that there were all sorts of opportunities if she could be a bit flexible on what she did. She tracked what worked, testing different elements scientifically to see the impact of changing a single ingredient or a different loyalty package. In the first year, she developed a range of strong relationships with local shops, charities and even the school, which she worked with on fundraising events.

At the end of the year, the four colleagues met to discuss how things had gone. They all assumed that since they were running the same business to the same model their success would be similar; they hadn't allowed for their fundamental differences in culture that each of them brought to their business. As they listened to each other outlining their successes and failures, it became clear that Andy had lost opportunities, particularly with the gym, because he wasn't adaptable. Pete had adapted, but because he didn't learn or have systems in place to track what worked, he didn't make as much as he should. Chloe had lost excellent staff and opportunities that the others had got because of her attitude to collaborating with local businesses and the community.

Only Maria was happy with her progress; she had adapted the business model as needed, learnt what was working and collaborated with the local community so that she felt accepted and had a great team of people working for her. Unlike the others, she thought she had a business that could go far and was already making a difference.

I hope this simple parable illustrates why I think these three elements of culture are so essential and how they work together. You will find more details about how to implement the principles in the coming chapters.

Chapter Thirteen

Adaptable

Creating a flexible culture

"The wise adapt themselves to circumstances, as water moulds itself to the pitcher."

Chinese proverb

What differentiates a successful business is its ability to adapt and change when the unexpected occurs, or circumstances alter. Being adaptable allows you to take advantage of change, seeing it as an opportunity rather than a threat, even if it is something as disastrous as the Coronavirus pandemic.

Being adaptable also means gradually updating rather than staying still. The examples everyone faces these days are technology updates, be they hardware like phones, upgrades of software or artificial intelligence.

If you update and adapt as changes occur, then you keep up smoothly with the latest technology. If you don't adjust, staying with your existing version, when finally you have to update because it fails or is no longer compatible, then the change is much more stressful because it is much larger.

Continuously adapting is much easier than a big change, with the caveat that the adaptation needs to add value. Again, technology illustrates that not every update does so!

"It is not the strongest of the species that survives, nor the most intelligent, but the one most responsive to change."

Charles Darwin

For example, Pfizer found that their drug for heart conditions didn't work. This could have been seen as a disaster, as the drug was to have had an essential strategic role in addressing a vast and profitable market. However, they had the sense to notice a side-effect on erectile dysfunction and acted on that. Instead of focusing on the failure, they adapted and seized the opportunity, investing millions of dollars in promoting and selling Viagra, with great success.

No one can foresee the future, but risk analysis, scenario planning plus open-mindedness and adaptability can mean that blockages and surprises are not fatal. Adaptability is particularly vital in innovation, as is rigorous testing and data collection.

Being adaptable is critical if you are to capitalise on being an organisation that pioneers learning; the learning is worthless if you don't change and adapt.

Adaptable staff

New technologies such as wearables, augmented reality and robots are changing the nature of work. It is becoming more complex and sophisticated, but also increasingly supported by technology.

What the job roles of the future will be is not clear. However, the characteristics of success will be very different. There will be a greater focus on flexibility and adaptability.

The fourth Industrial Revolution will have an impact on everyone, all professions, particularly service jobs in ways it is hard to predict but will inevitably require adaptability.

If most things are failing, look for the few successes, these can be a guide as to how to adapt.

Firstly, the culture must help people to move from seeing change as difficult and threatening to viewing it as exciting and an opportunity.

Being adaptable means being willing to respond to changes in attitude, other cultures, or different perspectives. Generally, adaptability links to a learning culture and curiosity. Everyone can adapt if required and motivated enough, even those who are most stubborn or set in their ways. Generally, humans initially learn to crawl and then they adapt as they learn to walk. You can find examples of how everyone has changed when motivated enough.

Openness to adapting can be encouraged by providing people with opportunities to try new things and different roles, so that they get other perspectives. I have found this will also mean they are likely to be more empathetic and adaptable when required.

Managers and leaders have a critical role in encouraging people to be adaptable and need to start with themselves:
1. Ideas and different perspectives need to be encouraged, not considered stupid so people are scared to speak or question when they don't understand.

2. People need to distinguish between what is actually happening and what they think might be happening. It's important to recognise the difference between fact and speculation. Sometimes, we base our beliefs on our feelings rather than reality, misinterpreting situations, attributing cause and effect to mere coincidence.
3. Do systems and procedures rule? Or do the values of the organisation override them, making people adaptable to the changing circumstances?
4. A manager needs to think that, if they left tomorrow, what would the person who took over do to improve things and then they need to do that now.

Everyone needs to be creative; suggesting improvements, responding to what they have learnt or are now experiencing.

You need to adapt based on reality, not perception. When I was head of sales and marketing at Dyno-Rod, I was told one of the problems was that we had very few commercial customers; we mostly were unblocking drains for consumers. It was an accepted fact and the marketing activity focused on raising the profile in the business sector to get more business customers. However, when I looked at the data, over 50% of the sales came from businesses, we were trying to adapt to address the wrong problem. The issue, in fact, was that we were not getting regular maintenance contracts with companies. What would make the big difference was to adapt what we did to attract regular maintenance contracts, and that became our focus.

Adaptable organisations

An organisation must be flexible at all levels, from individuals to departments to the entire company.

You need the resources to be able to adapt. Any organisation, whatever its size, should identify three sets of human and other resources:

- **The core staff/employees** who are mission-critical and will give the company its corporate culture; plus the equipment and space for them to do it. Staff that are adaptable in what they do. Gripple, whom I discuss more in chapter 17, can call the team from the offices to help if there is a rush in the manufacturing section.
- **Additional resources**; examples would be people who can respond to increased demand and seasonal fluctuations or additional technical or production capacity. The resource might be staff willing to work longer

hours, subcontractors or temporary staff, spare capacity in equipment and space, or a means of adding quickly, such as access to resources in the cloud. A solution that some companies use is zero-hour contracts to provide this additional resource, but this will have an impact on the culture and generally is not associated with a fundamental principle of the ROC© 'treating staff well'.

- **Outsourced activities**, provided by independent sources; these may include some mission-critical operations. I, for example, often write strategic plans for organisations, even though this is mission-critical.

To be versatile, a company needs flexibility in resources and how it balances its workload.

Covid and the international situation has led some companies, such as Gripple, to decide that they want to be less reliant on suppliers and to bring activities such as production of manufacturing machines in-house. Similarly, many organisations are turning to automation due to difficulties in recruitment and rising costs.

Zero-hours contracts

When I originally started this book, I did not think that these three levels of human resources were controversial. However, it is now apparent that many organisations use zero-hours contracts to manage their additional resources, with sometimes a small core set of staff.

If the balance is wrong, then this can have a radical impact on the culture of the organisation, with the temporary staff predominating. With no long-term loyalty in either direction, it is hard to create a values-driven culture. You may score highly on the 'adaptability' section of the ROC©, but at the expense of many other areas.

YOUR ROC© CHALLENGE

Is adaptability spread fairly across your organisation? Or is it those at the bottom of the business who have to do all the adapting?

Adaptable marketing

An adaptable company has brands that are not static but evolving. Consequently, because it is always learning and listening more than it is talking, it can move with agility and adapt. Being adaptable does not mean following every trend and chasing every opportunity – jumping on every shiny new object. Adaptable is within the context of a consistent set of values and clear vision.

Unless you are in touch with your markets and customers and understand their issues and goals, any change is likely to happen in a chance way. You will see something that merely looks good or follow others. But responsible companies evolve with confidence and agility, adapting to the needs of the market. They are continually testing and learning what works.

Hierarchies and the cult of personality

"Rigid hierarchies have their own special vulnerability to error… Errors at higher levels tend to pick up and combine with errors at lower levels, thereby making the resulting problem bigger, harder to comprehend and more prone to escalation."

Karl Weick and Kathleen Sutcliffe, professors at the Stephen M. Ross School of Business at the University of Michigan

Hierarchical organisations struggle to adapt well due to limited feedback from staff, who often tailor their input to suit the boss. Companies led by figures like Trump or Musk are often seen as authoritarian. These types of organisations are characterised by a personality cult that revolves around the leader, who is often seen as a strongman. Such leaders tend to be domineering and uncompromising, and they often use their power to suppress dissent and opposition.

People do not feel encouraged to give ideas or empowered to show initiative. The result is that the complexity of change that we all face is not adequately monitored or considered, as everything comes through the senior people, not those closest to what is happening.

A Case Study: How Hilti adapted to maintain sustainable profit[62]

A story – changing your business model showing ROC© principles
Hilti, a Liechtenstein-based manufacturer of high-end power tools for the construction industry, grew its business through selling high-quality machine tools directly to builders and tradespeople. It had built its success based on the

quality and robustness of its products, meaning not as much maintenance, better safety and a longer life. However, lower-cost competitors increasingly made the business model less profitable and growth hard to find.

Adaptable, innovative growth

Hilti decided to consider the broader market and the needs of the construction companies rather than just the direct users of the tools. It identified that the significant issues for construction companies, rather than the direct users, were the negative impact of broken tools, time lost in maintenance and theft of tools, on achieving the contract deadline for a build and avoiding financial penalties. A contractor makes money by finishing building projects on time. If the required tools aren't available and functioning correctly, the job doesn't get done. Contractors don't make money by owning devices; they make it by using them as efficiently as possible.

Hilti decided to address these needs by moving from being just a manufacturer to providing a service managing its customers' tool inventory. They did this by providing the best tool at the right time and quickly furnishing tool repairs, replacements and upgrades, all for a monthly fee.

The service sector was a very different market for them, as it meant ensuring that they had the right tools at the right place at the right time rather than just selling them. They had to adapt radically to achieve this. But it was very appealing to the construction companies because they lost no downtime, had no upfront investment and had predictable costs. All this allowed Hilti to compete with cheaper alternatives because it was no longer about the price.

Sustainable profit

The new service required a large amount of organisational investment and a significant move into the service sector. But it has led to higher margins, recurring revenues and a more robust niche and product differentiation away from cheaper manufacturers. It capitalises on the robustness of the Hilti products and their reliability.

YOUR ROC© CHALLENGE

What self-limiting boundaries does your organisation have? Would you consider a fundamental change in how you operate?

Managing adaptation

Adaptability is tricky; it's hard to decide when to act and when to wait while weighing potential consequences. COVID forced organisations to adapt, and it's fascinating to see which ones found it challenging to change. Personally, I expanded my market by adapting to online consulting meetings from all over the world at times to suit the client.

Any business consists of different systems, which are like the different parts of the human body: the bones, the muscles, the organs, the nervous system, the brain. If you injure your back, it may make your leg ache and have an impact on your hip, and so on. I regularly go for acupuncture and I am always amazed when the needle goes in and I feel a sensation somewhere different; the therapy is built on the connections across the body and highlights how everything is linked.

Similarly, an organisation has interlinked components, human and non-human, including buildings, organisational structures, processes, policies, values and vision.

Change something – for example, the office layout, so people no longer meet in the kitchen to make drinks – and suddenly the whole human dynamic can change, with reductions in informal communication and cross-departmental sharing. Move to home working and how do you build relationships and water cooler moments?

Some things are internal, but some interact with the external world. As well as the visible components, there are often cultural issues, such as politics and the 'way things are done around here'.

The impact on the 'system' is the first thing to consider when thinking about how and if to adapt. How widespread will the consequences of any adaptation be? Just in a department, across the company or wider? Systems thinking can then help you identify potential impacts to guide you to decide if the adaptation is a good thing.

To make sure that you are adapting wisely, you need to have clear goals and to understand how your business works. By doing so, you can effectively predict the impact of the change. You also need to be a learning organisation, as you will need the feedback and information on how things work. As you adapt, it is critical to get continued feedback in case more adaptation is required.

An organisation that effectively manages to be adaptable will have clear accountabilities so that people take responsibility, recognise the need for change, track the impact and adjust as necessary. The organisation must also encourage and be structured for cooperation and communication, so that the broader consequences of adapting are quickly identified.

All of this means you need a performance management system for the whole business, which isn't just about individual appraisals or departments, but which encourages and rewards company-wide success. Otherwise, a particular department may adapt or resist adapting, as that will make it successful while the company as a whole fails.

Small changes can make big differences

Matthew Syed, in his book *Black Box Thinking*, uses a great example to show that experience is only useful in guiding change if you track the results achieved. He talks about practising golf to improve your technique, and how as you practise on the driving range you adjust to improve your accuracy and the length you are achieving – the process of trial and error. Now imagine practising in the dark so you can't see where the shot goes – you can't improve, as you have no data to establish what result you achieved and thus what should be changed.

Your business can only adapt successfully if it has "the lights turned on", so that you are getting feedback about what is working and what isn't. The more immediate the feedback, the better, the more likely it is to be accurate and the quicker you can adapt.

A successful business empowers staff to adapt if something fails.

Sometimes it isn't obvious what needs changing. A classic example is a website which isn't converting. To improve website conversions, businesses should use science to test different hypotheses using randomised control trials. This involves having a control where the change or activity doesn't happen. By doing this, businesses can get feedback and adapt to get the best results.

Even small adaptations should be tested – marginal gains that add up to significant results. Google[63] in 2010 was carrying out 12,000 randomised control trials every year. These experiments identified what worked and what didn't. For example, they tested forty different shades of blue to use on the toolbar with 2.5% of Gmail users getting each shade and their response tracked. Scientifically, they established the blue to use and, according to Google UK's managing director, Dan Cobley, the colour switch generated an estimated $200 million in additional revenue.

David Brailsford was very successful when he worked with the GB cycling Olympic team. In 2000 they won just one gold medal, but after working with him they won eight in both the 2008 and 2012 Olympics. At the same time, Brailsford was working in road cycling to help the first Briton ever to win the Tour de France in 2012. He accomplished all of this with small adaptations that led to achieving big goals. His focus was not just on the cycling but on every aspect, including the mattresses, the cleanliness of the rooms and even the washing powder used for the kit. He optimised for comfort, sleep, reduced infection, etc. For him, it was about 'marginal gains', breaking down each goal into small steps, measuring the success of each and making adjustments.

YOUR ROC© CHALLENGE

What are your opportunities for marginal gains?

When we work with clients, we use a systemiser to break down critical processes in the business and to identify how they might be improved. Often, we find companies have got into a rut of doing something just because they always have. The habits can cover everything, from when they invoice to how they communicate. Small adaptations can have huge impacts. One web design agency we worked with was having cashflow problems. We suggested they adapt/adjust their payment terms from 30% upfront to 50% upfront and the problem was solved.

As a business, you need to track what you do, the results achieved and test adaptations on an ongoing basis. Adaptation is not a substitute for innovation; adapting the way you work in a market that has been overtaken by technological change is like trying to hold back the ocean with a sandcastle. My great-great-uncle matched carriage horses for a living. He could have started using colour charts to get a perfect match instead of using his eye, but the improvement would have been irrelevant, as everyone was moving to cars.

Similarly, as much as Blockbuster improved its video rental business, it was bound to fail when downloading took over. In contrast, record producers have survived in the world of streaming by adapting, offering short runs for small bands and targeting enthusiasts.

The skill you need to develop is to recognise when an event is temporary and you just need to monitor, when you need to adapt and when the impact is so radical that you need to be innovative.

Think in terms of a favourite piece of clothing; you lose some weight because you have been ill, so the item no longer fits. There is no need to alter it as you expect you will put the weight back on. Alternatively, you go on a diet/change to more healthy eating, lose weight and plan to keep it off, so now it makes sense to alter the item to fit because you love it and want to keep wearing it. You need to adapt it and it will also encourage you to keep the weight off. If, however, you are very successful at weight loss so that now not only have you lost inches but changed shape and now the item can't just be adapted, it no longer suits you, you would either have to innovate and change the item totally or give it away.

Similarly, with business, sometimes you need to wait to see if the change is permanent, but if you think the change is good, adapting may help to make it permanent.

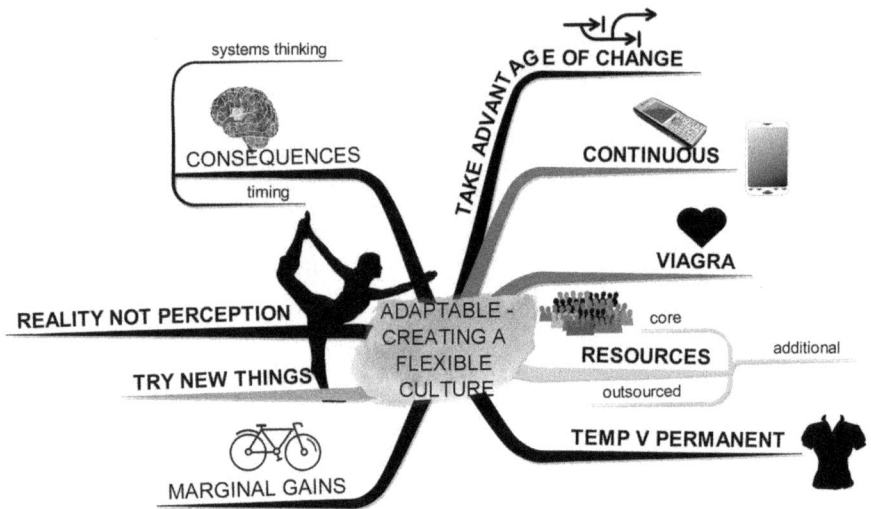

Figure 5: Adaptable – creating a flexible culture

Scoring yourself on the ROC©

Rate how adaptable the people and business are.

A score of ten would mean that the structure and the people adapt well within the context of achieving the broader vision. A low rating would indicate a fixed system and mindset resistant to change.

Chapter Fourteen

Pioneer Learning

Breaking new ground

"Learn from the mistakes of others. You can't live long enough to make them all yourself."

Eleanor Roosevelt

A culture of pioneer learning encourages people to try things and take the initiative to improve all aspects of the business – a learning culture has an impact on every element of the critical factors for success, from customer service to profit.

If you want to grow and thrive in the long term, you need a learning company that learns in 'real time' and that can adapt or innovate as the market changes. Having a culture of continuous learning will help you both attract and retain talented individuals, and also maintain a strong market niche.

It means learning from experience and the outside world as well as traditional learning.

Learning from experience

"We make sure we know where we are going wrong, so we can get things right."[64]

Toto Wolff, executive director, Mercedes F1

Learning from experience means from both successes and mistakes, including small errors. It also means having a culture where people can challenge their bosses and each other, rather than being scared to question those in authority. This is not to create a blame culture but a learning culture.

YOUR ROC© CHALLENGE

When things go wrong, do you ask whose fault it is, or do you ask how we learn from this for the future?

It can be easy to blame the corporate style for stifling learning from experience, particularly hierarchical organisations, but this is not necessarily so. The airline industry and healthcare are both hierarchical but are very different in how they learn, which has had a significant impact on them.

While healthcare professionals will look at medical journals and research papers, they are less willing to learn from their own or more junior staff's experience or even a patient's input. Often an example is dismissed as a one-off occurrence, an act of nature. They need scientific results and a significant volume of tests to be convinced.

In contrast, airline staff are encouraged to feedback from experience, with a reporting procedure designed to encourage people to report issues immediately. Consequently, most one-off failures and problems get reported and addressed, hence the deaths in air flights have proportionately plummeted, when avoidable deaths in healthcare have risen.

Estimates suggest that 1,000 patients needlessly die each month in the UK[65] from poor care, such as inattentive monitoring of the patient's condition, doctors making the wrong diagnosis or patients being prescribed the wrong medicine. In the USA, estimates are that over 400,000 people die annually from avoidable medical mistakes. In comparison, in the airline industry, annual deaths worldwide have fallen from 2,000 in the 1970s to as low as 44 in 2017. In 2022, 158 died but the majority of fatalities occurred in a single aircraft accident in China that claimed the lives of 132 persons.

Matthew Syed in *Black Box Thinking* discusses this in detail and talks about how, "Most large failures have multiple causes, and some of these causes are deeply embedded in organisations... Small failures are the early warning signs that are vital to avoiding catastrophic failure in the future."[66]

Unfortunately, whatever the sector, you need to keep focusing on the ROC© principles, they do not automatically happen. The airline sector, for example, has had a horrific example of not learning from experience. Boeing ignored the small failures pilots were reporting about the Boeing 737 Max, and it led to two major air crashes.

You don't get success without failure and it will often prompt another better route. There is no learning if you ignore or excuse the failure.

However, learning is only worthwhile if it is shared. It is no good a person learning but not sharing. The knowledge must be shared effectively, not just as an academic article as happens in the medical world, but instead, for example, in simple guidelines and checklists that are actionable and easy and quick to understand.

> "Someone who has never made a mistake has never tried anything new."
>
> Einstein

If your business is good at pioneer learning, then it is more likely to attract and retain people with a growth mindset who believe they can learn, get better and fulfil their potential. I hope I will continue to be endlessly curious.

Research indicates that people with a growth mindset[67] stretch themselves, take risks, accept feedback and take the long-term view. They are more successful and will make any business more successful if the environment supports them. In contrast, people with a fixed mindset believe they can't get better; their skills and abilities are fixed and so they take fewer risks and are resistant to learning.

Pioneer learning also means identifying what is working and copying it, learning from good practice.

The need for understanding all the data that a business creates has led to new roles, such as big data analysts or data scientists, but the data is meaningless if you don't learn from it and action that learning.

Learning from the outside world

The world is changing fast, so it is critical to keep up to date.

In 2006,[68] Facebook was in its infancy, X (formerly Twitter) had just launched and most people felt that they needed a camera separate from their phone. In the 2020s, the world is a very different place, and so is business. There is now a whole new set of jobs, which either fit within existing businesses or relate to new sectors.

In 2006, there were no app developers for iPhones or Android. Now, over half the world have smartphones and there are millions of apps. Nor were there cloud computing specialists. Now people use the cloud without thinking, and cloud management, engineering and strategising have become occupations.

Social media managers or their virtual equivalents are now considered essential by most large organisations and social media is a critical part of the marketing mix. Pioneer learning in this area can ensure you keep up with trends and don't miss opportunities or waste money. During the third quarter of 2023, Meta stated that 3.96 billion people were using at least one of the company's core products (Facebook, WhatsApp, Instagram or Messenger) each month.

Similarly, YouTube and TikTok have become essential tools for all businesses, not just large organisations. YouTube, as the second-largest search engine, is too big to ignore. Since launching in 2016, TikTok has skyrocketed as an app with three billion downloads. It is now the sixth most popular social media platform in the world and users spend on average ninety minutes on it every day. Actually run by ByteDance, it has been the most valuable start-up in the world and shattered records for growth.

ByteDance[69] is an inspiring tech giant that has revolutionised the industry with its innovative approach. With 1.9 billion monthly active users in 150 countries and a workforce of over 110,000, ByteDance has recorded an astonishing $58 billion in revenue in 2021. The company's success is driven by its unique innovation strategy, which relies on a shared-service platform (SSP) that centralises various business functions, enabling product teams to focus on serving customer needs and accelerating development and growth. ByteDance's broad exploration, rapid iteration and selective focus have enabled it to launch successful products quickly and terminate non-performing ones just as fast, making it a true inspiration for the tech industry.

Uber is an example of the new business models and opportunities. It was launched in 2009 and was the world's most valuable start-up at over $100 billion before ByteDance. Similarly, self-driving cars will create all sorts of opportunities for businesses who are pioneers in learning; as I age, I'll probably be glad that I'll be able to access a self-driving car.

Potentially, drones will offer fantastic opportunities; I dream of one that will be able to paint high ceilings. Amazon is now using them to deliver parcels and, unfortunately, they had a crucial role in the Hamas attack on Israel in 2023.

Every business needs to know about these developments and learn enough to see if they need to adapt or ignore them.

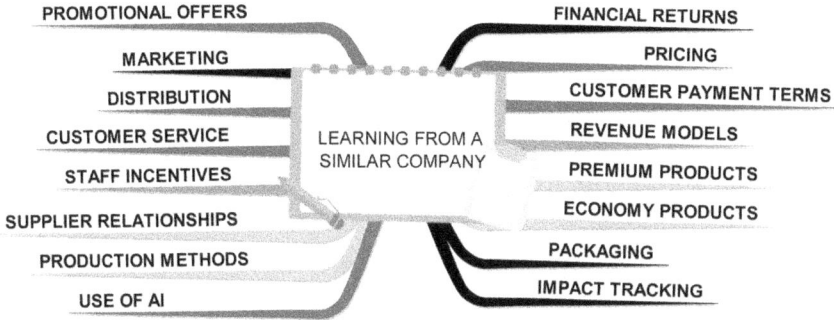

PROMOTIONAL OFFERS		FINANCIAL RETURNS
MARKETING		PRICING
DISTRIBUTION		CUSTOMER PAYMENT TERMS
CUSTOMER SERVICE	LEARNING FROM A	REVENUE MODELS
STAFF INCENTIVES	SIMILAR COMPANY	PREMIUM PRODUCTS
SUPPLIER RELATIONSHIPS		ECONOMY PRODUCTS
PRODUCTION METHODS		PACKAGING
USE OF AI		IMPACT TRACKING

Figure 6: Learning from other companies

Learning from others is particularly important when developing new products and services or entering new markets. It can save lots of wasted time and money if you can find an expert who has walked the same path that you want to take. However, take care that you factor in an understanding of their attitude to life and situation. The information needs to be filtered and considered.

For example, because someone has tried a particular thing which has failed does not mean it will always fail, any more than the opposite. Often, something has worked because of the person involved – they are a great salesman or well-networked locally – where it might not work for someone else. What success means also varies for different people as the story of the lettuces shows (see chapter twenty-four: Financial Success).

Toyota[70] empowers any employee who spots a defect to stop the assembly line. This power is part of the Toyota production system. Anyone can stop production across the plant if there is a problem. Senior management immediately looks to find the answer, assess the error and learn, and this has had a radical impact on Toyota's success. It's not about blame but learning.

Remarkably, this prompted the visiting chief executive of the Virginia Mason Health System,[71] Gary Kaplan, to realise he needed to change the culture in the health system. "If a culture is open and honest about mistakes, the entire system can learn from them. That is the way you gain improvements," says Kaplan.

He returned to the US from Japan and started trying to encourage staff to make a report whenever they spotted an error that could harm patients.

He set up online reporting and a twenty-four-hour hotline for his Patient Safety Alert System™, but the culture of blame and hierarchy was so strong, as is true in many medical settings, that few reports were made. It took courage to change the culture.[72]

Then a mother of four children, Mrs Mary L McClinton, died due to an error when she was mistakenly injected with a toxic antiseptic rather than a harmless dye because three identical stainless steel bowls were side by side. As stated above, deaths from mistakes in healthcare are not uncommon. However, Kaplan responded differently from the general medical norm of seeing it as a one-off error and keeping it quiet. Instead, he made a full and frank apology and said that they would learn from it. In addition, the organisation set aside its dozen or so goals for a single goal: To ensure the safety of our patients through the elimination of avoidable death and injury. Safety remained the single annual organisational goal for three years after Mrs McClinton's death.

It also set up The Mary L McClinton Patient Safety Award. Teams compete for it each year by submitting a rigorous application describing their safety-related work. There is a set of explicit criteria and a scoring legend that a multidisciplinary selection committee uses to score each application. The award goes to the team that demonstrates its safety work is patient-centred, has spread beyond a single work unit, has been sustained over time and been published or presented at regional or national conferences.

A month after Mrs McClinton died, the hospital learnt from a state health regulator that: "Every single hospital that they had surveyed in the month subsequent to Mrs McClinton's death reported that they had had the exact same situation in the procedure room and changed their process as a result of the tragedy." They also learnt that another hospital had a similar error two years earlier and did not have the courage to be transparent about it.

It signalled the culture change and, finally, the reports started being submitted. About a thousand reports a month from 5,500 staff addressed everything from errors that occurred because of colour blindness through to poor writing and processes that failed. Kaplan became CEO of the hospital in 2002, and by 2013 it was ranked one of the safest in the world. Since the new approach, it has seen a 74% reduction in liability insurance premiums – learning had a direct impact on the bottom line.

In Virginia Mason's culture, the system – not an individual – is to blame for errors, and leaders and staff know that they need to work together to made the system safer and better.

Encouraging risk taking

A culture of pioneer learning must involve pushing the boundaries and taking risks. Various companies encourage this in different ways.

Two examples: the first is Zappos, which is a company known for its culture as well as its innovative business model. The company built a fast-growing business because it encourages staff to take risks. They tell their employees to say what they think, even if it is controversial. They make tough decisions without agonising excessively. They encourage people to take smart risks and question actions that are inconsistent with their values. This culture extends to all their relationships, including customers, suppliers and investors whom they commit to "deal fairly with" as long as "everyone remains committed to (their) values." One of Zappos' core values is "we don't take 'no' or 'that'll never work' for an answer because if we had, then Zappos would have never started in the first place."

The other example is a software company in Boston, which gives each team member two 'corporate get-out-of-jail-free' cards each year. The cards allow the holder to take risks and suffer no repercussions for mistakes associated with them. At annual reviews, leaders question their team members if the cards are unused. It is a great way to encourage risk taking and experimentation, and results in a company full of people who are learning from their mistakes and coming up with great ideas.

If people are afraid to make mistakes, they won't try new things and learn, and the results across the business will reflect this. A business needs the intelligence and insights of everyone working in it to maximise its success, particularly the people at the front line.

Failing is an excellent way of learning. There was a famous story about IBM[73] in the 1960s when someone made a decision that lost the company $10 million. The CEO summoned the executive who had made the decision to his office and asked him why he thought he was there. The man replied he assumed it was to fire him. Tom Watson, the CEO responded, "Fire you? Of course not, I just spent $10 million educating you."

Integral to this is admitting that you have failed, and this is psychologically difficult, especially the more time and investment you have given the project or work that has failed. Technically, this is known as cognitive dissonance –

as humans, we want the outside world to fit our beliefs and, if it doesn't, we are more likely to distrust the evidence than change our beliefs.

Matthew Syed includes extreme examples in his book *Black Box Thinking*, where he shows how the UK police and justice system will argue against conclusive proof that someone is innocent once they have decided they are guilty. Even DNA data is ignored or explained away. Andrew Malkinson, fifty-seven, was convicted in 2004 of a rape in Greater Manchester, despite there being no DNA evidence and other clear evidence of his innocence. Having spent almost two decades trying to convince the authorities he was innocent, the court of appeal overturned his conviction in 2023 after fresh DNA testing linked another man to the crime.

The ignoring of evidence is generally not conscious; it is just that, for our mental health, we need to make the outside reality fit with our internal beliefs.

"To perceive the world differently, we must be willing to change our belief systems, let the past slip away, expand our sense of now, and dissolve the fear in our minds."
Professor William James, American psychologist and philosopher

In business, I tend to call it the 'Emperor's New Clothes Syndrome', where someone falls in love with a theory or new product or a way of working and, whatever the evidence, they keep going.

"Failure is simply the opportunity to begin again, this time more intelligently."
Henry Ford

Henry Ford had two firms go bust before he set up the Ford Motor Company. He learnt about pricing and quality from the first two failures and did not define himself by them, feel ashamed or try to hide them.

A culture that encourages people to learn from mistakes will be more successful and have fewer errors because it will learn. If people are scared and hide their mistakes, the performance can never get better. A learning culture accepts that people's beliefs can be challenged and failure does not define people.

Unfortunately, often the more senior you are, the harder it can be to recognise mistakes. The desire to reframe reality to make it fit with beliefs is overwhelming. If you change reality, this means that you can't learn its lessons. Not learning from experience can be a reason for getting an external perspective, though even that will be ignored if the belief is strong enough.

I spent some time coming up with the phrase 'pioneer learning', as it combines the willingness to benchmark and learn from others with the desire to take risks, try new things; pioneer learning from what works and what doesn't. It is not just learning from courses or books.

Learning from others

Most companies do some learning by looking at what is happening in the market, setting objectives and making some judgements based on what they achieve against those objectives. This learning tends to be ad hoc and doesn't automatically lead to the more fundamental knowledge that comes from questioning the basic operating principles, policies and procedures.

Just copying the best practice of another organisation without it relating to your vision and values will lead to confusion and undermine other critical parts of the Responsible Organisation Charter©.

For example, assume you find a company that seems to be successful because it motivates its sales staff by offering the use of a Ferrari for the top performer. You have learnt that this works, as it is the only change the firm made in the sales division to move it from poor to good sales. Obviously, it would be a good idea to implement it... but would it? Not if your values are about being environmentally friendly, your culture is to encourage collaboration and joint working, and you think the lifetime value of a customer is more important than the initial order.

Scientific testing

An attitude of pioneer learning means thinking like a scientist about lots of things that happen in the company, from ideas for innovation to marketing or production.

Pioneer learning means understanding what you want to test – your hypothesis – then observing what happens, recording the results, reviewing the results and then deciding how to proceed. If this is the norm, then the organisation will take learning for granted, it will be accepted as the way they are.

Lean manufacturing, lean start-up and much marketing good practice rests on continually testing what works and what doesn't. The aim is to move from assumptions to facts. There is a danger that we can make false deductions that an action or change caused a particular result, so it is critical that learning is structured rather than random.

All learning should include questions, theories and tests, followed by feedback and reflection, which may prompt more questions. Much of business is more art than science, but this is the one case where the scientific method is appropriate – techniques such as using control groups as in a scientific experiment, and meticulously recording results for both.

For example, imagine you want to understand if your customer values a new feature of your service. Traditionally, companies would often develop it, maybe test it with customers and then add it to the service and wait to see if sales go up. If they did, then it was a success, and if they went down, it was a failure.

This conclusion is a logical fallacy; just because one thing has happened, it does not mean it has caused the outcome. Some companies have tried to address this by asking customers, did you buy this because of the new feature? However, the customer will have made the decision based on a range of factors, so probably can't answer accurately.

To be a pioneer learning organisation, you need to undertake a split-test experiment. Split your efforts, adding the feature and promoting it to a random part of the market and having a control group who receive a similar level of promotion but not the new feature, so that the only difference is the feature. Then you can compare sales results and customer satisfaction to see if the new feature did have an impact on sales and please the customer. In a recession, sales might even decline with or without the new feature, but they might decrease less with the new feature. This testing allows learning, rather than guessing.

When you are launching or upgrading a new service, this learning can save a fortune. As practically everyone I know will testify, modern mobile phones have numerous features that we never use and don't want. Yet, engineers spend money and time developing them and adding them.

Microsoft has usability testing labs where developers can observe real users using their programmes. The key feature of being a learning organisation is that developers should not feel defensive about the issues with their coding. Instead, they should learn from what they observe and realise that success lies in finding solutions to the problems users encounter.

Benchmarking

Benchmarking can be exceptional learning, as it uses other people's experience to help set standards for your company. There are four recognised types of benchmarking:

- **Internal:** This is a comparison among similar operations within your organisation.
- **Competitive:** This is a comparison with the best of your direct competitors.
- **Functional:** This is a comparison of methods of companies with similar processes in the same function outside your industry.
- **Generic process:** This is a comparison of work processes of others who have innovative, exemplar work processes.

It should make sense to learn from the experiences of others rather than having to try everything new for yourself, making every mistake for yourself as well.

However, there are problems with benchmarking. One of the problems with benchmarking is that it can be subjective. It can be done in many ways and the answers will depend on how and by whom.

To be done effectively, it requires a significant investment of resources, including the time of senior managers. There can also be issues in terms of sharing information with competitors. Successful benchmarking requires trust between partners – it can be a beneficial outcome from collaboration. It is also going to be more successful if the partners involved share the same values and market.

When you are looking at cost reduction, the temptation is to only benchmark certain areas, often based on those seen as most critical or in need. However, there is a risk of missing out on valuable learning opportunities, which could have a greater impact on departments that seem to be performing well.

Some years ago, the University of Michigan undertook a study across a variety of industries. They approached the senior managers and CEOs and asked them to indicate the relative status of their company:

- 90% of the respondents thought their companies were above the average for the industry;
- 50% put themselves in the top quartile;
- 25% claimed to be among the top 10%.

These percentages are statistically impossible, but for many admitting or believing they are not top/good would be unthinkable. Recognise you are less than perfect, and then you need to change, and change is frightening, so it is easier to deny the need for change or the need to learn from others.

YOUR ROC© CHALLENGE

Where do you think you rank in your sector? What evidence do you have for this belief?

Unfortunately, not all benchmarking activities will challenge the perceptions of a company (or the management), particularly if you don't benchmark the areas where you feel you are performing above average.

Much benchmarking is an assessment at a given point in time and this is also dangerous – in a fast-moving world, things may have moved on before you even get the report.

Useful benchmarking is a continuous activity, not a one-off project. The learning can be applied and then new comparisons made to assess the impact and achieve further learning.

Another problem is that benchmarking can be antithetical to pioneer learning, as it can encourage you to copy what others seem to be doing well – not very groundbreaking.

Also, it can be challenging to work out precisely what has worked and why, and whether it will work in your company. Some things that work in one company could destroy another.

Superficial comparisons without in-depth understanding can be very dangerous. I call it the chocolate cake syndrome – you can see someone else makes a great chocolate cake, but unless you know the full recipe that achieved it, the quality of the products and equipment used, then you can't replicate it. Things work in context rather than in isolation, so to model the success of another company, it is essential to understand everything that contributed to that success.

If benchmarking merely gives you your relative position in a league table within your sector, it does not provide learning, as you will not know why you are where you are, what makes you better than some or worse than others.

Benchmarking is, however, useful for scoring and to identify areas of concern, notably in commercial issues. For example, there are benchmark percentages for direct food and labour costs in sectors like catering that are useful in setting operating parameters.

Benchmarking can also be useful for identifying what you might want to improve in an industry sector so that you have a focus for your innovation.

Informal learning

Learning from market need and how individual customers use your product or service can also help you identify a niche or significant market opportunities. One classic example in the mobile phone market is the Nokia 1100 – a story of an unexpected market, which I relate in chapter twenty-one: Life Changing.

YOUR ROC© CHALLENGE

Do you encourage staff to learn from customers? Do you really know how your customers use your products and services?

If a company has an environment of pioneer learning, then something called the reticular activating system kicks in. This system is a function of your brain that means you notice what you have identified as valuable to you out of the millions of things you see and hear each day.

For example, when you decide to buy a particular make of car, and you suddenly start noticing them everywhere – that is the reticular activating system kicking in.

If you ask staff, "If you see customers using our products in an unusual or unexpected way then let us know," then they will be looking for such incidents. Viagra is a great example. As discussed, it was initially developed for angina chest pains, but patients noticed side effects, which have made it a best seller when it didn't work for angina!

Learning happens all the time if you are open to it. Learning from someone who has solved the same problem or addressed the same issue as you is less formal than benchmarking but very useful. When I take clients to meet similar companies, I create a mind-map of all the issues that we might be able to find out about from them to act as an aide-memoire.

Pioneer learning is the easiest it has ever been. You can learn from local companies or a company doing the same thing anywhere in the world, particularly with modern technology.

Learning is all about the questions you ask.

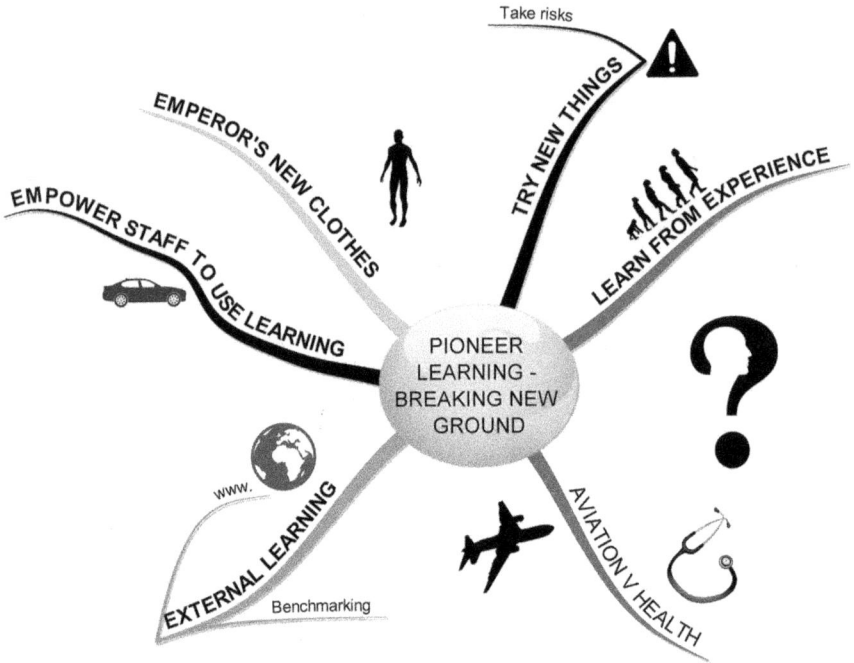

Figure 7: Pioneer Learning – breaking new ground

Scoring yourself on the ROC©

Rate how much you use pioneer learning as an organisation.

A score of ten would mean that everyone learns, and it is accepted as usual and exciting. A low score would suggest a lack of learning, either from what happens, what others are doing or how your industry is changing.

WINNING BY BEING GOOD

Chapter Fifteen

Collaborative

1+1=3

"The thinking and behaviour of almost all business managers in today's world reflects a world view grounded in the whole-equals-sum-of-the-parts and win-lose competitive principles of nineteenth-century mechanics, not the systemic, cooperative, win-win symbiotic principles of twenty-first-century cosmology and life sciences."[74]

H. Thomas Johnson, an accountant and professor,
Portland State University

My initial interest in collaboration was sparked when I was approached by a charity that had been told by a key stakeholder that it had to collaborate with a neighbouring charity doing similar work. They had been talking fruitlessly for seven months – could I help?

Interested in a challenge, I looked at articles and books on collaboration and found there was a lot on how to collaborate and nothing on why.

Collaboration is one of the best ways to scale up a business. A business can't do everything well, so collaboration allows a company to focus on what it does well and capitalise on the skills of others. It can also be useful to collaborate with your customer. Successful collaborations require clarity of purpose – why you are doing it, clear milestones, break clauses and a shared view of the world.

However, the real reason collaboration is growing exponentially is the speed of change and innovation, particularly in digital technology. To keep up with the needs of customers and the opportunities provided by new technologies requires new forms of collaboration, particularly given the speed at which innovation and disruption are taking place.

And this technology has also made collaboration in practical terms much more straightforward. Global platforms for crowdsourcing are emerging so anyone anywhere can work together; all of which means that talent, culture and organisational forms need to be rethought in the context of collaboration.

The pandemic showed the power of collaboration, as across the world, universities like Oxford, large pharmaceutical companies such as AstraZeneca, BioNTech, Moderna and Pfizer and the WHO and individual governments worked together to develop and deliver life-saving vaccines at speed and scale.

> "(The internet can) mobilise and coordinate the intelligence, experience, skills, wisdom and imagination of humanity."
>
> Pierre Levy, French Philosopher

To be collaborative you not only need to have a culture that will help you collaborate and can fit with your fellow collaborator(s), but you also need to have clear objectives, which both sides understand. In the case of the charities I mentioned, when I used a specialised decision-making tool, which I had developed, it became clear that the other charity had no goals that collaboration could help them achieve.

YOUR ROC© CHALLENGE

Would you want to collaborate with your organisation if you weren't part of it? Would you trust it?

Why the ability to collaborate is becoming more and more important

Collaboration can be internal or external. There are various levels of cooperation, from ad hoc activities or only working together on a project, through to setting up a joint venture or merging. Identifying an unmet need in your market or identifying how somebody could use your product in other markets is an ideal opportunity for collaboration.

> "Mergers are out, alliances are in."
>
> Gary Wilson, chairman of Northwest Airlines

Collaboration has always been essential. Nobody, be they a sole trader through to the largest company on the planet, should try to do everything themselves and it is more critical now than at any time before.

"No matter how capable its employees may be, no company can match the world's rapid innovation and improvement with internal resources alone."

Koch[75]

There are several reasons for this. The supply chain tends to be getting longer, involving:
- more people with differing job titles and perspectives;
- more businesses or divisions within a company;
- various processes and technologies;
- places potentially all over the world, even if sometimes they are in the same company.

Everyone has different viewpoints, but is mutually dependent and has to collaborate for success, or the chain breaks down.

Pressure on costs and the need to do more with less means companies must collaborate to increase productivity, efficiency and eliminate waste.

More and more workplaces are virtual, with fewer people working together in the same place and often a mix of time zones, cultures and languages, so the skills of successful collaboration are critical.

As businesses niche and specialise, they need to find collaborators who can support the things within the business that no longer are core and could/have to be done elsewhere.

Collaboration is becoming an incredibly powerful marketing tool – again driven by niching. Joint working means leads can be shared so that the potential customer gets the best fit. Also, 20% of customers want a premium product and collaboration can often be the best way to add and enhance a product or service to develop one. No company can be expert in every new technology but may need to access it, particularly for innovation.

The constantly evolving and complex world demands innovative and cooperative approaches to achieve success.

Collaborating to innovate

Collaboration is one of the most powerful ways to innovate. For example, Procter & Gamble[76] (P&G) have conducted research that shows that the majority of P&G's most profitable innovations have come either from internal collaboration across business units or from external cooperation with outside researchers.

When P&G's innovation success rate got stuck at 35% and the company was in trouble, the company's new CEO, AG Lafley, recognised that collaboration would be vital in helping P&G recover its value and improve its innovation performance. He launched a programme called 'Connect and Develop' and proclaimed that he was determined to make P&G known as the company that "collaborates, inside and out, better than any other company in the world."

Determined to encourage both kinds of collaboration, Lafley established twenty cross-functional "communities of practice" within P&G and declared that 50% of P&G's products, ideas and technologies would be developed by external sources. These collaboration initiatives paid off handsomely. P&G improved its research and development (R&D) productivity by nearly 60%, more than doubled its innovation success rate and lowered its cost of innovation. In eight years, R&D investment as a percentage of sales fell from 4.8% to 3.4%.

In 2021, a major Prosperity Partnership[77] was awarded by the Engineering and Physical Sciences Research Council (EPSRC) to a £5.6 million collaboration between Procter & Gamble, Durham University and Imperial College as part of the UK government's innovation strategy. The goal is to develop new, breakthrough scientific tools to reinvent the performance of everyday products, such as laundry detergents and household cleaners, addressing the complex environmental challenges. These tools will accelerate development of sustainable alternatives to current products and household tasks as part of P&G's commitment to make sustainable choices easier for the five billion consumers it serves every day.

New digital technology can allow collaboration between locations and departments that would have previously been impossible. By bringing together different groups, it facilitates more innovation and creative problem solving with differing perspectives. Used correctly, it can empower employees and make them feel more involved.

Collaboration, in the form of crowdfunding, also has an essential role in funding innovation. The Ocean Cleanup, which is developing an ocean-going plastic waste collecting device, initially crowdfunded £70,000, which allowed it to get seventy scientists and engineers to collaborate to create a 528-page feasibility study. This success then supported a second crowdfunding campaign that, within 100 days, had raised £1.5 million from donors across

160 countries. This campaign attracted support from wealthy people and now the amount raised has grown to £30 million.

Case study: Collaboration between business and learning to power a green innovation

A story – how BA is collaborating

British Airways, to celebrate their centenary in 2019, worked with Cranfield University to launch a challenge called BA 2119 to encourage academics to develop a sustainable fuel of the future.

The airline posed the challenge to British universities to develop a new or different pathway to achieve global leadership in the development of sustainable aviation fuels. Specifically, they asked for solutions to how to power a long-haul flight for at least five hours and produce zero CO_2 emissions.

Eleven universities submitted entries, which were judged on a combination of criteria, including carbon reduction potential, level of innovation, value to the UK economy and feasibility to implement.

University College London won with their solution to turn household waste into jet fuel. They proposed building plants to convert the waste near landfill sites across the country. The team estimated that this could deliver 3.5 million tonnes of jet fuel annually by 2050, resulting in negative emissions and the equivalent of taking more than 5.5 million cars off the road every year.

IAG, British Airways' parent company, is investing a total of $400m on alternative sustainable fuel development over twenty years.

British Airways is the first airline in Europe to build a plant to convert organic household waste into sustainable aviation fuel. They are collaborating with their partner, Velocys. They are also the first to bring together academics from British universities to work alongside them to create new solutions to this critical environmental issue.

Collaboration for growth

There are three ways to grow: organically, take-over, or collaboration.

Collaboration is one of only three ways to build a business. The others are organic growth, which is slow and capital intensive, or takeovers, which have a lousy track record. It is estimated that 80% of acquisitions never earn what they cost. For example,[78] when Daimler-Benz and Chrysler merged at the cost of $36 billion, the cultures didn't work, the merger failed and Chrysler ended up being sold for $7.4 billion after nine years, a loss of $28+ billion in shareholder value.

The foundations of successful collaboration

> "Trust always affects outcomes – speed and cost. When trust goes up, speed will also go up, and costs will go down. When trust goes down, speed will also go down, and costs go up."
>
> Stephen Covey[79]

All collaboration is built on mutual trust and respect, and works best with structured communication. It also works best when values and culture align.

Using the analogy of personal relationships, my experience has been that too often companies rush from an initial meeting to discussing marriage or living together, without really going through a courtship stage to establish that the basic understanding is there. Also, sometimes the collaboration won't work because one business is a 'loner', so however collaborative the culture of the other company, the relationship will be unsatisfactory.

Similarly, if a business with a manufacturing outlook wants to collaborate with a company that is sales focused then the likely significant differences in style and culture need to be considered very early on to see if a successful collaboration is possible. It can be a very potent collaboration but how to address the differences needs to be agreed upfront. Suppose companies have had a long relationship, maybe as customer and supplier, and share a common passion, mutual respect and understanding. In that case, the collaboration stands much more chance of success.

Like values, collaborative words are not enough; they need to translate into behaviours. The British Standard on collaboration, BS 1100, has some useful tools and guidance on creating strong collaborations. For example, they have a trust tool you can download from the inspire2aspire website. The tool allows you to map how much information you are happy to share with collaborators such as customer lists, suppliers' deals, business plans and strategies. The strength of your relationship will be reflected in the depth of the information that you are willing to share.

Anther practical indicator of the strength of a relationship is needing only a short and straightforward legal agreement that reflects a level of trust and understanding.

Successful collaborations are built on shared values, views of the world and attitudes to critical issues, such as customer service and the guarantees that support it.

A good place for potential collaborators to start might be to map together how they sit on the Responsible Organisation Charter© and talk through their positions on each of the principles.

Examples of collaboration

Morgan

Morgan, one of Britain's oldest carmakers, uses collaboration to improve its products, to reinforce its marketing messages and generate income.

Morgan has a niche of creating bespoke cars, still made by hand, and it has only recently stopped using whole trees to make its wooden frames for the cars. Each car is unique in that it is built to the customer's specific requirements. Genuinely environmentally friendly, each car literally rolls down the Malvern Hills during its production. They are hand-painted and hand-trimmed with real leather. Morgan offers over 40,000 colour options and over 500 different leathers.

It has collaborated with BMW for its retro-styled roadster using a three-litre straight-six turbocharged engine. Going forward, it is looking to collaborate with suppliers that can provide the elements for an electric vehicle, which fits their brand. This collaborative strategy has allowed it to keep up with market demands without the development costs or time delay of doing it in-house. Financially, it has worked; it announced almost doubled profits from its previous year, a record high in its 110th year of manufacture, 2019.

While it only sells about 700 cars per year, its historic factory in Malvern attracts more than 30,000 enthusiasts each year who spend money in their shop, buying collaborators' or partners' products, as they call them, which reinforce the brand.

As well as collaborations for leather goods, driving jackets, items to keep you warm in an open-top car and men's fragrance, they also jointly design watches with Christopher Ward, stressing the 'materials and the beautiful way each watch is put together' and the watches obviously have leather straps.

They have collaborated on several watch collections. One notable example is the C3 Morgan Chronograph, which features a silver-white dial inspired by Morgan car dashboards, a tachymeter, and the Morgan wings emblem. The watches are intended to provide a perfect blend of precision timekeeping and vintage motorsport styling, to appeal to Morgan enthusiasts who might not be able to afford the cars.

Nike

Business for Innovative Climate and Energy Policy (BICEP) was set up in 2008 with Nike as one of its founding members. It is a collaboration of companies sharing information on sustainability and committed to lowering the risks of global climate change by developing new ideas to reduce greenhouse gases and increase the use of renewable energy. It now has forty-eight members.

Nike also launched the Green Xchange with corporate partners to create a web-based marketplace to help collaboration, sharing intellectual property to increase innovation and new sustainable business models.

WWF

World Wildlife Fund (WWF) has looked to work with business to save the world's biodiversity. Rather than trying to collaborate across thousands of companies, it has identified the top ones making the most impact. So, for example, it looks to bring together the market leaders in palm oil, forestry, coffee, etc. It has shown that competitors can agree on shared standards, which protect the environment when they collaborate.

Multiple partner collaborations

Personally, one of the most potent collaborations that I was involved with included young people, charities, community representatives, social enterprises, a council (both staff and councillors) and a university. Over the years, a core group worked with me to create a youth centre and sports facilities in an impoverished area. The commitment to the end result was what made the collaboration work and it took years to come to fruition. They all shared the vision of getting young people off the streets and bringing different communities together.

Together, we developed the strategy and then we brought in the potential users to help us improve the design. I remember vividly one of the key things these young people from poor communities wanted: nice toilets. Think about school toilets and most youth club buildings where the opposite is the case. They wanted to feel good, they deserved nice adult toilets and they got them.

The power of the collaboration was the expertise and the perspectives from many different areas, which ensured it could address the complex needs of the community it was to serve.

Virtual Collaborators

"We are living in the middle of a remarkable increase in our ability to share, to cooperate with one another, and to take collective action, all outside the framework of traditional institutions and organisations."

Clay Shirky, NYU Professor

Crowdsourcing, not to be confused with crowdfunding, is a brilliant way of collaborating. It generally involves innovation, but TopCoder[80] was developed to identify great computer programmers. Problem statements are placed on the website and people compete with each other to solve them. The reason it works is because people want to be part of the community and it has many collaborative aspects.

It is a great way to solve problems; for example, a doctor wanted to analyse a massive amount of genetic information about the immune system. The community of 400,000 computer programmers was approached, and over 100 responded from nearly seventy countries. Sixteen of the entries outperformed the algorithm then used by the National Institutes of Health. It took two weeks and cost just $6,000.

Crowdsourcing can also be used to encourage collaboration by consumers to identify what charitable causes they want a company to support. Companies like Pepsi have got consumers to vote on what charities they fund on their website.

But it can also be a lot less sophisticated; each time I shopped at Waitrose, I used to get a green token to vote for which local charity I wanted them to give their monthly donation to, and I dropped it in a bucket to show my choice.

A Case Study: collaborating with competitors and charities to increase efficiency[81]

A story – how Google and Intel worked together

In 2007, Google and Intel came together intending to drive the IT industry towards greater efficiency regarding consumer energy use. After adding Microsoft, HP and WWF to the collaboration, they launched the Climate Savers Computing Initiative (CSCI). It built on the decade-long WWF programme to get major companies to set targets and reduce emissions, which had already resulted in a reduction of more than 50 million metric tonnes of CO_2.

CSCI became a non-profit group with nearly 700 companies as members, including 70-90% of the IT industry globally for hardware and software. CSCI worked with consumers and conservation organisations around the world to share knowledge and innovative tools to improve the efficiency of their products, thereby reducing emissions.

The collaboration has resulted in benefits for businesses, consumers and the environment. Across the industry, it has meant that companies developing energy-saving innovations are not penalised for their investment with a potential increase in costs.

Customers don't have to choose between sustainable and unsustainable options, since all the options can be energy efficient, helping to reduce their power bills and their carbon footprint.

A study commissioned by Natural Logic found that after just three years, annual CO_2 emissions from IT equipment had decreased by 32-36 million metric tonnes worldwide. It also identified that more energy-efficient products were replacing old parts. Its goal is to reduce global emissions from computers by 54 million tonnes per year, equivalent to the annual output of 11 million cars or 10–20 coal-fired power plants.

This collaboration has solved shared problems in a way that would have been impossible for a single business. It is now part of The Green

Grid (TGG), a non-profit industry consortium of end-users, policymakers, technology providers, facility architects and utility companies, collaborating to improve the resource efficiency of data centres. It has more than 175 member companies. Green Grid is the first industry initiative chartered to take a holistic view of the ICT ecosystem, with a focus on addressing the pressing issues facing data centre users. In 2019, TGG was acquired as an affiliate member of the Information Technology Industry Council (ITI), which is a premier trade association that works to advance public policies for the tech sector.

Internal collaboration

Collaboration is generally perceived as an activity that is external to a business, but it is also critical within. Often different departments and divisions compete for resources, success and influence, rather than collaborating to achieve more success for the whole company; classic internal politics.

Internally, collaboration is particularly useful for finding a solution where everyone feels that they have won. Frequently, people think that their specific concern is too significant to be compromised and, generally, they know most about it, so it is challenging to disagree. All insights and perspectives are valuable, so finding a solution through collaboration is essential in integrating all the aspects. It also helps people to understand each other and learn from each other. Knowledge sharing is critical and part of being a learning organisation.

For successful collaboration within a company, people need to come together because they all share a common vision and values. It can facilitate exponential growth and harness people's talents and energies to the full. It is truly inspirational when it works and creates a robust team culture.

Simple things like the physical layout of the workspace can help and hinder collaboration and interdepartmental working. If different departments meet in the kitchen and share a room for lunch, they are more likely to get to know each other. Similarly, open-plan spaces can encourage more joint working, as people overhear others' issues and can share their experience. The move to more hybrid working will have inevitably had an impact on how collaboration works.

A healthy corporate culture has people sharing ideas and learning from each other; everyone feeling united and collaborating.

Avoiding corporate loneliness

There is much talk about the dreadful impact of loneliness in our society; how it can cause mental health problems, such as depression and people feeling isolated.

I think that organisations can also suffer from loneliness; this is most obvious with those run by solopreneurs, but it even happens with larger ones. People in larger businesses can feel isolated if the culture does not encourage internal or external collaboration. If competition is the norm and people don't trust each other, then you will create a company full of lonely people and a company that has no friends. Beware.

Humans are social beings; we need to collaborate to succeed.

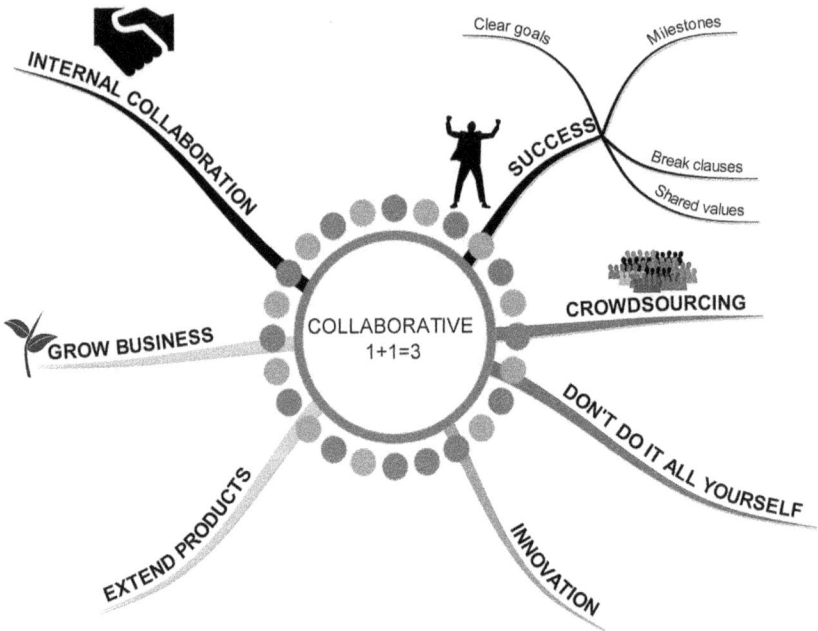

Clear goals · Milestones · Break clauses · Shared values · SUCCESS · INTERNAL COLLABORATION · CROWDSOURCING · GROW BUSINESS · COLLABORATIVE 1+1=3 · DON'T DO IT ALL YOURSELF · EXTEND PRODUCTS · INNOVATION

Figure 8: Collaborative – 1+1=3

Scoring yourself on the ROC©

Rate how collaborative you are.

A score of ten would mean that you have active collaborations in place

WINNING BY BEING GOOD

that are working and always consider collaboration as an option when developing strategies and plans. A low score would indicate a lack of trust or thinking about collaboration.

Chapter Sixteen

Relationships

Developing a win-win attitude

A company cannot thrive unless it is good at relationships. Generally, for many businesses, the customer relationship is the main focus in terms of relationships, as it appears to be the most important. However, a map of stakeholders for any organisation will identify a multitude of relationships that are critical to sustainable success.

There are direct relationships with staff, customers, suppliers, sponsored organisations and investors, and the less formal ones with potential customers and staff, neighbours and the local community. Then there are the critical influencers like politicians and parts of the public sector, such as officials who oversee regulations applying to the company, and national and international bodies such as trade associations, trade unions and other governments. Social media influencers and campaigning bodies and the media may not be seen as stakeholders, however, they also need to be considered in relationship management if only in terms of monitoring their comments.

Stakeholder management

Traditionally, stakeholder management has focused on mapping and then managing communications rather than thinking about the relationships as 'relationships', which need managing in a similar way to customer or staff relationships. It is useful to think about all relationships in terms of a sales funnel where you take someone who doesn't know you or like you and convert them into a raving fan.

Too often, stakeholder management is seen as the preserve of the PR department or is even outsourced to a PR agency; indeed, I have advised many companies and government in this area as a consultant.

Also, the stakeholder map can be too simplistic, as each individual may have multiple roles, some of which are voluntary and chosen and some of which are not. I might not have chosen a business as a neighbour if it opened after I moved there. It can be the case that, as the principal employer or monopolistic supplier, I also don't willingly choose them as my employer or supplier. The basis of the relationship will have an impact on how it is managed and also the potential quality of the relationship that can be achieved. Generally, a forced marriage is less successful than two people who meet, get to know each other and fall in love without any compulsion!

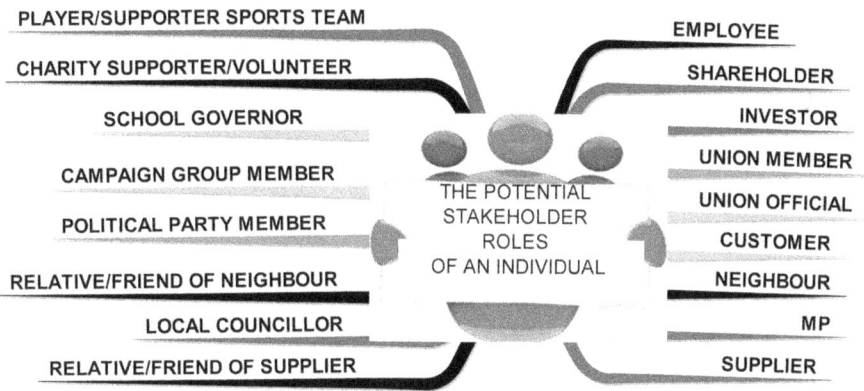

PLAYER/SUPPORTER SPORTS TEAM
CHARITY SUPPORTER/VOLUNTEER
SCHOOL GOVERNOR
CAMPAIGN GROUP MEMBER
POLITICAL PARTY MEMBER
RELATIVE/FRIEND OF NEIGHBOUR
LOCAL COUNCILLOR
RELATIVE/FRIEND OF SUPPLIER

THE POTENTIAL STAKEHOLDER ROLES OF AN INDIVIDUAL

EMPLOYEE
SHAREHOLDER
INVESTOR
UNION MEMBER
UNION OFFICIAL
CUSTOMER
NEIGHBOUR
MP
SUPPLIER

Figure 9: An example of the potential stakeholder roles an individual could have

As Figure 9 illustrates, one person may have multiple relationships with an organisation and their view will be coloured by how the organisation acts across all these relationships.

Many sponsorship deals are prompted by these complex relationships, as is much charitable giving. I could have made this map even more complicated by including personal relationships in more detail, such as parenthood, siblings and friends, both real and virtual on social media. Just as economics includes the multiplier effect where spending one pound can have a significant impact depending on how it is respent, the direct effect on an individual/organisation that is your immediate stakeholder ripples out. People tell/share their experiences directly and online. The impact of this is most evident with customers, particularly when they have complaints, but it is also true in many other contexts; we live by telling stories. Managing these stories is the critical role of stakeholder management.

YOUR ROC© CHALLENGE

What stories are your stakeholders telling about your organisation? Do you even know?

Learning from charities

In my experience, good charities are better at understanding the complexity of building stakeholder relationships than businesses. They are better for two reasons.

Firstly, charities tend to have a more extensive set of organisations or people that are involved in their financial success: donors, both corporate and individual; funders, such as trusts and the lottery; statutory bodies, such as the government and local councils where the relationship might be a commercial contract or could be about social impact.

Secondly, they are better at consciously thinking about and using all four levels of communication from platitudes to emotions. We feel closest to those people or organisations where we share an emotional connection. It is challenging to have a close relationship with a person or business where you only know facts about them, not what is important to them.

The four levels of communication

1. Platitudes: The simple ways we initially make contact with people, usually greetings, and the awareness raising publicity that businesses and charities undertake.
2. Facts: Building knowledge and understanding through the exchange of facts.
3. Opinions: For organisations, opinions are what the organisation holds to be important, such as its values, beliefs and purpose.
4. Emotions: Creating an emotional connection generally through showing how the organisation changes the world and often through how it promotes itself – people can be very passionate about brands.

Unfortunately, many businesses do not manage to communicate either their opinions or their emotions and this means that the closest connections don't happen. Where they do, people can become passionate advocates of the company; take Apple users who see themselves as creative and 'out there' or

Volvo drivers who share their passion for safety or Nike who have supported controversial athletes.

In the Responsible Organisation Charter©, the complexities of the customer relationship in terms of the service or product offering are captured in chapter twenty: Product Offering; specifically, how you change lives and in how you provide a consistent and reliable service or product.

This section on relationships focuses on the broader set of stakeholders, specifically addressing staff, suppliers and the wider community and being a good citizen.

As a business, your values and your vision will be the basis of your appeal and communications with all your stakeholders. If you achieve this, you will get the same benefits as good charities:

- public admiration and advocates that promote and support you;
- motivated, loyal and dedicated employees;
- satisfaction from knowing you are changing the world.

Why win-win

I get very depressed when I come across businesses that operate their relationships on the assumption that for someone to win someone else has to lose. For example, to provide good value for customers, it is necessary to drive down prices for suppliers, or to achieve strong shareholder return, staff have to earn less.

Firstly, this logic is flawed. For example, motivated staff who are fairly rewarded are much more productive and should increase shareholder value, a win-win. Secondly, in the world today, everyone is too well connected for bad treatment not to be exposed.

When factories in Dhaka collapsed in 2013, killing and injuring over 1000 workers who were making items for the western market, consumers and retailers knew within minutes and there was outrage. Even if the moral imperative was not overwhelming, the business imperative is obvious; consumers know and care. They will vote with their feet and tell their friends and the world through social media.

Healthy relationships are based on not seeing the other party as just a means to an end but in seeing them as an end in their own right with an essential role in the wider company. Part of the larger system that is the organisation.

Chapter Seventeen

Treat Staff Well

Creating a happy workforce

"The baseline rewards must be sufficient. Basic compensation should be adequate and fair – particularly compared with people doing similar work for similar organisations. Your (organisation) must be a congenial place to work. And the people … must have autonomy, they must have the opportunity to pursue mastery (get better at something that matters), and their daily duties must relate to a larger purpose. If these elements are in place, the best strategy is to provide a sense of urgency and significance – and then get out of the way."

Daniel Pink,
author of *Drive: The surprising truth about what motivates us*

Estimates are that up to 80% of people who are employed are doing jobs that don't inspire or engage them. This appalling statistic means that four-fifths of employees are not working to their full capacity, nor are they working in their passion.

AON Hewitt's[82] research indicates:

"A disengaged employee costs an organisation an average of $10,000 in profit annually; as a result, organisations with high engagement are 78% more productive and 40% more profitable."

They also found that companies with high engagement scores were more resilient to economic problems when the 2008 crash happened.

Think of the massive impact on the economy and wider society, as well as on the staff, if people were fulfilled and inspired at work because they worked for companies that believed *Being Good* and acting 'responsibly' would help them 'win'. Staff will be more productive and creative. They will inspire their families, acting as role models to their children. The businesses they work for will be happier, more successful, with more satisfied customers, who will know they can trust in what they receive.

The most visible parts of your business are the people who represent your company. While this chapter is about directly employed staff, it is also true of any people that act for you, for example, a virtual phone answering service or any other outsourced service, such as security, as well as whom you choose to collaborate with.

Every other element of the Responsible Organisation Charter© needs people to make it happen, and every other part of the Responsible Organisation Charter© feeds into treating staff well.

The most basic tenet in treating staff well is ensuring that they are physically safe. While this tends to be a given in the developed world, it may not be accurate for any third world subcontractors. Even in the developed world, people get injured or even die at work. During Covid-19 this was particularly true. For example, the pandemic presented the health and care sector with unprecedented challenges that exacerbated existing problems in the workforce. In its written evidence, the NHS Confederation[83] outlined a range of factors resulting from the pandemic that had an impact on the mental well-being of the workforce. They included:

- Increased workload and working hours.
- Intensity of working in different/COVID-19-safe environment.
- The impact of the heroes narrative, i.e., not recognising the human impact.
- Emotional strain from seeing large numbers of patients dying.
- Anxiety about their own and loved ones' health and infection risk.
- Guilt experienced by those shielding or working from home.
- Worries about being able to provide high-quality care.

NHS providers also emphasised that Covid-19 had exacerbated existing challenges around workforce, burnout and resilience.

Obviously, people dealing with the public can get verbal abuse or worse, particularly teachers, nurses and retail staff. In addition, retail staff increasingly face dangers from shoplifters.

However, treating staff well is much more than adhering to health and safety, employment and equality legislation and using rhetoric such as saying you regard people as your best asset. It includes creating a culture that helps staff to thrive, is fair and constructive, and provides meaningful ways for people to contribute. It is about actions, not words. It is now recognised that it is also important to endeavour to provide an environment where everyone whatever their unique needs should be able to thrive; this might be disability, neurodivergence or a particular style of working, for whatever reason. Currently, there are many articles in the press about the differences between Gen Z and baby boomers in the workplace, often suggesting this is a problem. In fact, differing perspectives need to be celebrated and accommodated in a winning organisation.

Staff rely on their employer for ongoing job security and it seems unlikely that a person on a zero-hour contract when they have no commitment from the company for ongoing work will feel engaged and committed. Similarly, low salary employers will struggle to get full commitment as people will potentially need to look for other ways to make money. In 2023, one in four people in the UK have a job on the side, mostly because of financial pressures, and in the US, 70% of Gen Z have a side hustle.

The level of care, trust and engagement of your staff will have an impact on both the short-term bottom line but also the long-term success of your business. What can seem to be a way of being a good employer can backfire if the broader context is ignored.

For example, when Tesco asked the staff at a store local to me about their bonus, they ignored the fact that it was shortly after making other staff who had been colleagues redundant. The bonus was not seen as motivational but rather as insensitive and uncaring.

> "As I grow older, I pay less attention to what men say, I just watch what they do."
>
> Andrew Carnegie

Often when a company is facing significant issues, the senior management ignores the staff and don't get their input, even though it is their future as well. It is vital to notice anxiety amongst staff and let them communicate explicitly, encouraging their honest feedback.

YOUR ROC© CHALLENGE

Would you recommend your child or a friend to apply for a job in your company? Why or why not?

More than money

Treating staff well does not equate to high salaries – money is not enough if the environment for staff is inadequate. Many lower salary firms can be good places to work if they treat their staff well and many high salary places are not good employers.

However, money can be an issue. Generally, the average annual pay rise equates to about 1-3% in additional spending power for an existing employee in the UK. But if an employee leaves a company generally, they can look forward to a 10-20% increase in salary and sometimes as much as 50%. Inflation, particularly in fuel prices, and rising interest rates can make even the most loyal member of staff consider moving for more money. Fulfilment is not more important than keeping your home if you can't afford your mortgage on your current salary.

YOUR ROC© CHALLENGE

Are you punishing loyalty to your firm and rewarding people who move regularly?

The absurdity of this is apparent when you think about the costs of employee turnover, including interviewing, hiring, training, reduced productivity. At the same time, new people have to learn the job, and there are lost opportunity costs and team disruption. Estimates have been made that the costs of replacing employees are:
* For entry-level employees between 30% and 50% of their annual salary.
* For mid-level employees upwards of 150% of their annual salary.
* For high-level or highly specialised employees, about 400% of their annual salary.

Keys to employee engagement

The four enablers of employee engagement[84] are:
1. **Visible leadership** – Empowering leaders who tell a compelling story about the organisation, where it has come from and where it is going.

2. **Engaging managers** – Managers who support their staff, give them focus and responsibility, treat them as individuals, coach, support, stretch them and praise them.
3. **Empowered employees** – Staff at all levels who are given a voice to either reinforce or challenge existing views and are valued as critical in finding solutions.
4. **Values which translate to behaviours** – Organisational integrity with values written on the walls reflecting day-to-day actions with no gap between 'what I say and what I do'.

Supporting these enablers and turning them into reality is likely to be a range of policies, procedures and training programmes, such as:

- Vision and values induction and awareness sessions.
- Management and leadership development and training.
- Clearly defined performance and promotion criteria.
- Staff development training.
- Volunteering opportunities.
- Time allowance to develop personal projects and ideas.

However, more important than these is a culture that empowers people in the workplace. When I have done work with teams, identifying their values as a team and how they can be turned into reality, morale has rocketed.

> "The person who sweeps the floor should choose the broom… We need to get rid of rules – real and imagined – and encourage independent thinking."
>
> Howard Behar, former president of Starbucks[85]

Management style

How your staff feel that they are treated will depend to some extent on how your company feels to be part of – most companies are a mix of these different styles:

Autocratic

Often a small business owner tends to be autocratic but charismatic leaders of more substantial businesses may also share this tendency – decisions are made by the top, be it a person or a small team, with little or no consultation. This can lead to dramatic sudden swings in an organisation; witness Elon Musk changing the working style and the name of Twitter to X.

Charities can also have this style. Critical strategic decisions are made by the charity trustees who do not work in the organisation and staff can feel they have little influence – even those in senior managerial positions. With this style of management, engagement can be maximised by ensuring staff feel they are listened to by the decision-makers and can have an influence.

Bureaucratic

Many charities can be bureaucratic, as can be public sector organisations or those who employ staff with public sector backgrounds – rules are the critical thing and what people follow. This style tends to stifle initiative but can ensure consistency. It is vital that the practices are continually reviewed to keep them up to date and people feel that they can influence the rules.

Technocratic

Many tech companies have a technocratic management style where computers or experts dominate – the machines may even monitor behaviour, or the finance people have control, as they control the numbers. In these companies, there is often a need to provide managers with people skills training or put in place staff who will look after the human aspects that keep staff engaged. As I write this book, it is still early days to assess the impact of artificial intelligence (AI) on how it feels to work in an organisation. Amusingly, AI in the form of Bing suggests this will be the impact:

> "Artificial intelligence (AI) has the potential to revolutionize the way organizations operate and make decisions. According to a report by McKinsey,[86] AI could enable automation of up to 70% of business activities, across almost all occupations, between now and 2030, adding trillions of dollars in value to the global economy. Senior leaders will also need to commit to building the required roles, skills and capabilities (now and for the future), so they can continually test and learn with AI and stay ahead of competitors. The situation is evolving rapidly, and there is no one right answer to the question of how to successfully roll out AI in the organization – business context matters.
>
> AI can improve organizational decision making, boost innovation

and productivity, and help organizations think bigger.[87] Businesses expect AI to have a positive impact on growth, productivity, innovation and job creation in their country and industry.[88] However, the implementation of AI requires organizations to think broadly about how it could affect their day-to-day operations and their people. Employees and managers should have a clear understanding of AI's strengths and weaknesses and how the use of the technology is linked to the organization's strategic objectives."

At the end of the information, Bing put, "Let's chat," but it didn't feel like an opportunity to catch up with a friend, even though their answer had been useful. I suspect, similarly, in an organisation, AI may let people delegate tedious tasks just as the introduction of spreadsheets automated counting, but just as I don't feel affectionate towards Excel, similarly, AI will not add to the atmosphere.

Joint working

The joint working management style is particularly prevalent in Germany, where workers and managers work together to run businesses. It should really engage staff, but sometimes staff fear that the consultation will only be on minor issues, not important ones. To be successful, everyone needs to feel that the consultation is 'real' and this will mean showing its impact on critical issues. It also means that staff need to be kept well informed.

Employee ownership

John Lewis is the most prominent example of employee ownership in the UK. Generally, in employee ownership, there are managers, but staff have varying levels of influence through their share ownership depending on the company. The ownership structure does not ensure that staff feel engaged, so it cannot be assumed that they are, just because they own part of the company. Often one of the styles listed above applies as well, with the issues identified.

Gripple,[89] a Sheffield company local to me, require their staff to buy shares. It is a 100% employee-owned company, meaning all staff own shares in the business. This has been the case since 1994 and was formalised in 2011, with the establishment of GLIDE, an employee-owned company that represents all the shareholder members who work in its partner companies. GLIDE is an acronym of: 'Growth Led Innovation Driven Employee Company Limited'.

The impact of this is a shared focus on success and they explain the impact:

> "Having engaged owners across every department of the business gives a commitment to the quality of our product and service offering that our competitors simply can't match. We're all working towards the same targets, and we all benefit when we meet them, so the focus on maintaining high standards is consistent at all levels."

Co-operative

Co-ops are based on the theory of joint management by everyone, with everyone having equal rights and involvement in decision making. Collective decision making can be slow and there can be problems of management by committee. As with employee ownership, this is not a magic bullet to staff engagement as the case study below shows, so it is critical to check staff feel involved.

Case Study: The impact of an egalitarian organisation structure

A story – how being equal made everyone unhappy

The organisational structure can have unexpected impacts on staff relationships. I consulted to an equal pay collective that was the unhappiest organisation I have ever come across. It worked in the housing sector and everyone from the architects and finance director to the receptionists were on the same salary.

Many of the staff resented the receptionists for earning so much for a generally lower paid role; the receptionists were aware of this and felt unhappy and defensive but could not leave as they were receiving so much more than they could get elsewhere. The more senior people worked less because they thought they didn't earn enough to work full time.

Because of the structure, no one felt that they had the right to praise or criticise and so people thought it was fundamentally unfair, as whatever you did, you got the same reward and no recognition. In essence, the structure had the opposite impact of what was intended.

Unfortunately no one felt able to change the structure and eventually it closed.

YOUR ROC© CHALLENGE

When did you last say well done or get praised yourself?

Empowering staff

Empowering organisations should reduce the direct day-to-day role of management. Nordstrom,[90] a US retailer, believes in empowering frontline team members to use their judgement in serving customers. For a long time, their one-page employee handbook read as follows:

> WELCOME TO NORDSTROM
>
> We're glad to have you with our company. Our number one goal is to provide outstanding customer service. Set both your personal and professional goals high. We have great confidence in your ability to achieve them.
>
> Nordstrom Rules: Rule #1: Use good judgement in all situations. There will be no additional rules.
>
> Please feel free to ask your department manager, store manager, or division general manager any question at any time.

This has been expanded but "use good judgement" still comes first. I would recommend their "code of business conduct and ethics",[91] which addresses lots of the issues of being a value-driven organisation.

Inspiration

To attract and retain the staff you want, you need to inspire them with a story of where the business is going and how they can be part of it, and how you change lives.

Without meaning, work is just a series of tasks and the time spent at work a period to be endured while waiting for the day to end, the weekend to arrive and to get a break for a holiday.

Staff need to be as committed to the business cause as a volunteer is to the charity they support. Whatever you believe, like a volunteer, staff can leave, particularly in sectors where demand exceeds supply like hospitality, healthcare, engineering or technology. If staff stay under sufferance, they are a threat to the business.

Job satisfaction ranks highest on most surveys of what people want from work. Here are other examples of what people want from their work:

- Personal freedom and autonomy in determining how they will do their job.
- The respect of colleagues and being part of a team that is passionate to achieve results, and is unified around a common goal and set of values.
- Opportunities to learn something new and build skills in something worthwhile.
- Challenging opportunities, including chances to try and fail.
- Helping other people and a feeling of purpose, which preferably is within the business but could also be achieved by activities such as volunteering.
- Clear results, such as completing a project or producing a distinct output – the happiest people I have ever worked with were drain cleaners who responded to the emergency call for a blocked drain, got the satisfaction of solving the problem, thanks and good financial rewards.
- To feel involved, valued and consulted.
- Very important: appreciation and recognition – sometimes all it takes is a thank you.

Money ranks pretty low down the list of important things – it is necessary but not necessarily motivational. However, the lack of it can be demotivating, causing resentment, low morale, poor customer service and a lack of effort and productivity. Even more demotivating is apparent unfairness in reward, where similar jobs get different bonuses, or the difference between the top and bottom is vast.

A motivational environment

There are all sorts of ways of providing an environment that motivates staff. For example, Charles Handy in his book *Inside Organizations* describes one company that gets the people in the factory who make a machine tool to deliver it in person to the customer. While this disrupts the workflow in the factory, the motivational effect on the staff more than compensates and it provides a better service for the customer who gets an expert at the installation. Also, the team are always striving to ensure the equipment is perfect since they will be there at installation.

Staff can be motivated by their working environment and the facilities, such as an onsite gym, pleasant rest areas, etc. Staff events, such as parties and trips, can build a feeling of being part of a team. Others go further, with employee ownership schemes that mean everyone 'owns' part of the company – a real team.

Gripple exemplifies all these elements, with a great manufacturing environment where the shop floor is as pleasant as the offices. In the agricultural section, for example, there is a huge cow with staff handprints from the team all over it.

There are relaxing staff rest areas with games, computers, papers, food and drink facilities and a restaurant cooking and preparing fresh food that can be delivered to staff at the different sites and simply paid for and ordered on terminals in each location. Their staff turnover is very low and their success is very high. Interestingly, they do not have defined job descriptions and, when an order needs to get out, everyone will lend a hand if it is required.

Some benefits can cost little or nothing. Ben & Jerry's ice cream, for example, allowed each employee three free pints of ice cream a day and free massages. The impact was high, showing a company that cared, but the cost to the company was relatively low.

The physical space where people work is important and can alter how they interact and feel. Noise, light, the quality of every aspect from the toilets to the coffee machines will, in practical terms, indicate how much an organisation cares about its staff.

When I visit a restaurant I don't know, I will go to the toilet and, if it is run down or dirty, I probably won't stop. Similarly, a good employer doesn't let staff use old, broken or dirty facilities or even worse have one standard for the senior team and another for junior staff.

The physical environment can even have an impact on how much staff feel that they are heard and appreciated. If you as a manager generally talk to staff from behind your desk with a computer monitor, which takes your attention, and is also in the way, this can give out a message that you, the manager, are not listening or caring. Add in answering the phone if it rings and you are, in practical terms, showing how much you care. Merely moving the monitor or meeting somewhere else and diverting calls will improve how much people feel heard. Gripple has its board table in an open-plan office as it is employee owned and this is a physical manifestation of the openness – there are no secrets.

Many businesses provide volunteering opportunities for staff. Volunteering opportunities help with recruitment and retention. People also want diverse career experience and enjoy the possibilities that volunteering gives, particularly if they can support a cause they feel passionately about. NatWest encouraged its staff to take on voluntary national roles in JCI UK, the international personal development organisation. This support was a win-win, with staff feeling supported while improving their leadership skills, which helped the bank.

Other employers allow staff to feel more in control of their own time. Many larger companies let staff spend part of their working week on their own projects. For more than seventy years, 3M's unique 15% culture has encouraged employees to set aside a portion of their work time to proactively cultivate and pursue innovative ideas that excite them. In 1948, long before Google and Hewlett Packard, they started giving staff 15% of their time to explore their own projects. The most famous output of this was the Post-it note, but many of 3M's 22,800 patents are derived from its 15% programme. The programme is available to everyone, not just researchers. Remarkably, even after many years, in 2014, 3M was still selling $1 billion worth of Post-it notes a year.

The foundation of 3M's collaborative and organisational culture[92] started with William McKnight, who served as president and then chairman of the board for thirty-seven years. He was a visionary in his perspective on people and innovation: "Hire good people and leave them alone. Delegate responsibility and encourage men and women to exercise their initiative. Management that is destructively critical when mistakes are made kills initiative. And it's essential that we have many people with initiative if we are to continue to grow," said McKnight. 3M actively seeks to promote McKnight's principles in its ongoing efforts to solve tomorrow's problems.

Google introduced the 20% Project to get new ideas for the company. This scheme resulted in Gmail, Google Earth and Gmail Labs. There are conflicting reports about whether it is still going.

LinkedIn[93] has had [in]cubator, a programme that gives engineers time away from their regular work to work on their own product ideas; Apple Blue Sky allows some workers to spend a few weeks on pet projects; and Microsoft created The Garage, space for employees to build their products using Microsoft resources.

As well as keeping staff motivated, the personal time to think and do projects can help in attracting people when all else is equal in recruitment.

When MTV surveyed millennials on their work habits, they found that 78% believe it's important to have a side project that could become a different career. Companies of all types, from investment banks to advertising firms, are now known to be explicitly tolerant of side-entrepreneurship.

Here are three different models that have been tried:[94]

Huge, an ad agency, gets workers to pitch ideas for start-ups and the winners get funding and office space, with the agency acting as an incubator with a part share in it. "It's also a way to test ideas that could be good for clients," says Huge CEO Aaron Shapiro.

Adaptive Path, a product design company, lets staff have ownership of any idea they come up with on their job, to incentivise them to be as creative as possible in solving problems for clients.

Ideo, a design firm, regularly puts out calls for 'white space projects'. These can be tasks as varied as event planning or data visualisation, which employees from any department can join in on. "They're meant to get people involved in what they're passionate about, not necessarily their core competency," says Ideo partner Duane Bray. "If they have a hobby on the side, it's a way to bring that skill to work."

In reality, everyone would like a job where they are recognised and respected as an individual, their needs are met and where they are working in their passion – successful companies facilitate this.

Finding staff that fit your values

Your staff will have a view of your company before they even apply for a job. They may have come across it as a customer or in the traditional or social media. When they see your ad for the job, that will also set the tone – is it formal or chatty? What characteristics or skills do you focus on?

Your job titles also indicate the culture of the business, as does the pay, other benefits and the working style. Developing a list of questions that lets you assess a candidate's cultural fit with your business can help to avoid hiring anyone who may not hold the same core beliefs. Sharing your values with the outside world can also help attract people who support and share your values.

Iceland, the UK-based supermarket chain, is known for its unique and inclusive culture that values diversity and teamwork. According to their website,[95] they are "one big team" of "a diverse group of people who get stuck in to help each other out." They have a strong focus on employee engagement and have developed a culture that encourages employees to be proud of their work and to make a difference.

WINNING BY BEING GOOD

"Be part of our family
We're different. We care.
We're not a dull, stuffy corporate.
We're Iceland."

Heading on Iceland careers page

Iceland Foods recruit happy people who will bring their personality to work. They are clear about their culture:

"OUR CULTURE

There's no other business quite like Iceland. No frills. No fuss. Lots of fun. Very down to earth. And big on personality and getting things done.

The pace here is lightning quick. We value our colleagues. And together we work hard, challenge the norm and go the extra mile to make our customers happy. That's what it's like to work here every day. Iceland isn't for everyone. It can be challenging and the pressure can be on. But if you're friendly, customer focused and always positive, Iceland is for you!"

A TV programme on Iceland Foods showed how they tested the ability of candidates to stay positive under stress during the recruitment process and how seriously they take the recruitment of every member of staff, even a part-time shop assistant or driver. A part-time driver, for example, needed to do a group exercise to see how they would work in a team under stress. Each candidate had a member of staff to observe how they behaved; those shortlisted then had an interview and a test delivery run in an area they didn't know to make it even more stressful. Iceland Foods invest a lot in getting the right staff who will thrive in the culture, give excellent service and consequently stay, even though the wages are not high. Iceland has been voted the best firm to work for against many more glamorous firms.

Getting this fit correct does not only mean that you will provide a more consistent experience across your company, but you will also have happier staff, as they will be working with like-minded people. The fit should not be confused with hiring all the same type of people – this is about having a similar attitude, e.g. fun, formal, relaxed, etc. I explain this more in the section below about Kolbe.

Who you recruit and how you treat them will be fundamental to what sort of company you have.

> "Recruitment is the hardest part of running a business."
>
> Bob Brown, inspire2aspire

Bob Brown, who is both my husband and business partner, believes people are not rigorous enough in their recruitment processes, frequently recruiting a person like themselves, which is often the wrong thing to do.

Everyone is more productive if they are working in their passion. A manager should be delegating what is not their passion to someone who does have that activity as a passion, be it selling, bookkeeping, cleaning or serving customers. It is improbable that someone the same as you will love doing something you hate.

A Case Study: Using innovation to recruit

A story – getting creative in recruiting

Legacy Sport is a social enterprise that focuses on improving the health and fitness of children under eleven. They are growing very fast and needed to hire a new instructor. They received lots of CVs and interviewed quite a few people but could not find the right mix of attitude and skills to provide the inclusive and practical fitness training that they wanted.

As their consultants, we discussed possible solutions – short term, they managed to increase the hours of an existing member of staff, but if they were to continue to expand, they needed to find a way of successfully recruiting.

First, we defined what attitude was needed. Candidates should have a desire to help every child reach their fitness potential. Consequently, a critical ability was an understanding of body language, so that an instructor would notice if any children were turned off/disengaged and would, therefore, be able to respond and ensure that everyone was included immediately. Providing engagement for all is a fundamental part of the Legacy Sport ethos, ensuring all children in a class are engaged, rather than the memories some of us have of school sports where it was the fit and athletic children who got to do all the fun things.

We played around with where we might find the right sort of people – where you fish affects who you catch. However, a shortage of candidates was not the problem – how to screen and find the right ones was. So, we came up with the idea of using short videos of sports sessions with children for candidates to review and comment on with the aim to screen out candidates who couldn't interpret body language and didn't realise when a session needed adjusting. This screening should reduce the numbers to interview and improve the fit with the corporate culture.

Help with recruiting

I first took a Kolbe A™ test over twenty years ago and I still use the results now. Kolbe tests the way you instinctively solve problems and respond to situations.

We ask the people we work with to do the test so that our relationship with them can be more successful. After a Kolbe profile, we'll know if people like lots of facts, structure or a more relaxed, quick, creative style. It helps people working together to understand each other. It's great for teams such as boards or project teams and people in partnerships, particularly living and working together couples. It reduces the frustration of working with people who have a different style, as you can understand it.

When recruiting, it gives an objective way of identifying who will fit well in your team so that you get the best balance.

What we like about Kolbe is that it celebrates who you are, gives tips on coping with things that you're less good at and doesn't expect you to change.

IQ tests tell you what you can do. Personality tests tell you what you want to do... the Kolbe A™ Index measures what you WILL or WON'T do. It is a quick and easy thirty-six-question instrument, giving you a greater understanding of your instincts and allowing you to begin the process of maximising your potential. Kolbe as a conative test helps you get the right person in the right job so you can provide a reliable service and be consistent with every aspect supplied to the highest quality.

Choosing the right employees is critical and, if your business is changing, the types of staff needed will also change.

Some employees know how to bring new products and services to life and are happy working in a changing environment, while others like stability and are great at selling and maintaining existing customers and products. Putting someone in a role that instinctively doesn't suit them is a recipe for failure when, in another position, they might be a great success. Getting the role which naturally fits is why we like to use Kolbe profiling rather than a personality test affected by emotion.

But emotional engagement is essential, which is why job descriptions should ideally also include the social purpose of your company, how you change the world. If someone isn't excited and inspired by what you want to achieve, then they are not likely to be right for your organisation.

The person or the role

When you are recruiting or appointing someone to a role, the role may need to be adapted to play to the strengths of the new person performing the function. The previous incumbent might have been great at administration; the new person isn't but fits the role in every other way. It is important not to set them up to fail by giving them tasks that are not their passion when, with a small change, they could be doing a great job, which they can feel passionate about.

Just because, in the past, a job included specific roles and responsibilities, it is not sensible to assume that it has to continue in the same structure. If you don't feel you can do this, then there is no point appointing the person. This is why it is essential to understand what is critical to a role and what is just nice to have. Losing a potentially great member of staff because you can't adapt shows why adaptability is included as a vital principle of the ROC©.

YOUR ROC© CHALLENGE

Do you really know what your staff feel about your company? How engaged they are? How do you know?

Like other parts of the ROC©, it is crucial to track the health of your staff relationships, using a mix of quantitative and qualitative methods, such as staff turnover figures and staff surveys. Probably more than any other area, it can vary from person to person and change very quickly. It is almost certainly the most complex area to track, as individuals are affected by non-work events and may not always want to share their issues. It is critical to have a culture where people feel able to be honest, so you can understand what the problem is.

Good staff relationships are fundamental to good business

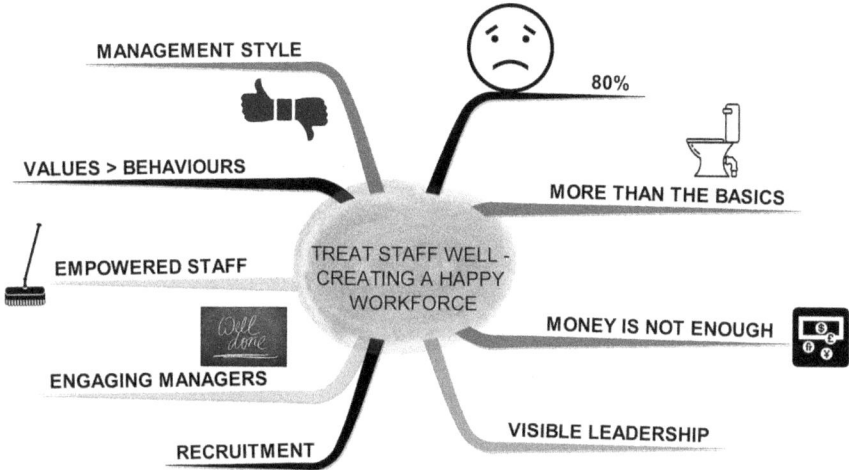

Figure 10: Treat Staff Well – creating a happy workforce

Scoring yourself on the ROC©

Rate how well you treat staff.

A score of ten would mean that everyone feels empowered whatever their role; staff are engaged and happy. A low rating would indicate a workplace with low productivity, disengaged workers and high staff turnover.

Chapter Eighteen

Treat Suppliers Fairly

For good value and service

"The greatest change in corporate culture – and the way business is being conducted – may be the accelerated growth of relationships based... on partnership."

Peter F. Drucker

Writing this chapter has been one of the most challenging parts of writing this book. I didn't expect it to be, but as I tried to find companies who treat their suppliers well, I saw too many stories of businesses that appear elsewhere in the book as examples of good practice that then fall down in this area. Unfortunately, companies that would never dream of treating staff or customers poorly seem to treat their suppliers as though they should be grateful for the honour of selling to them.

But just as bullying staff may achieve short-term results but creates lots of problems in the long term, so does bullying suppliers. Instead of suppliers looking for ways to help your business grow because they feel it will result in joint success, they will look for ways to take shortcuts or make a quick profit from you. Badly treated suppliers won't trust that they will benefit from any growth they help to achieve or ideas they provide if you are the sort of company that always seems to be looking for the cheapest supplier rather than showing loyalty.

Similarly, as with employees, if supplier relationships and communications focus on rules, regulations and warnings, then you will stifle all their initiative and the supplier will do just what is required and no more. Often, contracts and purchasing guidelines seem to be all one-way requirements and penalties for the supplier. A balanced contract is not about accepting poor behaviour from a supplier; it's about understanding that a good relationship has shared commitments.

Every business has suppliers and they have a critical and often ignored role in many of the principles of the Responsible Organisation Charter©, particularly underpinning growth. It is very short-sighted and self-defeating to ignore their role.

Your suppliers are as much stakeholders in your business as your customers, employees and investors. The way that you treat them will say as much about your company as the way you treat any other stakeholder, and getting it wrong can lead to highly public problems.

Supply chains are getting longer and more complicated. Even small companies can be reliant on global relationships with suppliers and these can often be critical.

During the time I have been writing this book, supply chains have become more complex. The UK has exited the European Union, the long-term stance of the USA in the world is uncertain and relations with Russia have broken down. Relations with China have deteriorated, and a pandemic has had an impact on trade. These world events will potentially affect many supply chains and existing relationships in ways that it is difficult to predict, so it is a particularly appropriate time to be thinking about supplier relationships.

There are also additional pressures like the Modern Slavery Act in the UK. It requires large goods and services firms to display a 'slavery and human trafficking statement' online, indicating the steps that they have taken to ensure their supply chain is slavery-free.

Successful supplier relationships

"Our supplier partners are our allies in serving the interests of our other stakeholders in bringing to market the safest, highest quality products available. We treat them with respect, fairness and integrity at all times."

Whole Foods

Intelligent companies treat their suppliers like partners.

"There are three vital steps to partnering success:
1. Determine what it is you need but don't have: customers, capital, special expertise, products, production capacity, or distribution channels,

2. Determine who has what you need,
3. Ask them for it, but first make sure you have something they want or need (this last point is the most important)."

Curtis E. Sahakian, managing director,

Corporate Partnering Institute

In an ideal world, suppliers should be partners who can help you grow and provide a consistent service to your customers. They should offer competitive high-quality products and services that ensure you as an organisation can provide consistently high-quality products and services and generate sustainable profits.

As step three lists above, think beyond the value of the contract to your supplier to what else you offer them; it might be an opportunity to develop a new product line, prestige from you as a customer or access and understanding of a new market. Don't guess, ask them what they want from the relationship.

Supplier lead relationships

It can be the supplier that prompts a good relationship. Georgia Pacific(GP), the paper company, improved their business performance by building closer relationships with their retail customers, such as Costco and Walmart.[96] For example, they introduced joint business planning. Capitalising on their understanding of their products, they focused on giving retailers the best knowledge on how to understand consumer behaviour, including which products to select, merchandising and marketing investments. This improved returns for the retailers and for the company. As a result, they changed from being perceived as the "worst" partner to being a "valued collaborator with significant knowledge about how to improve a retailer's business."

I was appointed as partnership manager when the UK government wanted to employ charities and social enterprises to help people open bank accounts. The title reflects the relationship, which indicated that we needed the expertise of the organisations who understood the people we wanted to reach and help open bank accounts. While we had a tendering process, it was designed to allow the organisations tendering to specify the method they wanted to use; we wanted to know the potential outputs for the money but recognised the organisations as the experts. We also didn't want people forced to open a bank account; they needed to have the capacity to run a bank account, so our tendering process allowed for this.

It's critical in good supplier relationships that you don't get any unintended consequences by the way that you tender or structure the contract. If we had made the tender payments based on the number of bank accounts opened then people who shouldn't might have got bank accounts. This meant a level of trust between both sides and a more detailed discussion before getting to a contract as we were not paying for guaranteed outputs. We also needed people to get enough support and to understand what they were doing, so we didn't want the focus to be on doing it for the lowest price. I spent much time as the overseer of the tendering process understanding the methods and process of each tendering organisation and their reasons for why they thought that it would work. The government needed results but not at the cost of vulnerable people being convinced to do something inappropriate.

YOUR ROC© CHALLENGE

Are you sure the way you tender or pay your suppliers isn't leading to them act in ways that don't fit your values?

Laying the foundations – it's not luck

Some might think that a company is very fortunate if it has good, trustworthy suppliers, but this does not happen by chance. It happens because there is trust and respect between the two sides. It doesn't happen if the supplier is just seen as a cost that needs to be managed and controlled or a customer is just seen as a 'cash cow'.

If you force a supplier to match the lowest costs in the market, now often Chinese price levels, then it is likely that quality will suffer and, in the end, this can be highly costly as the many product recalls in the car industry have shown.

Constant renegotiation and swapping suppliers to get the cheapest deals means that, in a crisis, your suppliers are not likely to show you much loyalty. Similarly, a relationship based on price will not encourage a supplier to be proactive in offering other support. If new products or innovations occur, the supplier will offer them to someone who has treated them well, not the company that has acted as a 'bully'.

Alternatively, in a partnership where you work closely with suppliers, you can involve them in your innovations and new product development and they can contribute their expertise and ideas. This classic crowdsourcing can be effective and speed up the time to market.

While not every supplier has the same value or importance, like every customer, they should all be treated with respect.

However, you need a stronger relationship with key suppliers who offer something that is difficult to get elsewhere or is mission-critical. In sectors with lots of competition, it depends on the importance to your business, e.g. there are lots of cleaning companies, but in the catering sector cleaning is mission-critical, so a healthy relationship is essential. The importance of suppliers varies and should be mapped.

If you are a valued partner rather than just another customer, then in a crisis when you need help and a creative response, you are more likely to get it. You will get the best staff working on your account, better deals and greater flexibility. A good relationship takes less work to manage. Disputes take time and reduce efficiency. Good relationships are built on strong communications, which lead to trust and openness, which reduces the number of misunderstandings. Initially, they take time to develop, but the investment is worthwhile.

Companies that chase the cheapest deal never make that investment in the supplier relationship. Consequently, they never reap the benefits of a partnership where both sides understand each other's strengths and weaknesses and the supplier can provide a more effective service.

The test of whether you have a healthy relationship generally comes in a crisis. For example, if there is a petrol strike, as happened in France, and a supplier has limited fuel to deliver, who gets the delivery?

YOUR ROC© CHALLENGE

In a crisis, would your suppliers choose your company as a preferred partner or leave you to struggle?
If you were around, did they help you in Covid?

Areas of concern

FedEx, who rank highly in customer satisfaction surveys and are focused on achieving their values, see their suppliers as critical in achieving this:

"Delivering on customer value expectations, FedEx actively partners with suppliers who share an exceptional focus on quality, service and customer value."

However, in 2014, the headlines across the States were about how FedEx was finding cheap suppliers and subcontracting to them as a source of cheap labour with worse conditions than their direct employees. It's not clear if this had an impact on their sales, but it has had an impact on their image as an ethical business.

Similarly, elsewhere, Iceland, who have strong values and treat their staff well, as I have highlighted elsewhere, are identified by the Groceries Code Adjudicator (GCA)[97] as the company who treat their suppliers worst overall. They have got better, but are still notorious for slow payment and about a fifth of their suppliers say they do not comply with the code set up to protect suppliers from abuse. The story was reported in the press and has undermined their image.

Asda, part of Walmart, do great stuff in the community, with their community champions based in each store having total freedom to spend 30% of their time doing what they think is important to support their local community. Their activity and support creates a very positive image locally. However, in 2017, they were identified as the worst supermarket in terms of treatment of their suppliers, receiving complaints about incorrect deductions from invoices without notice, requesting lump sums to make up profit margins and conducting 'abusive' forensic audits of suppliers' accounts.

Contrast this with the approach taken by Timpsons, based on John Timpson's early experience as a buyer:

"If you are purely purchasing a commodity then the major considerations must be price and payment terms. As a result, e-auctions are bound to play an increasing part in the buying game. But we still rely on several suppliers whose service level is just as important as price. Personal relationships play a big part in the way one company deals with another.

My first executive job was to buy women's shoes. I was lucky to share a buying office with two experienced campaigners who taught me how to forecast fashion and how to negotiate a good deal with good manners. I was also fortunate to find some suppliers who sold the best-selling shoes and were a pleasure to deal with.

I have never forgotten the importance of treating suppliers in the way you would wish to be treated yourself. That is why I invite all our key providers to a regular lunch that is the nearest we get to an AGM. I use the opportunity to give these important stakeholders a frank update on trading.

To ensure that the ethical approach I learnt when I was a buyer continues, we have written a suppliers' guide to explain how we do business. The guide makes clear that we stick to every deal, tell the truth and pay on the nail. We are not a soft touch, but we think it is important for suppliers to feel they are members of the team."[98]

John Timpson

YOUR ROC© CHALLENGE

If you set up on your own, would you want your current employer as a customer?

Who you are as a business – part of your image

Even if a company thinks it has done everything legally and it is not their 'fault' but it was the supplier's, this is no longer enough to protect a business's image and brand. When someone died after eating a Pret a Manger sandwich, the fact that the company blamed a supplier did not register highly with customers who just heard the name they knew.

The costs of failure are high and building strong relationships with suppliers can help minimise risk, pre-empt crisis and protect your brand.

Tesco, as well as facing potential charges concerning how it adjusted figures, has also been found by Ms Tacon, the Grocery Code Adjudicator, to have mistreated its suppliers.[99] Ms Tacon's investigation found that even when money owed to a supplier had been acknowledged by Tesco, on occasions the money was not paid for more than twelve months, with some amounts taking two years to be repaid. "I found that delay in payments was a widespread issue that affected a broad range of Tesco suppliers on a significant scale," Ms Tacon said. "The delay in payments had a financial impact on suppliers, was an administrative burden to resolve, detracted from the time available to develop customer focused business and had a detrimental impact on some suppliers' relationships with Tesco."

This case has been high profile in the press and illustrates the broader impact that treating suppliers can have. Memories can be lengthy and when Marks & Spencer moved its clothes manufacturing from Yorkshire to cheaper overseas companies, it had an impact on both its image and sales, particularly locally in the county.

OSI, a Chinese supplier to McDonald's and Yum!, was involved in a food safety scandal. Both Yum! and McDonald's took the view that they had done everything that could be expected of them, and that the failure was 'legally' OSI's responsibility. The media and lawyers agreed that it was OSI's failure, the quality of the products supplied, not the purchasers' fault. However, consumers still voted with their purse, with McDonald's reduced to a vegetarian menu in many of its North Asian stores as they were unable to serve beef. Yum!, who had found alternative suppliers, saw its traffic go down significantly as it was their third food crisis in two years. When the OSI scandal became public, McDonald's stated that they would suspend all orders from the Shanghai supplier, only for it to become public that they were going to move the orders to another factory of the same supplier. This becoming public further dented consumer confidence, hence the need for the vegetarian menus.

Both companies saw their stock prices fall on the New York Stock Exchange. Part of the given for both brands was that they were safe places to eat and the consumer expected them to honour that and not blame someone else.

In contrast, Green & Black's have created international supply chains that have enhanced their image. When Craig Sams launched Green & Black's, it came naturally to him to work with suppliers in a partnership arrangement that was fair, respectful, sustainable and organic, having done this with Whole Earth Foods. Green & Black's was the first company to win the Ethical Consumers Award and gained the important support of the Women's Environmental Network in 1992. Green & Black's paid fair and fixed prices and the growers were not exposed to dangerous chemicals. The Togolese matriarchs they worked with benefited from the sale of every bar. Green & Black's also benefited from good PR. For example, a headline in *The Independent* summed it up: "Right on – and It Tastes Good, Too." This supply chain strategy resulted in strong distribution and sales.

Even when supply chains are relatively local, issues can arise. In the UK, the horsemeat scandal might have been caused by meat processors, but I expect few people remember their names. However, they can name the supermarkets and their products that were implicated.

Part of managing a supply chain is ensuring that there are foolproof quality assurance and audit processes where, for example, meat testing is done regularly. However, more important is the quality of the relationship with suppliers, so that a level of trust and commitment to shared goals is in place.

If a business is continually driving prices down from its suppliers but says it wants high quality, it logically must know this is impossible on the rates it is paying. The supplier is more likely to believe the action of low prices than the words of high quality. Translating values into behaviours applies in every aspect of business life.

The supplier is likely to cut corners and reduce quality as much as possible because it feels forced to by the procurement pressures. Legally they may be at fault, but morally the wider world will make their own judgement.

Generally, building a strong relationship with a supplier so that you develop a long-term partnership will save a business time and money and potentially lead to collaboration opportunities and perspectives that may help with innovation.

It will also provide greater consistency, to support customer service.

When working with your supply chain, it is useful to jointly develop measures that will identify that the relationships are doing well. Examples might be the number of times senior management have met, tracking of problems and frequency of communication.

Creating strong supplier relationships

First, it is useful to know what your suppliers think of you as a customer. You can do this by asking how they think you measure up across all the principles of the Responsible Organisation Charter©, and seeing what score they give you for treating suppliers fairly.

You can then ask them to explain why they gave that score and how you could improve it. But other scores are also instructive. If they rank you low on innovative growth when you want to score highly, then this can prompt a discussion about how they might be able to help you to innovate. If they don't think you have a clear vision or values that translate into behaviours, then they cannot help you achieve either.

A Case Study: Being really open about supplier relationships

A story – how Procter & Gamble manage their supplier relations

Support from the top

Procter & Gamble publishes sustainability guidelines for supplier relations on its website.

In the introduction, there is a commitment signed by the chairman. The intro explains that they base their supplier relations on their corporate purpose, values and principles. They are very clear about what they expect and what suppliers can expect, specifically mentioning:

> "P&G always seeks to treat suppliers honestly, ethically and fairly. We believe that any relationship works best when a foundation of trust exists between the parties."

Clear guidelines

As part of their ethical treatment of suppliers, they are guided by the following:
- We tell the truth. We do not intentionally mislead others.
- We do not take advantage of honest supplier errors.
- We treat proprietary supplier information in a confidential manner.
- We do not reveal suppliers' pricing, technology, or other information without prior written permission.
- We resolve issues, claims and disputes on a factual and fair basis.

Proactive development of a supplier base

Since 2003, P&G has wanted more minority suppliers to grow in scale and scope. They have encouraged joint ventures, strategic alliances and mergers and acquisitions to bring greater diversity and inclusion to their supplier network.

YOUR ROC© CHALLENGE

How much do you know about your suppliers, their values and vision?

In developing a healthy relationship, it is useful to use the Responsible Organisation Charter© as the basis of a survey to establish how each supplier measures up and how they align, for example, on values, vision, attitude to the environment and behaviour as a good citizen. Public sector procurement includes some of this, with its questions about added value, but it is not comprehensive enough.

The product offering part of the ROC© is particularly relevant in terms of consistency and what makes each supplier's offering unique. The environmental impact is also essential as this is part of your ROC© score in this area.

Suppliers that score highly on the Responsible Organisation Charter© and align closely are potentially likely to be good prospects for close collaboration or at least preferred supplier basis. If you care about treating your suppliers fairly, for example, but they mistreat their suppliers or staff, then it will reflect on your business, as we have already identified.

Suppliers need to not only be assessed on their processes such as quality standards but also on their business ethics.

Before any factory can become a supplier to Patagonia, the outdoor clothing company, they are assessed with four criteria: quality, social standards, environmental impact down to farm level and production/sourcing. On an ongoing basis, they audit suppliers and look to build a collaborative relationship so that they treat their suppliers fairly. For example, they have in place internal controls to prevent last-minute order changes or demands for price cuts.

The integrity of Patagonia's supply chain can be directly investigated by outside sources, thanks to their innovative transparency effort, the Footprint Chronicles, which details the exact social and environmental conditions in their supply chain.

The interactive website includes profiles for over seventy factories and twenty-eight textile mills, which are also linked to product pages, allowing shoppers to trace back the exact product that they would like to purchase.[100]

Prompt payment

In the UK, you can sign up for the Prompt Payment Code (PPC).[101] The goal is for code membership to act as a badge of honour, inspiring confidence, enhancing reputation and demonstrating a strong relationship with suppliers.

The code sets standards for payment practices and best practice, including:

Pay suppliers on time
- Within the terms agreed at the outset of the contract.
- Without attempting to change payment terms retrospectively.
- Without changing practice on length of payment for smaller companies on unreasonable grounds.

Give clear guidance to suppliers
- Providing suppliers with clear and easily accessible guidance on payment procedures.
- Ensuring there is a system for dealing with complaints and disputes, which suppliers know about.
- Advising them promptly if there is any reason why an invoice will not be paid to the agreed terms.

Encourage good practice
- By requesting that lead suppliers encourage adoption of the code throughout their own supply chains.

Pay within sixty days maximum
- Signatories also undertake to pay suppliers within a maximum of sixty days (in line with late payment legislation), to work towards adopting thirty days as the norm, and to avoid any practices that adversely affect the supply chain.

The Small Business, Enterprise and Employment Act 2015, makes it a statutory duty for large businesses to report on payment practices. However, following the law is not sufficient to create an excellent supplier relationship, which will support you in being a responsible organisation and having a good future; this takes the proactive building of a partnership that will work for both sides.

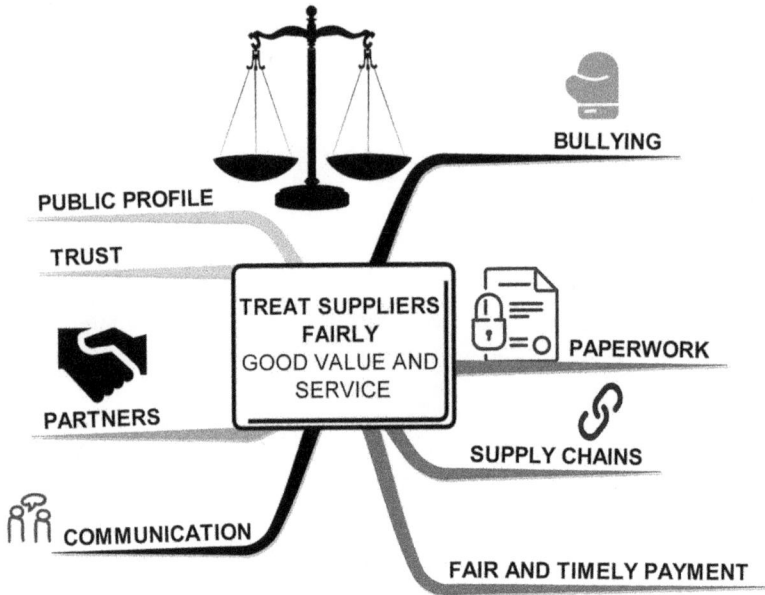

Figure 11: Treat Suppliers Fairly – good value and service

Scoring yourself on the ROC©

Rate how well you treat suppliers.

A score of ten would mean that they are well treated and recognised as integral to your business. A low rating would indicate a focus on cost, lack of loyalty and late payments.

Chapter Nineteen

Good Citizen

Helping the wider community

"The perception that businesses must choose between turning a profit and improving the communities where they operate is outdated and irrelevant in our interdependent world."

Bill Clinton[102]

The first step to being a good citizen is to consider on whom you want to have an impact, plus what fits with your values and ethics. I am taking as a given that you obey the laws of where you are based, though even that can be difficult in areas where bribery and corruption are endemic in the business world. Paying taxes in the places where you work is also fundamental to being a good citizen.

The complexity of being a good citizen

You need to focus and have a strategy for being a good citizen just as you do for every other part of your business. Even Bill Gates focuses, as he knows he can't cure all of the world's ills.

A good starting point for identifying whom you should consider having an impact on as a good citizen will be your stakeholders. They could be local, regional, national and potentially international, and often their needs will conflict with each other. Hence, you also need to map them in terms of their importance to you and your values.

You decide whom you include – for many who feel part of one world, it's not stakeholders but the whole world and everyone. For others, they want to be more focused on how they can act as a good citizen.

"It is in the interest of the enterprise to take care of the economic and social environment; to create value for shareholders but also to create value and wealth for customers, employees and regions where the companies operate, because our company is an economic and social project."

Franck Riboud, former CEO Groupe Danone

Life is complicated in terms of how you rank your priorities. We lived and worked in a small village where the local quarry wanted to reduce their carbon footprint by installing a wind turbine. While this fits with national and international agendas on reducing greenhouse gases, their local neighbours were less keen in terms of noise and possible interference with TV and mobile signals, which are poor already. For any business, the need is to fit with their values and mission. In this case, they couldn't get planning permission, so the decision never had to be made.

However, the quarry, run by Breedons, is generally a really good neighbour both to our village and others, so much so that when they needed support for a planning application I and other locals spoke on their behalf at a planning meeting.[103]

Being a good citizen is about where you make your social impact; social impact has been defined as:

"A significant, positive change that addresses a pressing social challenge. Having a social impact is the result of a deliberate set of activities with a goal around this definition."

Center for Social Impact, University of Michigan

In terms of social impact, an employer in an area has significant social impact by just being an employer, as this injects money into the local economy by creating jobs and worthwhile activity for people.

The local multiplier effect, first identified by John Maynard Keynes in his 1936 book *The General Theory of Employment, Interest and Money*, means that money spent locally is worth almost 400% more to the local economy.[104]

Supporting the local economy is one of the most powerful things a company can do: spending in the local economy creates more jobs and reduces the burden on statutory services. The reality is that people on benefits who are not in work tend to be less healthy, have more accidents, have more social problems, need help with housing, etc., so providing good jobs is a powerful way of being a good citizen.

The introduction of the Public Services (Social Value) Act in the UK has helped to make how a company is a good citizen more commercially relevant to companies. The Act places a duty on Commissioners to consider Social Value. Unfortunately, the Act neither defines the meaning of 'Social Value' nor supplies guidance in its measurement. Public sector bodies just know that they need to think about social value when they buy things, i.e. both securing a reasonable price and meeting the more extensive social, economic and environmental needs of the community.

> "Companies need to build social issues into strategy in a way that reflects their actual business importance."
>
> Ian Davis, managing director, McKinsey and Company

Fundamentally, being a good citizen is not just about money; it is also about backing causes in which you believe. There is tremendous power in such actions.

Julian Richer of Richer Sounds not only treats his staff well, but he has also transferred 60% of his shareholding into an employee ownership trust. He gives 15% of profits to charity and has a more significant cause financing an independent watchdog Taxwatch looking at the finances of multinational companies.

The elements of being a good citizen

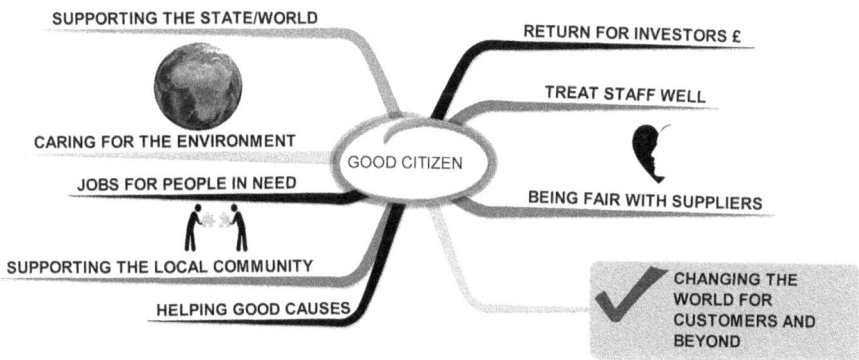

Figure 12: Elements of being a good citizen

Many of the fundamentals of being a good citizen are fulfilled by addressing other principles of the Responsible Organisation Charter©.

For example, treating staff well and being fair with suppliers is part of being a good citizen. The broader impact is that if you pay staff enough and ensure that they have a good pension, they don't need state support. Well paid staff have a positive impact on the public sector.

Giving staff time to volunteer or take public roles, such as being a councillor, is not only fulfilling for them but is also part of being a good citizen as a company and supporting the local community. Patagonia in 2018 shut its stores so staff could vote and convinced over 400 other companies, including Walmart, to sign on to its 'Time to Vote' campaign.

Similarly, minimising environmental impact not only helps the planet, but if it involves buying locally, this supports the local economy. If it also consists of selling products that can be repaired, this helps create more jobs as well as reducing waste.

As well as treating suppliers fairly, which means that they thrive and can employ more people, your relationship can also encourage them to be good citizens and uphold the principles of the ROC©.

Many companies sell Fairtrade products, which should ensure that the suppliers that they buy from are paying living wages. It allows consumers to choose ethically produced products, though again, it needs to be managed and carefully overseen. For example, the Co-op and Sainsbury's were selling roses from Kenya trusting the Fairtrade certification when, in fact, the workers were only earning 48p an hour, not a living wage, and were expected to pick 2,400 flowers in an eight-hour shift.

Changing the world with money

One of my frustrations with the charity sector is their relationship with money. Unfortunately, many people equate profit with wickedness and, with pride, charities are described as the 'not-for-profit' sector. There is a dislike of money unless it has been donated. And unease about making a profit to the extent that a widely used computer model in the charity sector for working out how much to charge for public contract provision has no profit margin included, i.e. no margin for error and no return on investment.

Creating a good return for investors is a critical part of being a good citizen. Companies on the stock market will be part of pension fund investments and investments for charities. If these investments do well, the better the return and the better pensioners and charities will do.

Many firms donate to charity either directly or via local community funds who identify good causes or by setting up a charitable trust themselves. These trusts, such as Joseph Rowntree and Standard Life, often fund key research and innovative projects in the charity world, which otherwise wouldn't happen. I am currently applying to such funders for a charity that wants to launch a groundbreaking digital platform, which will transform the lives of the poor.

Traditional corporate social responsibility

Much of being a good citizen tends to be the apparent part of corporate social responsibility, i.e. giving to charity. But it is worth reviewing if you are maximising the impact you can make.

Instead of just donating to any charity, can you work with ones who could benefit from your expertise or share similar markets? Do you know what are the significant expenses of the causes you support, and could you purchase more cheaply for them because of your scale? Could you help by selling services or products for a charity or social enterprise or passing them leads which may fit them better than you?

For example, a social enterprise offering IT services could work with a larger IT company picking up the clients that would be too small for them.

In supporting the local community, could you provide meeting rooms for community groups or do you have any waste paper that would be useful for playgroups, for example?

Do you support the local schools with work experience, interviewing practice for pupils and inspiring them to join your business and industry?

Using your business activities to be a good citizen

Adjusting your business practices can also be a great way to be a good citizen. Can you provide routes for people in need to get jobs with you?

For example, in my work with charities who support people from poor communities, I know that many from non-English backgrounds are desperate to work but are incredibly nervous about their English skills and interviews. Many have minimal contacts outside their community, so could you offer interview skills, training for adults or just informal opportunities for them to meet your company and build their confidence?

Timpsons trains people in prison and then employs them on their release. Employing ex-offenders might not be for you, but could you be more flexible so people with caring needs could work for you?

Can your business expertise be valuable in advising charities or the public sector? Can you use business speeches or your blogs to promote your values? As well as promoting the values you think are valuable, you will also be deepening your relationships as people will understand you better as a business.

The next step would be getting involved in public roles that support your values.

YOUR ROC© CHALLENGE

Do you have a clear strategy about how you work with and contribute to stakeholders and would your stakeholders agree?

A Case Study: How CSR can have an impact across an organisation

A story – fulfilling your values using ROC© principles

TARGET[105]

Good Citizen

Target, the US discount retailer, has a history of donating 5% of its profits to local, national and global good causes. They listen to and involve both their staff and their customers. Based on this listening, their focus was on education. Their 'Take Charge of Education' programme aimed to donate an additional $425 million to schools by the end of 2015. These funds could then be used by schools in any way they choose, which makes them incredibly valuable.

Target wanted to support children from preschool through to high school and beyond, believing that a focus on education is critical for the USA if it is to remain innovative, stay globally competitive and build leaders of the future.

It was particularly keen to address the gap in attainment between white and minority students, with only 68% African-American and 73% Hispanic students graduating from high school compared to the national average of 81%.

In 2017, Target decided to reinvent their approach to corporate responsibility, moving from a portfolio of philanthropic priorities to a new philosophy that shifts corporate responsibility to the core of the business, calling it Future at Heart.

Collaborative

To support their commitment to education, Target has collaborated with other organisations to champion the cause of at-risk students and help improve graduation rates. They sponsored a report titled 'Don't Call Them Dropouts', based on research with teenagers. They then publicised the issues in *The Washington Post* to raise awareness and encourage more involvement.

Behaviour driven by shared values

"Being locally relevant is really important if an organisation is going to be purpose-driven and values-based...

We believe business can be part of developing solutions for pressing social issues, and we strive to create shared value through initiatives that provide solutions for guests (customers) and meaningful benefits to both business and communities."

Laysha Ward, president of community relations for Target

Target has training and external support for senior management as part of its commitment to values-based leadership.

Treat staff well

Treating staff well and developing them is seen by Target as part of their commitment to the communities where they work. They believe that developing the skills and leadership abilities of their staff has a ripple effect out into the community. They work hard to support and nurture strong teams and obtain feedback from them about what matters to them and their communities.

The company encourages team members to become involved as volunteers in their communities equating to more than one million hours per annum.

Minimising environmental impact

Target has a range of sustainability initiatives, including:

- providing "more responsibly sourced, wellness-focused food"
- using the Higg Index – a sustainability measurement tool used primarily by apparel and footwear companies
- assessing the thousands of vendor partners
- achieving LEED (Leadership in Energy and Environmental Design) certification for 124 stores opened in Canada

Innovative Growth[106]

In 1992, Target was a regional retailer turning over $3 billion. It aspired to grow by being different and creative and, in the next fifteen years, it achieved this, rising to $63 billion. It has become known for innovative design, which is both hip and cheap. They achieved this by recruiting key individuals such as Robyn Waters who had worked at an upmarket department store buying designer goods like Armani and Versace. She came in with the role of 'ready to wear' trend manager, with little authority or resources. She managed to change the culture by finding buyers who would innovate and showing how successful it could be. She wouldn't just use the statistics to make her argument but also engaged the emotions by showing what the colour would look like in situ and how other companies such as Apple were using colour. She also used photos of how the boutiques were doing things to help people see how things could be different, to help spark their creativity and innovation.

YOUR ROC© CHALLENGE

Do you have a range of corporate social responsibility (CSR) activities across your organisation like Target?

Explaining what you are doing

Many larger businesses seek to explain how they are serving the wider community and being a good citizen in their annual corporate social responsibility report. However, for many readers, this has little credibility because it is seen as a self-serving document.

You can improve this perception and improve relationships with stakeholders by including their views and asking them to rate *your* performance as a neighbour/in your relationship with them, even when the views may be challenging.

Alternatively, a more twenty-first-century solution is to provide a digital real-time report; for example, including air and water quality, data about community involvement and provide opportunities for stakeholders to comment.

The traditional way of being a good citizen

Traditionally, many businesses have supported charities as part of being a good citizen. These donations, plus volunteering, are tremendous and can have an unusually large impact on smaller local charities. However, in my experience, the most potent way charities and businesses can work together is in a collaboration where they each benefit, and it can work long term.

For example, when I was working with Colgate-Palmolive, we did an on-pack promotion on Ajax products to donate to an older person's charity and also provided cleaning products to the scouts to go into older peoples' homes to clean for them. The collaboration gave us a promotion which supermarkets liked and ensured we continued to get shelf space and helped two different voluntary organisations.

Businesses can have a significant impact, especially on smaller charities, by supporting them with technology. Many non-profits have been slow to adopt new technologies due to focusing their funds on their causes. This creates an opportunity for technology-focused businesses to collaborate with non-profits, helping them integrate innovative solutions and achieve their goals more efficiently.

The Fourth Sector

However, a fundamental change is happening with the emergence of what has been coined the 'fourth sector'.

The fourth sector[107] is a convergence of the public, private and non-profit sectors and is changing the way charities operate, approach social issues, and relate to one another.[108] They are moving to one that is neither wholly profit-drive nor social impact-driven.

During recent times, there has been a gradual shift in the business models of commercial businesses, the public sector (particularly at a local level) and charities. Traditionally, larger income-driven companies have progressed from donating money through corporate social responsibility programmes to more substantive partnership roles with charities, but any size company can do this.

Local councils with reducing budgets have moved from giving grants to working with charities to identify how together they can improve services for local people. On a larger scale, governments are using public-private partnerships for everything from health to education and, frequently, these can be with charities.

To win by *Being Good*, businesses are going further and integrating social impact into their business models, linking it to their values, encompassing both earned income and some degree of social benefit into their business model. In reverse, charities are thinking more about being sustainable long term by earning income.

In the USA, TOMS Shoes was founded in 2006 with an integrated business strategy: for every pair of shoes purchased TOMS would donate a pair of shoes to a child in need – One for One®. The name even came from thinking about how shoes can create a better tomorrow, which got shortened to TOMS Shoes. As well as making sense for a shoe company, it also addresses a significant need, as almost a quarter of the world's population suffers from soil-transmitted infections.

Ninety-five million pairs of shoes have been donated, protecting children against infections, as well as injury and disease. Many communities reported a massive decrease in foot disease since the distribution of TOMS Shoes. The reduction is, on average, over 60%. They have also extended what they sell and give. In 2011, they launched TOMS Eyewear, partnering first with the Seva Foundation to expand the One for One® model. Through this partnership, they help provide medical treatment, sight-saving surgery and prescription glasses to those in need. In 2014, they launched TOMS Roasting Co® in conjunction with Water For People. TOMS coffee sales have helped to provide safe living conditions and economic prosperity to developing communities through sustainable water systems. By 2019,[109] it had had an impact on over 96.5 million lives giving shoes, sight, safe water and impact grants.

"We are committed to dedicating at least one-third of our annual net profits to a giving fund managed by our very own Giving Team. We will then distribute shoes and grants according to an annual investment plan that reflects the needs of our Giving Partners, as well as the causes our community cares most about."

Spreading the impact of the Fourth Industrial Revolution

Many businesses have the ideal opportunity to ensure that, like the previous industrial revolutions that preceded it, the fourth Industrial Revolution raises global income levels and improves the quality of life for populations around the world.

However, to date, those who have gained the most from it have been consumers rich enough to access the digital world.

A Case Study: An inspiring story of fishing and phones

A story – Nokia changing the world

I have always believed that many businesses do much good even while they are making money; not all, but many of the inspiring stories are unknown.

This story is about the most impoverished fishermen working in India, who for generations have struggled to survive. They use rudimentary boats, risking their lives to catch fish to sell and feed their families and communities.

After catching the fish and returning to port, the amount they used to earn was dependent on what the local wholesaler would pay. Without refrigerated boats, in the heat of India, they couldn't sail to another port or wait for a better offer, so they stayed poor and hoped for a miracle or change of heart where wholesalers would feel more generous.

The miracle came in the form of technology. It cost almost a month's wages when one fisherman, Rajan, bought a mobile phone in 2003, but it changed everything. Now he has his phone with him as he fishes, and it rings as wholesalers enquire about his catch. "When I have a big catch," Rajan reports, "the phone rings sixty or seventy times before I get to port." Rajan receives offers from competing wholesalers, agrees the best price and sails to the relevant port to deliver. In ten years, his family income has tripled, allowing him to get electricity, television and schooling for his children.

And the mobile has also changed the lives of farmers, addressing the problem that over one-third of India's fruit and veg output would go to waste due to market failures caused by lack of information. Now, mobiles provide information such as prices, which people in the developed world take for granted.

How did it happen? Well, Nokia developed a phone that met the needs of the poor, building in options that we in the West would have considered useless or irrelevant. For example, it could store multiple contact lists – essential in a phone that may be shared by many users in a village. A particular call could be price limited – necessary in a shared phone, and you didn't have to be able to read to use it.

It also included a flashlight, radio and alarm clock. And Nokia did well with it. Two hundred and fifty million Nokia 1100s were sold in the first five years of its life compared to 174 million iPods in its first five years. It made Nokia the largest selling consumer electronics device in the world at the time.

Nokia understood the market, created a product to meet its needs at an affordable price and changed the world for millions of people. As a person who is passionate about marketing, this makes me a little emotional.

YOUR ROC© CHALLENGE

How could your products and services change the world for the better?

If we understand the problems people face, we can create products and services that can help them change their lives, giving them dignity and control.

What else can be developed? Charities, social enterprises and companies can all play their part by matching the needs of those who are most vulnerable in our world.

I read the Nokia story in *Demand* (Slywotzky and Weber, 2011), which is full of inspirational companies changing the world.

As the case study illustrates, some businesses such as Nokia have used technology to improve the lot of the poorest people. Technology can be a force for good, but an alternative view is that technology could lead to mass unemployment, as robots and machines take jobs and the gaps in society widen.

I prefer to think that, like revolutions before this, new roles will be found, such as robot wheelchairs liberating people with disabilities. Every opportunity includes a threat and vice versa.

Global business can open new markets and drive economic growth if companies and the political environment allow it. However, this should be set in the context of global warming and the environmental impact of travel, so using local technology and suppliers is also becoming more critical.

Being a *Good* business requires thinking beyond your immediate stakeholders to the broader society for all the reasons outlined elsewhere – it appeals to customers, staff and makes economic sense.

The future is likely to create a job market increasingly segregated into 'low-skill/low-pay' and 'high-skill/high-pay' segments, which in turn will lead to an increase in social tensions, for which everyone has a responsibility and reasons to address.

Inequality threatens stability, as recent political elections in the USA and UK illustrate. Most people don't want to live in gated communities because poor people around them threaten them implicitly or explicitly.

More broadly, more people having more wealth means that they can spend more, and this provides opportunities for everyone, as well as improving the world.

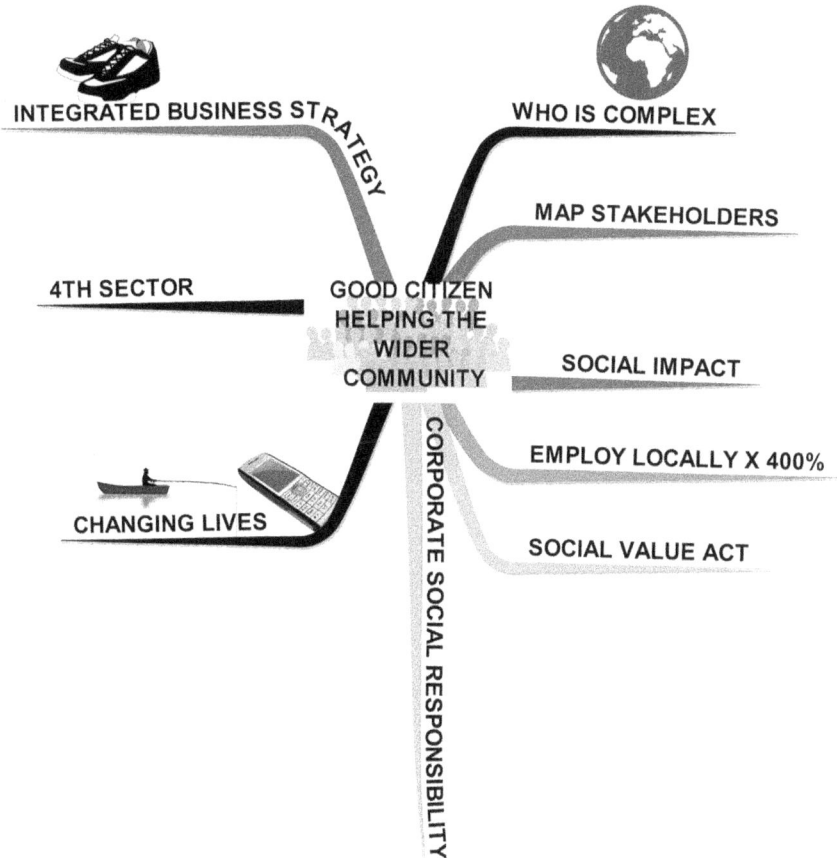

INTEGRATED BUSINESS STRATEGY

WHO IS COMPLEX

MAP STAKEHOLDERS

4TH SECTOR

GOOD CITIZEN HELPING THE WIDER COMMUNITY

SOCIAL IMPACT

EMPLOY LOCALLY X 400%

CHANGING LIVES

CORPORATE SOCIAL RESPONSIBILITY

SOCIAL VALUE ACT

Figure 13: Good Citizen – helping the wider community

"Profits are not always possible when business tries to serve the very poor. In such cases, there needs to be another market-based incentive – and that incentive is recognition. Recognition enhances a company's reputation and appeals to customers; above all, it attracts good people to the organisation."

Bill Gates

Like every element of the ROC©, being a good corporate citizen should fit with your vision and values and work with all the other parts. The investment you make should give you a return not in money but in how you change the world, particularly in areas that are important to you.

The impact might be in supporting your staff, your local community or a passion such as access to clean water or sight, as in the case of LensCrafters.

Whatever it is, it is more than just spending money in response to different requests; it needs to fit with your role in the world and be proactively planned.

Scoring yourself on the ROC©

Rate your score as good citizen.

A score of ten would mean that you have a strategy and it fits with your vision and values. A low rating would indicate that you may give in an ad hoc fashion to charity, but you haven't thought beyond that.

Chapter Twenty

Product Offering

Making your vision and values real

So many people have a great idea that they believe will change the world, but it never happens. It is never launched as a product or service, so it never becomes a reality. All the visions and values in the world are meaningless if they don't translate into something that exists: a business, charity or social enterprise offering a service or product.

What you actually do is essential to *Winning by Being Good* and how well you do it is even more critical.

Product offerings need to reflect the needs of customers or users. A lot of lip service is given to this, but over time, a business often gets caught up in its systems and processes and forgets the customers' needs and wants, such as talking to real people on the end of a phone when they have a problem.

Jeff Bezos of Amazon puts an empty chair in internal meetings to remind participants about the customer:[110]

> "In a typical company, if you have a meeting, no matter how important it is, there is always one party who is not represented: the customer. So, it's very easy inside the company to forget about the customer."
>
> Jeff Bezos, Amazon

In this digital era, the implication is sometimes that the brand and marketing is more important than what you provide. However, to create a long-term sustainable business, your product offerings must be what people want/need, i.e. that will change their lives consistently and consume the minimum amount of natural resources.

There is now global competition in most markets. Fail with your product offering and there will always be someone there to take your place.

There are three principles in the section of the ROC© on product offering:

- Life changing
- Reliably consistent
- Minimising environmental impact

These reflect the key elements of a successful product or service and how you need to run your operations. What you do, how you do it and the impact you have.

Firstly, if you do not change lives, how can you be doing *Good*? How you change lives is what you reflect in your vision, and your product/service is the way you do it. And how will you make any money, as why would anybody want to have what you offer? Either you must be addressing a need that helps someone with a problem or helps them achieve a dream or desire. To be truly successful, you need to be able to measure how you change lives, and this will give you the messages for your marketing.

However, a life-changing product or service needs to be reliable. If you think in medical terms, if the ventilators that Dyson created in response to the Coronavirus pandemic didn't work consistently, then however good they were, they were no good. The ultimate success as a business or a charity or public sector body is providing products or services that consistently achieve your vision, reflect your values, change lives and can be produced economically and sustainably.

This success relies on having reliable products and services supported by systems and values that embed reliable consistency; otherwise, there will be an intermittent failure, which won't achieve your vision or values and will also be very expensive.

Every other principle of the Responsible Organisation Charter© requires reliable consistency.

In essence, there can't be long-term success without reliable consistency.

Consistency is hard.

Achieving reliable consistency is all about the processes and systems in your business, as well as a culture that encourages consistency.

Consistency comes from the top and it is a critical characteristic of successful leaders and managers. It helps them achieve their goals and create a culture of action and achievement. And being consistent is vital for a winning corporate culture, i.e. one that is fair.

Consistency in your offering only comes if staff are treated with consistency and teams act in a measured and conscientious manner. It comes down to creating the right habits in the business based on your values. It also requires the right people to be in place.

One of the significant challenges for the world is the environmental crisis we are facing and *Winning by Being Good* has to involve minimising your ecological impact. You should consider the environmental impact not only of the products and services you offer directly, but also the impact of all the supporting activities. What is the ecological impact of how you operate? Your marketing and selling, where you work, how you remunerate and incentivise your staff? These are all part of the environmental footprint caused by offering the products or services you do.

The three principles underlying your product offering need to be balanced. You may be able to create a more significant life-changing impact, but it could be more harmful environmentally; this can be a particular challenge when trying to provide cost-effective solutions where plastic, for example, is the simple solution. Remarkably, a hypnotherapist friend has struggled to find recycled and environmentally friendly products for the hygiene changes she has had to make with the pandemic and the products she has seen have been a lot more expensive. If she wants to offer a cost-effective service, then it is difficult to be environmentally friendly – this is even more of a challenge for charities. You need to ensure that your values help you to decide what is the priority. Your values need to be ranked to ensure that they give you practical guidance and criteria for making decisions that everyone can follow.

If someone pops down the shops to get some more coffee or washing up liquid, do they buy organic, fair trade, environmentally friendly, the quality brand or the cheapest? The work you do with the ROC© should help everyone when they have to make these simple decisions. In fact, as I will show, they are not simple. For example, is a good quality washing up liquid more environmentally friendly because you use less? Could it even be cheaper? What about the packaging and how well it works?

All your operating decisions are directly or indirectly part of your product offering. When someone uses something you offer, the impact is dictated by how you act and your values and what your organisation stands for as well as what you directly do, as I hope you will see in the following chapters.

Chapter Twenty-one

Life Changing

Making a difference in people's lives

"If you have a product adding value to the world, you have a product that can add to the fight against poverty as well."

Jeffrey Sachs

Changing lives has always been part of the ethos of the charity sector, however small the charity, but companies have not tended to think in terms of how their products or services change lives. Early on in my marketing career, I had a leaflet to review. I had to use a highlighter to identify what were features and what were benefits. How you change lives will be based on these benefits, but it takes it further and generally includes how you do things, your behaviours based on your values, as well as the actual product or service.

In the charity sector, how you change lives is known as social impact, but it doesn't have to be solving the big things. It could be as simple as solving how someone accesses public transport.

Life changing depends on the circumstances. For example, for someone in sub-Saharan Africa, getting a means to charge a mobile and provide light at night is life changing.

In the developed world, a search for 'life-changing products' on the internet brought up speakers, headphones and a book weight (something to hold the pages down). Pretty depressing. In fact, you can change lives in the developed world just as profoundly. Simple examples are local businesses that are welcoming and provide human contact for lonely people, or cruise companies that think about the needs of the disabled so that they can go on excursions ashore rather than be stuck on the ship.

Identifying how you change the world
In assessing yourself on the Responsible Organisation Charter©, one of the

most challenging areas to quantify is how you change the world; in business terms, what are the broader benefits you provide? How does what you do change the world both directly and more widely?

YOUR ROC© CHALLENGE

Have you asked your customers how you change their world?

What you do versus its impact is the difference between features and benefits – changing what you do into the effect it has has always been of critical importance to successful marketing. I am just extending that principle so that you consider the impact on the wider society.

In the charity world, this is called the Theory of Change (see Figure 14).

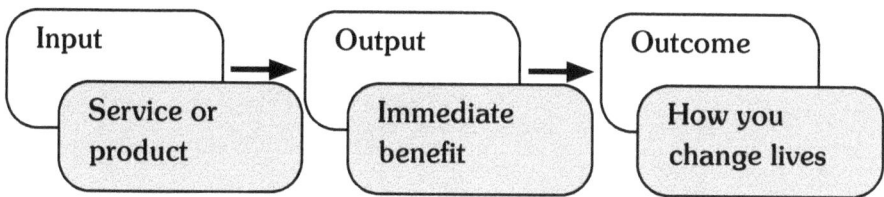

Input	Output	Outcome
Service or product	**Immediate benefit**	**How you change lives**

Figure 14: Summary of the theory of change

In the charity and social enterprise sector, understanding your 'theory of change', i.e. how you change lives, is expected by many funders and social investors. However, in the business sector, it is not something I have ever come across.

I think understanding your theory of change has a value, whatever type of organisation you are. For a charity, clarifying the theory of change means moving beyond a passion for doing good to understanding how you change lives, what the impact is and how you track/prove that impact.

For any organisation, there are four reasons to work out your theory of change:

Reason 1: It reduces the danger of being all things to all people
A theory of change requires that you think about who you are serving and what is valuable to change in their lives. The first thing you need to do is

to decide your focus; are you going to focus on a limited set of people or a limited type of change?

In the charity world, Cancer Research UK focuses on research into cancer, not every disease that might kill people (as the name exactly says). MacMillan nurses don't look after anybody who is ill, just those with cancer. In both cases, this means they get more support because it is obvious what they do. Every organisation can benefit from that clarity; in the commercial world, this is your niche. If you want to be successful in a sustained way, the cause will also fit with your passion.

Reason 2: It requires you to be really clear about what you offer

A theory of change is like a scientific theory: "You do x, causing y to happen, which has the result of z."

By writing it down, it generally becomes clear how you can increase your impact by adding ingredients.

For years, we have used this general theory of change:

"Our Success Formula
Tools x (Creative Strategy + Inspirational Coaching)
= Greater Success for YOU"

This book is a result of identifying that we needed to bring together and explain the strategies that underlie the tools that we use every day with organisations.

Reason 3: It allows you to test what you do

Like a scientific experiment, you can test a theory of change, looking at each part of the equation, which gives you data to improve. With no explicit formula or result, how can you identify if you are achieving what you want or improve?

Reason 4: It provides you with marketing messages

Just like Cancer Research UK, a clear theory of change gives you powerful messages and your testing gives you evidence that what you do works. NB: the powerful messages always come from the impact not the inputs, hence for Cancer Research UK, the messages you first see on the website[111] are:

"Together we are beating cancer."

"Help us bring about a world where everybody lives longer, better lives, free from the fear of cancer."

These messages are repeated across the site, for example, in explaining their strategy.

Working out and tracking how you change the world

Explaining how you change the world can be incredibly challenging when the results of what you do are not immediate or are not easy to measure objectively. For example, you make people feel better or happier, but how do you track that? Could you have a happy index or happy factor that goes with your product or service? More importantly, how do you measure happiness?

We have a Sunflower of life© explicitly designed for business owners that measures how they feel about different areas of their life, including happiness. It has no hard criteria and, interestingly, we find that often people make lots of progress and then score themselves lower when they next do it because their aspirations have expanded.

If you provide goods and services that enable communities to flourish, it means that you're making/doing things that are useful for people. As a result, you will earn more, both in terms of finance and well-being and, consequently, success.

It's easier to see how a charity or social enterprise creates a social impact or changes the world, as they are often either working with people in need or employing people with needs.

Identify impacts as precisely as possible and quantify them to make them as powerful as possible. Use the effect in how you explain or even name the product or service, and even develop a service package with additional ways to increase the impact. You can look for social impact in all sorts of areas, as Figure 15 overleaf shows.

Lots of this is in 'charity speak', so let me explain in reality what some of the more unusual terms mean.

Financial Inclusion

Many disadvantaged people do not have access to the financial products that the general population take for granted, such as bank accounts or debit/credit cards. Addressing this is called financial inclusion. I was involved in a large project for the government when they wanted to start paying people benefits and pensions directly into bank accounts and found that 15% of the people did not have an account to pay into. My task was to identify charities, social enterprises and businesses that could help people open accounts. Many people found it very difficult to open an account because they did not have utility bills, driving licences and passports to provide sufficient proof of who they were are and where they lived. Without a bank account, lots of things are impossible, so people had meters for electricity, meaning no bill and higher charges, which leads to more poverty.

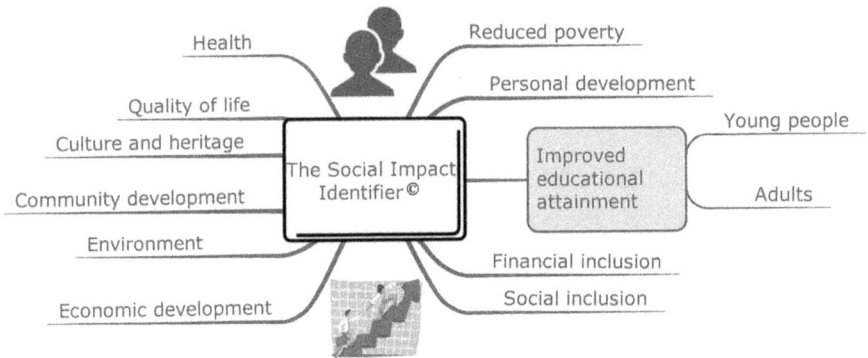

Figure 15: The Social Impact Identifier©

Social Inclusion

The other less well-known phrase is 'social inclusion'. People can feel socially excluded for many reasons, from mental health problems that stop them going out or being in places with lots of people, to lack of English skills or money, creating practical reasons to be excluded.

Social impact can also come from what you *stop* happening. An unusual example is camel racing, which is one of the wealthiest sports. It takes place in the Middle East, and it used to be that to get a very lightweight rider, children were used as jockeys. Many died or were injured. A solution had to be found if the sport was to continue giving employment and social benefit. Now, foot-high robots weighing five to eight pounds ride the camels. They look like humans and even wear silks and include speakers so that the owners can give commands to the camels. Social impact can happen in bizarre ways.

A Case Study:[112] Changing lives by just changing processes

A story – improving breast cancer care showing ROC© principles

A clear vision

Laura Esserman, a surgeon and associate professor of surgery at the University of California at San Francisco (UCSF), had a vision of better treatment for women with breast cancer.

In the 1990s, the typical treatment outlined in a Stanford case study for a woman finding a lump in her breast was first seeing a GP, who then referred her for a mammogram and then she waited for the results, with gaps of days and weeks between each appointment.

Assuming there was no cause for concern, then there was an appointment with the surgeon who hopefully had got the mammogram results. If not, there was a delay while they were found. Then the surgeon took a biopsy and the woman waited for the results.

If cancer was detected, then there was generally surgery, then radiation treatment with a radiotherapist and chemotherapy with a medical oncologist, all requiring separate appointments. The process could cause weeks of anxiety.

Esserman's vision was of a breast care clinic where a woman with a lump could walk in, within the day of her visit establish if there was a problem and, if so, get a treatment plan.

"Everything under one roof... putting the woman at the centre."
Switch by Chip and Dan Heath p76-81

Behaviour driven by shared values

Esserman was not senior enough to have much influence, but she inspired with her vision and found people who shared her values of wanting to improve the experience for women.

It started small, with a four-hour clinic once a week where different departments were encouraged to work together. It then gradually grew to two days a week with more surgeons, nurses, counsellors and support staff involved.

An identifiable market niche

As the success grew, the Breast Care Center was offered an entire floor in a new cancer centre being constructed by UCSF.

As well as everything under one roof needed for the treatment of breast cancer, the centre also has a relaxing healing garden and a café. The boutique sells not only flowers and gifts but also wigs and scarves for patients undergoing chemo. As the centre has expanded, it offers even more:

- Art for recovery.
- Breast cancer decision services.
- Cancer exercise counselling.
- Cancer resource centre.
- Cancer survivorship programme.
- Core and more class.
- Healing through dance class.
- Meditation and guided imagery for cancer patients.
- Oncology social work.
- Peer support programme for cancer.
- Qi gong.
- Restorative movement class.

The Breast Care Center works to heal the whole person, caring for both their physical and emotional well-being, but with a clear niche of only working on breast cancer.

Life-changing, reliably consistent and sustainable profit

To achieve her vision, when Esserman found that the radiology department would still be located elsewhere, she gave up a third of her space to have a mammography unit on the same floor.

The new kind of care attracted patients. Numbers grew from 175 to 1,300 per month in six years from 1997 to 2003. It has become a significant source of revenue for the UCSF and a recognised leader in breast cancer care and research.

The centre has achieved its vision, changed lives and does so consistently and profitably. It continues to update its service and now uses UCSF MyChart, an online patient service. Message your provider, request medication refills, view some test results and more.

This is how Esserman now describes the patient's experience:

"When a patient comes into the Breast Care Center, I can walk around the corner and look at her films that day. While she's in the room, we can do a biopsy and get the diagnosis in five minutes. We have a gynaecologist on staff that specialises in fertility issues for women with breast cancer, and I have a genetic counsellor on staff that is one of the nurse practitioners. The patient stays in the same place and doesn't need to go anywhere."

Switch by Chip and Dan Heath

NB: in writing this case study, I looked at recent reviews on Yelp and some were not positive about the customer service. Staying *Good* is an ongoing process and these reviews are another example of why constant work on being *Good* is essential.

Measurably life changing

Make your wider social impact part of your marketing strategy.

If you can, it is most effective if you have an objective measure of how you change lives. The prominent examples of this are products or services that save money, such as discount stores, or improve productivity or results such as the One Acre Fund or the Nokia phone.

These are quantifiable and the broader impact can then be explained, such as being able to afford to educate children or live better.

Like any part of business, the goal should be to continually be looking to improve how you change lives and be seeking to innovate to increase the impact.

Some businesses that focus on providing cost-effective services may use the amount of money they save people as part of their marketing. This message is a classic case of where something simple could be made more potent by doing some research.

For example, consider the difference between saying: we save our customers 10% and we know that with the money we save them our customers can have better holidays and help their children through university. One is a bit of money; the other is life changing.

Identifying how you change lives will inspire everyone involved with your organisation. It also gives meaning to tasks that contribute to the life change indirectly and makes people feel they are doing something worthwhile, so that you change their lives as well.

Changing lives is life changing for those who do it.

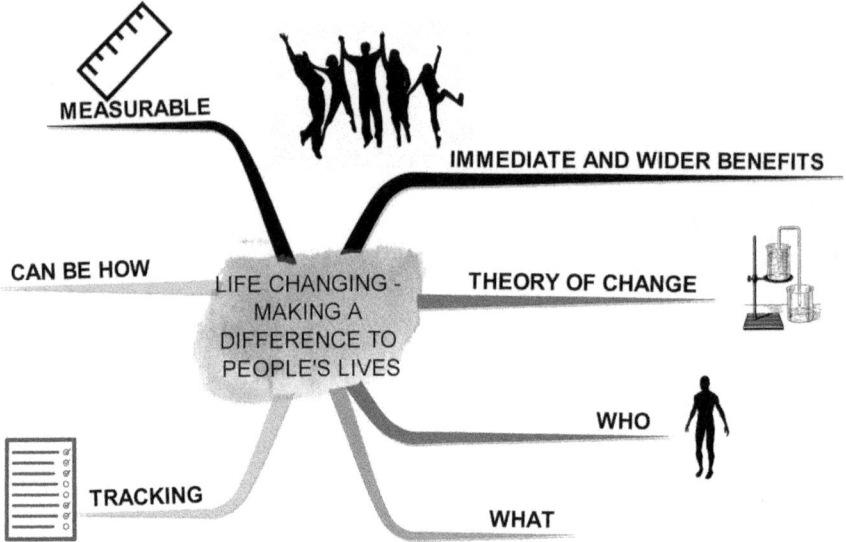

Figure 16: Life Changing – making a difference to people's lives

Scoring yourself on the ROC©

Rate how much you change lives directly and more widely.

A score of ten would mean that you change lives and know how you do it, with a clear theory of change. A low rating would indicate you sell stuff but don't know how it changes lives; it probably will because otherwise why are people buying it, but you need to work out what you are doing.

Chapter Twenty-two

Reliably Consistent

Successful every time

Why consistency is important

Research indicates that the main reason businesses lose customers is not price, but poor customer service.[113] And poor customer service equates to you doing something that the customer does not expect and betraying their trust, i.e. a lack of consistency.

Research by McKinsey[114] indicates that: "It's not enough to make customers happy with each individual interaction," it's about consistency and that if you manage that, it can increase customer satisfaction by up to 20% and lift revenue by up to 15%, while lowering the cost of serving customers by as much as 20%. It makes sense, fewer problems cost less money.

A customer is four times more likely to defect to a competitor if the problem is service-related than price or product-related.

Worse, now, not only are they likely to leave but they are also likely to leave a comment on a review site or tell their friends on Facebook or mention it at business networking in the business-to-business arena.

Estimates vary about how many people someone shares a bad experience with, from at least ten to over twenty-six, but this is just face-to-face; amazingly, social media and review site data is not available. What is known is that, unfortunately, only one in twenty-six customers will tell a company about their negative experience according to research by Esteban Kolsky. Complaints are better because they can get sorted but they cost money. The Institute of Customer Service (ICS) found more consumers were experiencing service issues in 2022 than at any point since its customer satisfaction index began in 2008. The ICS calculated that UK firms were having to spend a total of £9.24bn every month in worker hours covering complaints handling.[115]

Airlines provide some of the clearest examples of how visible lack of consistency can become. For instance, in 2018, Ryanair failed the consistency test by cancelling flights for 700,000 people without being very clear on their communications; this caused a social media storm as well as mainstream media headlines.

However, if you have a good product or service that is reliably consistent, then social media becomes your friend, with people recommending you and sharing your success.

Financially, keeping customers is of paramount importance. A 2% increase in customer retention has the same effect as decreasing costs by 10%.

Bain & Company calculate that a 5% reduction in the customer loss rate can increase profits by 5-95% and a 10% increase in retention can increase the value of the company by 30%. The financial gain is not only because there is no additional cost of acquisition, which is six-to-seven times higher than the cost of retaining an existing customer, but also because the probability of selling to an existing customer is 60-70% compared to the likelihood of selling to a new prospect, which is 5-20%.[116] Customer profitability tends to increase over the life of a retained customer.

Feedback is critical. Research[117] indicates that 70% of the best companies in customer experience management use customer feedback to make strategic decisions compared to 50% of industry-average organisations and 29% of laggards.

What customers want
Generally, customers have some relatively simple requirements, which you need to supply consistently:
- Respect.
- Honesty.
- A personal relationship: to be heard, not treated as a number but an individual, particularly if they are feeling vulnerable. Consequently, customers like to deal with the same person if they have an issue, not be passed from person to person.
- Companies demonstrating a desire to help and support existing customers: some companies seem to give the impression that only new customers have value.

I have spent several years writing this book, using it as an excuse to go on longer cruises where I could write on the days at sea. It has allowed me to experience many different levels of service from the ships where staff recognise you and offer you the coffee you like before you ask, to those who have decided that digital technology is the way to go.

One company now uses a tablet to take drink orders, which then go to a central serving point where anyone may end up coming back with the drinks, not the person who took the order. The method is designed to increase efficiency, but unfortunately, on several occasions when we ordered, the drinks we received were incorrect. It wasn't the person who was delivering them who had made the error and it was frustrating as a customer. It had not improved the customer experience, it had depersonalised it and had not enhanced consistency.

As I finalise editing this book I am yet again on a cruise that exemplifies inconsistency, all human based. A fellow passenger noted that over a twenty-day cruise, every time they had a café frappe it was made differently, cream/no cream, ice/crushed ice/no ice… Unfortunately, the nice ship, the good entertainment and food will not be what I share with my friends or blog about. I don't blame the staff but rather the training and management.

Being consistent in what you offer means you can be trusted, and this is fundamental to being *Good*. Consistent so each time a person purchases a widget, they get the same quality widget, and also consistent in terms of the quality of the relationship from beginning to end – 'walking the talk'.

If you say you offer a quality caring service, but the moment the customer has left the shop you are unwilling to listen or they have to contact an impersonal help desk if there are any problems then this is not consistent with your stated value of quality caring service.

Being consistent in service does not mean learning a script repeated without meaning every time, such as, "Have a nice day." It is about the underlying attitude, wanting to be helpful, really listening to the customer, building rapport, remembering a name.

Consistency is fundamental to trust and it is vital in assessing your business. The internet, review sites and social media mean that any inconsistency is likely to be publicised very rapidly, particularly if it makes people angry, like a cancelled flight with no warning.

YOUR ROC© CHALLENGE

How do you know if you offer consistency? Would everyone in your organisation agree on what consistency looks like?

My experience in franchising taught me that it is useful for everyone to think like a franchisor. If you run a franchise, you know that you need to be clear about what each franchisee must offer so that the brand offering is consistent everywhere. In a franchise, this means that typically there is a 'bible', which encapsulates how to run the business. This manual tells you how long to cook the hamburger or in Dyno-Rod's case to take your boots off when entering a customer's property. Unfortunately, non-franchise businesses rarely see the need for a manual for much of what is seen as apparent or straightforward. It is assumed that the corporate culture and management will inculcate the right standards. Even if the values are clear and translated into behaviours consistently, it is not guaranteed.

Achieving consistency is not consistent

Consistency is fundamental to your relationship with your customer. How you will achieve your consistency will vary depending on the type of service you are offering – consistent creativity requires a different methodology from consistent hamburgers, for example.

If you can guarantee better service, then 55% of customers would even pay extra, according to research by Defaqto. However, get it wrong and it takes twelve experiences to make up for one negative experience that hasn't been sorted satisfactorily.

Deal with a problem correctly and sort out a complaint, and a dissatisfied customer is more likely to remain loyal and even become an advocate promoting your business.

If you do nothing to make your customers feel loved and don't provide a consistent product within five years, you are likely to have lost at least 50% of them.

A Case Study: How Rackspace gets to benefit in differing areas

A story – using ROC© principles to achieve consistency

Rackspace[118] hosts internet sites for other companies and has won awards for its customer service under the slogan 'Fanatical Support'. However, its service wasn't always so reliably consistent. It changed when one customer was pushed from pillar to post, trying to get a response to quite a simple query. He had phoned and emailed and, in the end, contacted the MD in desperation.

Rackspace took action to ensure consistently excellent service from then on. First, they recruited David Bryce as head of customer support and he created an aspirational banner with the vision:

"RACKSPACE GIVES FANATICAL SUPPORT"

Providing exceptional service was recognised to increase costs, so Rackspace adapted its business model to remain price-competitive. It did not attempt to offer cutting-edge technological expertise but rather a focused and standard offering, backed by fantastic service.

The most radical change was in how they handled phone calls; they got rid of the call queuing system. Changing the system forced a change in behaviour to reflect the value of customer service.

> "When a customer calls, that means they need our help, and we've got to answer the telephone… When a customer has a problem, we shouldn't deal with it when it's convenient for us. We should deal with it when it's convenient for the customer."
>
> Graham Weston, founder of Rackspace

The focus on service converted into profit, with Rackspace being the first internet firm to generate one in 2001. Over the next six years, it averaged 58% annual growth and, by 2008, Rackspace had passed AT&T as the highest-grossing firm in the industry.

By 2007, the company was talking to its customers three times per week. The company launched the 'Straitjacket Awards' for employees who'd been so fanatical about service that they'd become downright insane. By 2008, Rackspace was one of the top places to work in the US.

Getting it right

The business-to-business sector tends to have more complex customers. There is a range of people in the customer organisation looking for reliable consistency from their supplier. Consequently, a company-wide pervasive values-driven culture is essential. For example, if the finance department of a customer receives poor service from the accounts department, then this can jeopardise the relationship, however excellent the product or service received by the business.

A classic example of inconsistency often is in the area of customer service. The first step to addressing this is to identify what you think excellent customer service looks like – preferably working with customer service personnel, maybe doing mystery shopping and also looking at your competition or examples in other sectors with exceptional service.

For many people, estimated at 9-10 million per day,[119] Amazon is the benchmark of excellent service. It focuses on the customer experience. Customers get used to the speed of delivery, ease of payment and suggestions tailored to them as individuals. The Amazon service feels like personal service even though it is automated. It may seem unfair for people to have such expectations from other suppliers. Still, in many cases, Amazon can supply a product if another company fails to measure up and generally with very few clicks, even 'one-click'. They cleverly use Prime, which charges people to be part of their loyalty programme, to help pay for the consistent service and to encourage more purchases, which may include any company's products.

You need to develop a system to ensure consistently excellent service every time. Your system might be a checklist to follow, it might be training for staff and/or software, it might start with something simple like implementing some standards, e.g. every call is answered within three rings by whoever is available.

Consistency and quality has an impact on business: Amazon identified that even a one-tenth of a second delay in a page loading could reduce sales by 1%.

Consistency in customer service will also depend on your supply chain. This is identified as one of the reasons for the high level of customer complaints identified by the ICS and mentioned above.

I used internet firm Zooplus for my cat food for over a decade when we had cats. They were excellent and very consistent, too consistent as it happens. I once got close to running out of cat food (I had been away) but I didn't worry because I knew they delivered quickly. Enter a new delivery firm, DHL, who on both the Friday and Monday provided very specific hour windows when they would deliver. The first day, the note on the tracking was 'wrong address'; the second day, the note on the tracking was 'couldn't find'. So, I attempted to contact them. No phone number, just an email form to complete and at no time when trying to deliver had they rung. The result: I didn't think highly of DHL, but also my trust in Zooplus had been reduced; they were no longer consistent. If the delivery hadn't arrived by the end of the week, I would have bought from elsewhere and may not have gone back if the new supplier was good. Over ten years of good service undermined by a supply chain issue.

Your organisation needs to provide amazing life-changing product consistently. NB: this can be as simple as turning up on time. To achieve that takes every principle of the ROC©, from staff who care and can be adaptable, to enough profit to ensure you have the cash flow to supply on time.

Consistency is the foundation of trust on which you build success.

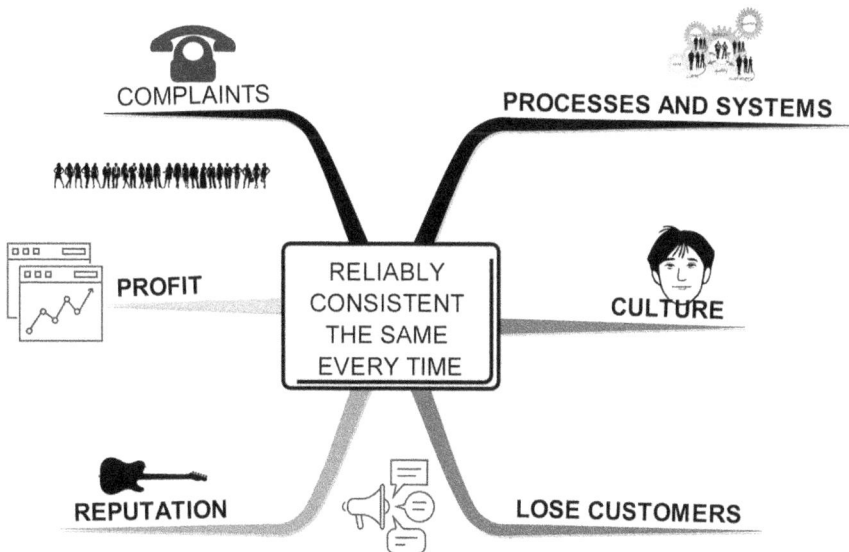

Figure 17: Reliably Consistent – the same every time

Scoring yourself on the ROC©

Rate how reliably consistent you are.

A score of ten would mean that everyone gets the same quality, not necessarily the same thing and you can prove it by what you track, feedback and customer retention. A low score would probably indicate issues across a lot of the ROC© from values to staff and profits; hopefully, you already knew you had a problem and you're working on it.

Chapter Twenty-three

Minimising Environmental Impact

Ensuring a neutral carbon footprint

When I tell people I have been writing a book on *Being Good* in business, many of them automatically assume that means being more environmentally aware. It is a given that being ethical in business means considering your impact on the environment.

In the long term, there's no alternative to sustainable development if we are to survive and satisfy the needs of a world that has a current world population of 7.6 billion, which is expected to reach 8.6 billion in 2030, 9.8 billion in 2050 and 11.2 billion in 2100, according to the United Nations.[120] NB: in 2015, the estimate was just 9 billion population[121] by 2050, so there has been almost a 10% increase in the estimate in less than a decade!

Evidence that our environment needs better protecting includes:
* The frequency of extreme weather events like flooding.
* Increased poor quality of air due to human activities.
* Increased incidents of forest fires due to global warming.
* Decreased ice caps of earth.
* Increased deforestation.
* Increased death of sea creatures due to excessive plastics.

Environmentalism is very high profile. "The People and Nature Survey for England"[122] conducted by the UK government found that 83% of adults surveyed said they were going to make changes to their lifestyle to protect the environment.

Even so, there are still companies that are convinced that the more environmentally friendly they become, the more the effort will erode their competitiveness. They comply with their legal requirements if they are big enough but still believe it will add to costs and will not deliver immediate financial benefits. They then fear that they will lose out to competitor companies, particularly in the developing world, who may not consider the environment and do not have the extra costs. It can mean that the need to become sustainable like corporate social responsibility, is divorced from the core business objectives, when it needs to be part of the mainstream.

In contrast, companies like Unilever now look at all their providers' environmental policies, not just those of their raw materials suppliers. So, even if you are an advertising agency, your environmental impact and strategy will have a role in how attractive you are to customers like them.

It's not easy; often, suppliers can't provide green inputs or transparency and sustainable manufacturing needs new equipment and processes, but there can be huge benefits as well.

Currently, there are only rules for large companies about reporting their environmental impact, but they are likely to begin to apply to smaller ones because, if they supply the bigger organisations, they will need to provide data to them. There is legislation that is collectively lumped together as ESG, which the British Business Bank explains as:

> "ESG is a collective term for a business's impact on the environment and society as well as how robust and transparent its governance is in terms of company leadership, executive pay, audits, internal controls and shareholder rights.
>
> It measures how your business integrates environmental, social and governance practices into operations, as well as your business model, its impact and its sustainability.
>
> The three components that make up ESG are environmental, social and governance."[123]

In terms of environment reporting in the UK, the Companies (Strategic Report) (Climate-related Financial Disclosure) Regulations 2022 requires some companies to disclose climate-related financial information in their annual reports and the Companies Act 2006 includes the need for large companies to include in their annual report a strategic report with information about their ESG policies and practices. Regulations are constantly evolving, and all organisations, whatever their legal structure, will need to stay up to date with the latest requirements to ensure compliance.

How being environmentally friendly can provide competitive advantage
Environmentalism can be good for any organisation.

A study[124] of the sustainability initiatives of thirty large corporations identified that sustainability is "a motherlode of organisational and technological innovations that yield both bottom-line and top-line returns."

Some companies such as Patagonia have made their environmental stance part of what makes them stand out as a company. They have built on the tradition of make do and mend, which contrasts with the throwaway attitude to cheap clothes that is common.

Patagonia, who make outdoor clothing, push the five R's: reduce – buy less, even with advertising campaigns stating "Don't Buy This Jacket"; reuse – encouraging people to swap or resell; repair – they offer online repair guides and in-store repairs; recycle – where they get reprocessed; reimagine – changing the use of a garment. They encourage customers to send clothes back to facilities that will reprocess them into new garments, therefore keeping those items out of landfill. They also ask customers to pledge not to buy things they don't need. To help combat the climate crisis, Patagonia also try to significantly reduce the amount of virgin material they use. For example, in one season, 94% of Patagonia's line used recycled materials, allowing the company to avoid 4,300 metric tonnes of CO_2.[125]

> "We design and sell things made to last and be useful. But we ask our customers not to buy from us what you don't need or can't really use. Everything we make – everything anyone makes – costs the planet more than it gives back."
>
> Patagonia public statement, 2012

Patagonia also works with Blue Sign, a third-party organisation that vets products for chemicals and residues, and through The Footprint Chronicles, customers can track the overall impact of their products from design until delivery.

Consequently, Patagonia has a loyal customer base willing to pay more for clothes they know are made to last, and this has resulted in a 40% increase in sales.

> "If we wish to lead corporate America by example, we have to be profitable. No company will respect us, no matter how much money we give away or how much publicity we receive for being one of the '100 Best Companies', if we are not profitable."
>
> Yvon Chouinard, Patagonia's founder

Patagonia[126] started as a small company selling tools for climbers and has grown into a wide-ranging outdoor apparel enterprise, nearly doubling its turnover to $1 billion in the five years leading up to 2018. As a company that targets consumers who care about the environment and the outdoors, Patagonia has been highly effective at creating alignment between its business and operational model.

The business model is to create value by selling high-quality, high-utility outdoor products, especially for low impact sports like hiking, climbing, snowboarding and others. They do this while maintaining corporate ethics that have made it one of the 'World's Most Ethical Companies' for over six years in a row. Patagonia roots their business model in four core values – quality, environmentalism, integrity and innovation – all of which they convey through their operational model. Staff turnover is just 4%.[127]

They see everyone as responsible for sustainability, so in 2014 Patagonia got rid of their sustainability department and made it part of the business.

Part of Patagonia's business model also includes an emphasis on helping to protect the very thing that their top consumers care about most: the outdoors. It's best summarised in their 'Reason for Being', which emphasises the connection between their customers' love of outdoors and Patagonia's dedication to protecting it.

> "Our values reflect those of a business started by a band of climbers and surfers, and the minimalist style they promoted. The approach we take towards product design demonstrates a bias for simplicity and utility. For us at Patagonia, a love of wild and beautiful places demands participation in the fight to save them, and to help reverse the steep decline in the overall environmental health of our planet. We donate our time, services and at least 1% of our sales to hundreds of grassroots environmental groups all over the world who work to help reverse the tide."[128]

In 2018, they even endorsed two candidates, Democrats representative Jacky Rosen in Nevada and Senator Jon Tester in Montana, for their stances on protecting public lands. Both won their election battles.

Other companies like Tesco have become more environmentally aware over time and have realised that it can give them a marketing edge. They have developed a range of initiatives to cut food waste. These have included leading the way in selling oddly shaped fruit and vegetables, which would have previously been rejected, to creating an opportunity by selling small avocados in cardboard egg boxes. Their snack avocados not only created a new market but also stopped them being thrown away, which was happening because they were too small to be sold.

The King Charles food waste project launched in 2023 is an initiative that aims to reduce food waste by ensuring edible surplus food and waste produce goes to charities supporting those in need or is reused. The king has donated funds to help hundreds of food banks and charities across the UK store more food by providing them with fridges and freezers.[129]

The danger of ignoring or responding slowly to environmental impact is illustrated by what happened to Nestlé when they committed to reducing their purchases of palm oil from companies involved in deforestation but said it would take five years.[130] Greenpeace and consumers were not satisfied with this and developed a spoof 'Take a break' advert showing someone unwrapping a Kit Kat and then eating a bloody orangutan finger. While Nestlé got it taken down from YouTube, it had already been copied and reposted 180,000 times in the first twenty-four hours, rising to 700,000 within days. *The Sun*, the largest circulation newspaper in the UK, then covered it, calling it a 'Kitkatstrophe' and *Forbes* labelled it a 'Kat fight'. The stats again show the power and impact of social media. They also show the need to respond speedily.

Why being environmentally friendly makes sense

Using less saves money and, to achieve it, you have to be innovative, which encourages one of the fundamental principles of the ROC© and supports business success. Innovative and better products sell well and, marketed correctly, give you a competitive edge, as Patagonia illustrate.

Many companies have started to become more environmentally focused because they have been forced to. Still, it is essential to recognise that even having to comply can provide a market opportunity.

A simple example in the UK happened when supermarkets were forced to charge for plastic bags to reduce landfill and pollution. Many have taken the opportunity to create well designed 'bags for life' that promote their companies and that consumers are happy to pay for. We have become walking ads for them and pay for the privilege.

As companies take environmentalism more seriously, they begin to audit their supply chain, then to innovate with new products and then even develop new operational and business models. All of this can get you ahead of the game; often, the legislation will follow and give you a competitive advantage.

Companies[131] in the vanguard of compliance naturally spot business opportunities first. In 2002, Hewlett Packard learnt that Europe's Waste from Electrical and Electronic Equipment (WEEE) regulations would require hardware manufacturers to pay for the cost of recycling products in proportion to their sales. Calculating that the government-sponsored recycling arrangements were going to be expensive, HP teamed up with three electronics makers – Sony, Braun and Electrolux – to create the private European Recycling Platform. By 2007, the platform, working with more than 1,000 companies in thirty countries, recycled about 20% of the equipment covered by the WEEE directive. The platform's charges are 55% lower than its rivals, partly because of the scale of its operations. Not only did HP save more than $100 million from 2003 to 2007, but it enhanced its reputation with consumers, policymakers and the electronics industry by having come up with the idea.

Getting multiple benefits

Working from home can have significant positive environmental impacts as the pandemic has shown, reducing travel time, travel costs and energy use, pollution and saving business office space and the associated costs. It can also be very popular with staff, adding to their job satisfaction. It provides flexibility and can also increase the pool of potential recruits; for example, people with caring duties can find home working very useful.

Some businesses in the UK give their returned stock to charity. It may have nothing wrong with it; the customer may just have changed their mind and the charity can sell it to make money and help others, and it keeps it from being wasted and costing the company in disposal fees. This returned stock transfer happens with clothes and particularly furniture. Others give close-to-obsolete food and old stock to charities to reduce waste and the cost of disposal.

It's not easy

Minimising environmental impact is good business sense as costs rise. It makes sense to reduce waste and the materials used and particularly energy usage, as it reduces costs. What is more complex are decisions about what constitutes being environmentally friendly. Paper production is one of the most complex environmental areas; for example, is recycled paper better environmentally than paper certified by the Forest Stewardship Council (FSC)? Until I saw a presentation, I didn't even know there were different standards.

There are pros and cons. To recycle a tonne of paper uses the same power as an average home consumes in nine months, creates one metric tonne of CO_2 and uses 7,000 gallons of water. In fact, much paper that claims to be recycled may only contain a small percentage of recycled material.

The Worldwide Fund for Nature (WWF) considers FSC the only credible certification (above purely recycled). Still, it's not straightforward and many people don't understand FSC, while recycled seems easy to understand.

Even more complex are business sectors that are potentially destroying themselves – the prominent examples from the past and present are fishing and farming. By taking too much out of the environment, you destroy it, so you cannot continue.

However, while it is difficult, it is not an excuse to do nothing.

YOUR ROC© CHALLENGE

Are you even doing the basics in terms of the environment? Does everyone turn off lights, only boil enough water for the drinks required and think before they print? Is it in your culture?

What is sustainability?

Everyone needs to think about sustainability. Sustainability (Savitz and Weber, 2006) has become a buzzword for an array of social and environmental causes. In the business world, it denotes a powerful and defining idea: "A sustainable corporation is one that creates profit for its shareholders while protecting the environment and improving the lives of those with whom it interacts." You need to operate so that your business interests and the interests of the environment and society intersect. A sustainable business stands an excellent chance of being more successful tomorrow than it is today, and remaining successful, not just for months or even years, but for decades or generations.

Using a financial analogy, sustainable organisations and societies generate and live off interest rather than depleting their capital. Capital, in this context, includes natural resources such as water, air, sources of energy and foodstuffs. It also includes human and social assets – from worker commitment to community support – as well as economic resources, such as a licence to operate, a receptive marketplace, and legal and financial infrastructure. A company can deplete its resources for a while, but generally not for long. A firm that honours the principles of sustainability, by contrast, is built to last.

Sustainability in practice is now recognised as essential for doing business in an interdependent world. Sustainability in the broadest sense is all about interdependence, which takes several forms.

Sustainability respects the interdependence of living beings on one another and on their natural environment. Sustainability means operating a business in a way that causes minimal harm to living creatures and that does not deplete but instead restores and enriches the environment.

Everyone can play their part

Even if you are a service company, you can minimise your impact on the environment by driving more efficient cars. We had a hybrid and a tiny vehicle, which attracted zero road tax because it is so fuel and emissions friendly. We needed to buy a new car to replace the hybrid. We discovered that disposing of the batteries in hybrid cars was not good for the environment. Modern diesel cars are now very environmentally friendly for the long journeys we do, so we have swapped to a diesel, despite many headlines suggesting this is wrong; another example of the complexity.

Everyone can recycle what they can, minimising energy and water usage and just being more aware. Reuse is also essential; can your old equipment be valuable to a charity or other community groups?

A Case Study: Using Tech for Good

A story – a business with ROC© principles anyone can use

Ecosia, an environmentally conscious search engine set up by Christian Kroll in Germany, now means that every time you do an internet search using their service, they will plant a tree. Each search removes around 1kg of CO_2 from the atmosphere because of their solar plant and the Ecosia forests.

As of November 2023, over 186 million trees had been planted. It calls itself the world's largest green internet firm and has 20 million users, including me. Each time you go to search, you see the tree count ticking over, it's inspirational.

It collaborates with rivals currently using the algorithms developed by Bing, Microsoft's search engine, and getting a share of their ad revenue. Initially, it sought to work with Google. Ecosia collaborates with experts and locals to run its tree planting. It wants to ensure the maximum impact with trees not just soaking up CO_2 but also solving other problems. In Senegal, Ecosia's trees have replaced a mono-culture of peanuts and maize with 'forest gardens' where the trees are surrounded by fruit, vegetables and medicinal herbs.

It works in an environmentally friendly way, its servers are all powered by renewable energy and its offices include a balcony where they grow herbs, walnuts and fast-growing paulownia trees. While it has to store some data on users for cybersecurity, it only keeps four days' worth. It also is trying to find a way to steer search results to get more environmentally friendly results.

Changing your business model

But can you go further? Can you change what you offer, to reduce your environmental impact? In *Triple Bottom Line* (Savitz and Weber, 2006) they talk about how some companies are moving to 'dematerialisation', a second element in the evolving concept of sustainability.

Dematerialisation is based on the realisation that consumers don't necessarily *want* or even need the physical materials used in manufacturing, shipping and many products. When you buy a television, you don't want a box of electrical components – so many pounds of glass, plastic, metal, silicon and other materials. No, you want the fun, information and entertainment you derive from watching programmes on TV. The physical elements are irrelevant and even *undesirable,* not only to the consumer but to the manufacturer, the shipper, the merchandiser, the retailer and whoever must dispose of the broken or worn-out TV set a few years down the road. At every stage, the extraction, processing, shaping, shipping, handling and disposal of those materials creates costs, depletes the environment and produces streams of waste. If the materials could be reduced or eliminated while keeping the benefits TV provides, everyone would be better off.

Building on this insight (and driven by the availability of computer chips that enable dramatic size reductions for electronic components), many companies are finding ways to reduce the physical presence of the goods they produce. Today's computers, music systems and telephones are a fraction of the size of their counterparts from twenty or thirty years ago. Today's large, flat-screen televisions contain much less material than the small-screen, big-cabinet units in most living rooms a generation ago. When we went to Japan in 2011, we saw a prototype of a system where your wall became your TV, computer, book or photo album. Sadly, I haven't yet been able to buy one.

Cars are becoming lighter (and therefore less costly to manufacture, service and ship, as well as less expensive to run), as steel is replaced by aluminium, and metals by new ultra-strong plastics. Offices are gradually replacing costly, bulky paper with electronic data flows; vinyl records (while making a comeback in a niche way) have given way, first to smaller CDs and then to completely dematerialised online streaming. Paper books are in rude health (maybe you are reading this as a published paper book) and, of course, digital downloads are also growing. However, print-on-demand technology is ensuring that print runs now fit demand rather than a need for wasteful long print runs, which are then remaindered and pulped.

Pushing dematerialisation further, many kinds of companies are exploring ways to transform the goods they sell into services, thereby providing the same value at less cost, or more value at the same price.

Dematerialisation moves us into the realms of marketing. How can we meet customers' needs most effectively – are there innovative ways that we can offer what they want, which increase their satisfaction, increase our profits and help save the planet?

The airline industry has particular environmental challenges. Sustainable aviation fuel is the only realistic near-term option for long-range jets, but will be lucky to reach 15% penetration by the mid-2030s. Hydrogen looks good but is decades away. Oil companies are not currently investing enough in developing cost-effective alternatives to the products derived from their existing oil wells.

However, paradoxically, a design concept that has been around for 100 years could be the answer. Still at the prototype stage as I write, blended wing aircraft[132] may be the way the airline industry meet the net zero targets. The aircraft design blends the wing and the body of the aircraft into a single structure, which makes it more aerodynamic and fuel-efficient than traditional aircraft designs.

The blended wing design allows the entire airframe to provide lift, which reduces the weight of the aircraft and enables it to carry the same payload as traditional designs while consuming less fuel. The design also eliminates the need for a tail, which reduces drag and noise. Blended wing aircraft have several environmental benefits. They are more fuel-efficient than traditional aircraft designs, which means they consume less fuel and emit fewer greenhouse gases. According to a study, blended wing aircraft designs are estimated to reduce carbon emissions by up to 30% compared to current airliners. The design also reduces noise pollution, which is a significant environmental concern in areas surrounding airports. JetZero hopes to have a prototype airliner that can use existing airport gates by 2027. It has been awarded a $235 million contract by the US Department of the Air Force to build a working prototype of its revolutionary blended wing body (BWB) aircraft. It believes its all composite material design will deliver 50% fuel efficiency.

YOUR ROC© CHALLENGE

Is environmental thinking seen as core to your business or an add on? How much do you consider it when thinking about innovations?

Toyota and Volkswagen have moved from thinking about cars to thinking about transportation and, consequently, car sharing with partner companies, KINTO and MILES Mobility respectively. They are exploring how you could get instant access to a car when you needed it without having the capital outlay, the insurance, maintenance or storage issues. This will surely link in the future to driverless vehicles.

Thinking about the environment and current environmental challenges can potentially give you a new market niche or competitive advantage. In sub-Saharan Africa, the shortage of trees due to deforestation has caused an architect[133] to revive a 3,500-year-old building technique, the Nubian Vault. The method, which uses locally produced mud bricks, is much more environmentally friendly than importing modern materials such as concrete or corrugated metal. Granier, the architect, claims that it creates a much more durable and comfortable home.

By training local people to use the technique, La Voûte Nubienne, an NGO, provides them with a new source of income. Granier says the plan is for the project to kick-start independent markets for house-building, which will then spread naturally to other areas and communities.

"Our organisation gives an architectural solution to transform housing in Africa in future," he says. "The goal at the end is to give people the tools and the capacity to build by themselves."

Over 2000 Nubian Vault homes have been built and every year 500 Nubian Vault buildings are now being built by 400 specially trained masons. The majority of projects are rural housing, but there are also some schools, clinics, churches and mosques, as well as a small amount of urban housing.

Competitive advantage

Many of the companies mentioned in this chapter are using a focus on being environmentally friendly to create a niche and a competitive advantage or to future-proof their company or an industry.

Thinking about the environment can result in totally new business areas. Celtic Renewables is creating biofuels from the by-products of Scottish whisky production. It has attracted £43 million of investment for its new bio refinery, which will be able to produce one million litres of sustainable biochemicals annually. Initially, it has focused on using residues from the Scotch whisky industry. But this platform technology can be applied to a wide range of by-products from other industries worldwide, including food production and agriculture. They have received letters of intent from several global chemical companies, and demand for products from their first plant is already 300% oversubscribed based on its capacity.

In Japan and the UK, a bacterium has been identified that can 'eat' PET, the most common single-use plastic, allowing for potential reuse, but commercial development is still pending.

Climate change is part of the current operating environment and most of the world realises it cannot be ignored.

But it goes beyond just the climate. The London Hilton on Bankside in London opened its first vegan-only suite in 2019. The room is wholly made from animal and cruelty-free materials and the minibar and room service is vegan.

Seeing it as an opportunity and challenge is part of being a *Good* company and recognising it is part of the broader sustainability of any organisation.

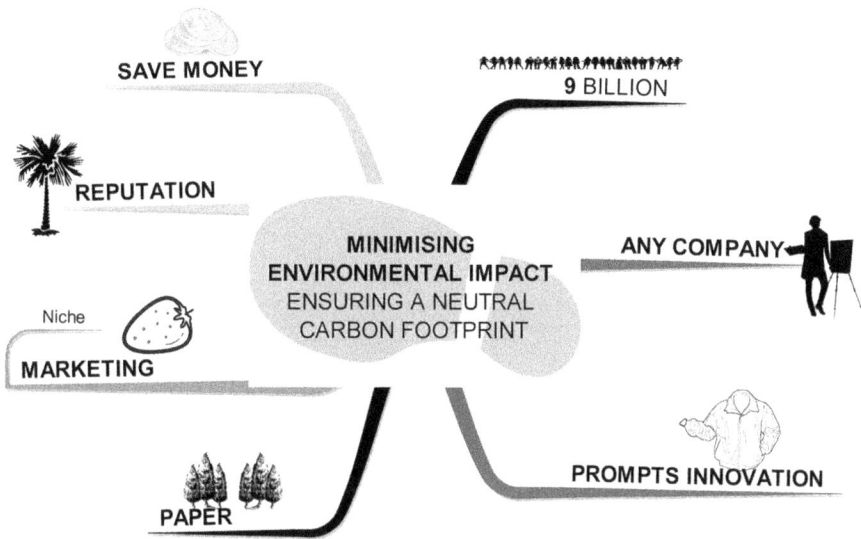

Figure 18: Minimising Environmental Impact – ensuring a neutral carbon footprint

Scoring yourself on the ROC©

Rate how environmentally friendly you are.

A score of ten would probably mean that you take this seriously and already are monitoring and reporting on your carbon footprint. A low rating would indicate that this has not been a priority, maybe because of your industry or because you have not thought it was critical to business success.

Chapter Twenty-four

Financial Success

Ensuring a long-term future

And finally, we get to where the majority of business books about success start: money.

There is no objective definition of financial success; it depends on your vision for the business, the scale that you want to achieve and how much money that will take.

> *Being good is good business if you have a clear definition of financial success,*
> *which meets the needs of all your stakeholders and not just shareholders.*

The three fundamental principles for sustainable ongoing commercial success reflect the need to have strong marketing, i.e. a niche, linked to innovative growth, products and processes, and a financially sound way to run your organisation.

Only one of these is directly about money, and the other two are key drivers to ensure ongoing financial success.

The following parable illustrates why I chose these three principles. It has several themes that are relevant to financial success and strategy. I wrote it many years ago in response to people who didn't seem to understand strategy and thought it was irrelevant to their organisation as what they did was too straightforward to need it. I chose the simplest product I could think of – the lettuce – and a simple family setting initially with three sons, which grew to seven, all wanting to compete with their father to run a more successful business. I like using parables, as generally everyone loves a story, and it allows one to consider some hard questions.

This parable is about how, even if you are only growing lettuces, you can create exciting niches. Still, it is also very relevant to the overall area of financial success as, for each of the brothers, commercial success and success overall has a different meaning. It illustrates how turnover and profit are very different and how your strategy, niche and, particularly, innovation all contribute to your financial results.

A parable for our time: The lettuce growers

Once upon a time, there was a lettuce farmer and he had seven sons. They were all very competitive, wanting to beat their father and each other. They all went into the lettuce business with a determination to achieve financial success in their own way. Without knowing it, this meant each was creating their own specific niche.

Alfie, the eldest, thought, "How can I sell more?" He recognised that his father had focused on just the local town, so he decided to sell to the next village as well. His financial success was to double his turnover, though the cost of delivery meant his profit didn't go up that much. His niche was geographical; he dominated the local towns in terms of lettuce growing.

Bertie, the second son, was interested in the environment and being *Good*. He saw that many people were concerned about the quality and source of their food. Hence, he marketed his lettuces as local and, as soon as he could, he qualified for the organic mark. Bertie didn't sell more in volume, but his turnover and profit went up, as the average price for organic lettuce was 350% more than for standard lettuce. The combination of fewer chemicals and higher sales price meant his financial success was considerably more profit. He could also take on apprentices and the long-term unemployed, as the production system was more labour intensive, and yet he still could make a profit. His niche was being organic and very ethical. His ethical stance has increased his success, and he now gives a share of his earnings to support relevant charities, including one that works with him to employ people with learning disabilities in the growing process.

Son number three, Colin, wasn't really interested in lettuce growing; he was very bright and thought a lot. He thought about how people use lettuce and decided that they often used it as a garnish or part of a sandwich, then ended up throwing away the rest of the lettuce. Also, people complained about having to wash the lettuce and the inconvenience of having to try to dry lettuce leaves after washing. He also liked technology, so working with a packager, he invented a system that would keep bagged leaves fresh and created a new industry and sector, which is now multi-billion pound and worldwide. (Update: the global packaged salad market size was valued at $10.78 billion in 2020.[134]) He created a multinational business with the average price per weight of lettuce 500% higher than for a simple unbagged whole lettuce. He had substantial financial success in terms of the size of the business and created the bagged lettuce niche, but it took a long time to develop the technology and lots of investment. Colin didn't grow any lettuces directly, instead managing the packaging, distribution and sales; he was an expert at supply chain management.

Son number four, Donald, liked to travel. He realised that people were getting more adventurous in the food they would eat. He started growing Lollo Rosso and other foreign varieties, selling to restaurants and consumers, also securing a price 500% higher than a simple cos lettuce. His financial success was in higher profits and turnover in the niche market of specialist varieties of lettuce.

Eric, son number five, learnt from his elder brothers, identifying where the most profits were. Working with Bertie, Colin and Donald, he developed a range of speciality bagged lettuce, some of which was organic. He didn't grow lettuce himself but made good profits as by weight he could get eight times the price of standard lettuces with no capital investment. His financial success was in his income and the design of his business meant he could run it from a laptop anywhere in the world, so he went on lots of long holidays. His niche was in speciality bagged lettuce.

Freddie, the sixth son, looked at market trends and identified an opportunity with the growth of 'grow your own' and people living in cities with no gardens. He developed living lettuce, so people could buy and keep a small tray of growing lettuce on the windowsill and have fresh lettuce leaves as they needed them. His baby leaf salad in a plastic tray sold weight for weight at fifteen times the price of standard lettuces and involved less labour and maintenance as it was sold younger. Overall, he made the highest percentage profit on turnover, which made him a financial success and the leader in the living lettuce niche.

The final son, George, as the youngest, was the one who learnt to get on with everyone, so he was a natural collaborator. He set up collaborations with other salad ingredient growers, egg and pig farmers, and sold ready meal salads with egg and ham. He saw this as an opportunity, as people were looking for convenient and healthier lunches rather than the standard sandwich. His financial success and niche was to create a new ready meal category and get it into supermarkets.

The moral of the story is that their areas of interest and skills led them to ask different questions, thus to different business models, different sorts of financial success and levels of profit and market niches. Even though they all started from the simple lettuce, they all took very different routes and all of them felt that they had achieved more financial success than their father. Whatever the business, there are always a multitude of paths to take. The choice depends on which fits with your vision and values, and this will have an impact on how and what financial success you achieve and your niche.

YOUR ROC© CHALLENGE

Is there a clear definition for success in your organisation?

The story of the lettuce growers illustrates the range of niches that can be created for even something as simple as lettuce. To have ongoing financial success, you need to have a strong market position. Whether you are a large business, smaller business, start-up or charity, this means finding a clear niche market or market proposition.

Chapter Twenty-five

An Identifiable Market Niche

Stand out from the crowd

The importance of having a niche has increased as marketing has changed with the growth of the digital world. Potential customers now have so much more power as they search the internet for solutions. They need to feel attracted to you as a business; you can't just rely on a big marketing campaign. Having a niche makes you stand out from the crowd.

It has always been useful to have a niche, but in the digital era and the global market, it is essential. In today's highly competitive landscape, it's clear that businesses are facing immense challenges in standing out among countless others. It's important for your market position to be clearly defined so that you can make the most of every opportunity and truly shine.

The opposite of having a niche is being all things to all people, a classic error that many start-ups make when they think that they should pursue every opportunity or they might lose out.

But it can also happen with more substantial companies; one of the largest was Woolworths. It failed because it was not clear why you would go there. What was its niche? For some of the items it offered, discount shops like Poundland took its place and initially thrived, which shows Woolworths could have survived if it had clarified why it existed – what its niche was. However, even the pound shops are now struggling as 'cheap' is not a great niche.

What is a niche?

Generally, an identifiable market niche means that you are serving a group of people or businesses with particular needs, who often actively need the solution you are offering. Many lucrative niches are ignored because companies target broader markets but providing they meet vital criteria smaller niches can be very successful. Particularly today, very targeted niches are possible because geography has become less of an issue for many businesses. What, without the internet, might have been too small a market, can become viable if it is global.

Digital technology and big data now mean that targeting and satisfying the specific needs of individual customers is now possible and often expected, but this should not be confused with creating a niche for your business.

A niche is what makes you unique and your brand stand out. It does not necessarily mean targeting a specific market; it can be the way that the business operates. John Lewis has been renowned for its strategy of 'never knowingly undersold'; that is its niche linked to a strong customer service ethos. They have now scrapped it. It will be interesting to see whether their reduced commercial success has anything to do with this.

While writing this book, I met a woman who built a very successful travel agency using the same strategy – never let a customer find that a fellow traveller has paid less and, if they did, she refunded the difference. She also got her staff to organise flowers to greet people in their hotel rooms when they arrived and to treat each trip with the importance it could have for the traveller, arguing that after a house and a car, holidays are the next major purchase. If at any point the customer returned and was justifiably dissatisfied then the travel agency would book them another holiday free, the ultimate in good marketing and cheaper than advertising.

A niche is more about the business model than individual products and services. Most large companies will have more than one niche. It is critical to stay adaptable.

As Rita McGrath[135] in her book *The End of Competitive Advantage* argues, companies must develop the ability to rapidly and continuously address new opportunities rather than search for increasingly unsustainable long-term competitive advantages. If you do adapt or change your niche, you need to do it within the context of a consistent set of values and your theory of change.

Kodak had a very flexible niche in capturing memorable moments but lost sight of it as it became obsessed with the income it generated from printing photos. It became fixed in seeing itself in a niche of 'photo printing' and 'film selling'.

Developing your niche

The starting place for creating a strong niche is knowing your market and understanding where you fit in it.

A useful question to ask in developing a niche can be: what can we do to contribute more to our customers, our community and the world, which will also meet the vision and values of the business?

Firstly, you need to map where you and your competitors sit against identified needs in the market, to see if there are any immediate gaps.

The niche could come from any element of what you offer at each stage, from purchasing, product/service or after purchase, see Figure 19.

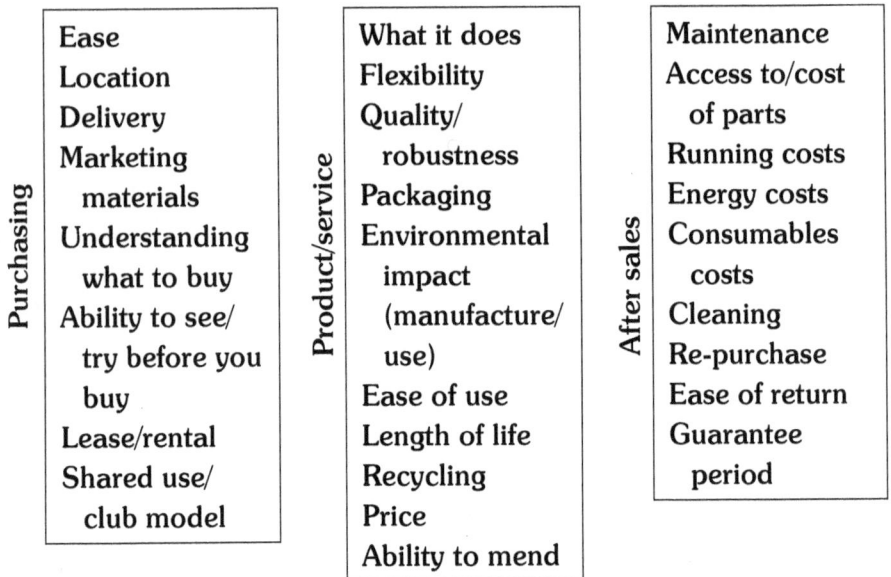

Purchasing	Product/service	After sales
Ease	What it does	Maintenance
Location	Flexibility	Access to/cost
Delivery	Quality/	of parts
Marketing	robustness	Running costs
materials	Packaging	Energy costs
Understanding	Environmental	Consumables
what to buy	impact	costs
Ability to see/	(manufacture/	Cleaning
try before you	use)	Re-purchase
buy	Ease of use	Ease of return
Lease/rental	Length of life	Guarantee
Shared use/	Recycling	period
club model	Price	
	Ability to mend	

Figure 19: Potential parts of an offering that can create a niche

Amazon stands out with its niche based on making the purchase easy at every stage from search to payment and delivery. In contrast, Dyson has niched on innovative products that provide a high-quality result. It is harder to find a well-known brand that has a niche based on after-purchase benefits, such as low running costs. Ongoing, this looks like a significant opportunity to create a niche, as all sorts of crucial commodities become scarcer, including energy. Patagonia (mentioned in Chapter 23) has capitalised on the potential to repair, reuse, recycle, reimagine and reuse its products as a niche. But incredibly, no single car firm has decided to niche on the cheapness of maintenance and running costs.

Identifying the unmet needs of existing customers and markets
You can also think beyond your specific offering to the broad questions of life and how what you do could maybe help address them as unmet needs for your customers.

Fulfilling unmet needs is how to create changes in the world.

If you can identify an unmet need, then you will have the opportunity to create a great niche.

Addressing the unmet needs of people is doing *Good*. Either it will improve their lives, or it will allow your business to grow and provide worthwhile employment for more people and/or you will generate income, which can be used for doing *Good*.

You can either look for unmet needs using your existing products in new markets or develop your products to meet unmet needs in your current markets. As you identify unmet needs, identify the wider *Good* that addressing them will achieve. There are a set of minimum standards that you need to achieve to satisfy a market. If you aren't meeting them, you either need to address them first or consider another market. Only when the obvious needs are met can you then begin to look for unmet needs. For example, I have an unmet need for a hairdryer that I can use with an arthritic shoulder, which also creates great results for someone who is useless at blow-drying their hair. However, if the dryer does not effectively dry hair, then it is pointless no matter how much it addresses my specific needs.

Finding unmet needs in new markets

You can find a new niche by taking an existing product or service and offering or shaping it for a new market that is not being served, or a market that may have just arisen.

Brad Burton set up 4Networking, a business networking organisation, as a response to the fact that more and more people were setting up as sole traders, often working from home, and were looking for supportive organisations they could belong to. There were other networking groups, but their focus was not as supportive. 4N's motto was "Meet, Like, Know, Trust" and its aim to be 50% social and 50% business, providing people with micro-businesses the opportunity to share issues and create a support network. It grew to over 250 groups (his goal) with over 5000 meetings a year. But its niche has not been easy to protect with lots of other competitors starting up free versions, and its sustainable profit has come under threat. With the pandemic, it shifted its model to virtual networking and has never gone back to the large number of meetings it used to hold each year.

"It's not the product that makes a business, it's the offer presented to solve a very painful problem. Once you find the golden combination of a hungry market, a believable promise (offer) and proof that you can and have delivered on that offer, you have the foundation for a very successful business."

Rich Schefren

A Case Study: Creating a market niche by how you change the world

CareMore was named to reflect its philosophy of proactive care and a caring touch. It is an inspirational American healthcare provider offering state-funded care, which changes lives and saves the state money. Their simple, common-sense routines are focused on the patient as a person and, because they work, they save almost 20% on overall costs. They want to provide care that families would give themselves to their loved ones.

Looking at the market, Sheldon Zinberg in the late 1980s identified an ageing population with many specialists dealing with individual bits of their care but no coordinated care or simple support to prevent problems. Even then, he was prompted because of pressures on finances, and now it is even more relevant. The unmet need identified was for coordinated person-centred care, ranging from preventative measures to acute care. It took him several years to develop the service, which initially was not just for the elderly, but then became focused on this sector because of financial constraints.

What developed is not rocket science but does meet unmet needs. CareMore works with the elderly. It identified unmet needs often just by watching. For example, up to a third of older people failed to show up for appointments, not through wickedness but lack of transport. So, initially, they provided free transportation to get people to appointments. Now they predominantly visit people in their own homes and the payment model allows their care team to spend half an hour or more consulting with each patient. Home visits enable them to identify non-medical problems that are not addressed in medical school, such as no fridge to store insulin or dangerous rugs that might cause a fall. It might be that monthly they need to get a frail older person's toenails cut to reduce dangers of tripping and provide access to exercise sessions to increase muscle strength and stability. They aim to solve the root causes of health issues, whether they are behavioural, economic, or social.

They also are more proactive in their treatments and were early adopters of technology, providing talking pillboxes to remind people to take pills. They give people with congestive heart failure scales linked to the surgery and get them to weigh themselves daily so that they get early warning of problems with the heart, which are indicated by sudden weight gain. In the first six months of using the scales, hospital readmissions for congestive heart failure fell by over half.

A subject close to my heart is their focus on diabetes. For example, instead of leaving wounds or treating in an ad hoc way, they set up a wound clinic. The clinic is staffed with nurses caring for small cuts and providing regular monitoring to prevent the deterioration that can be the start of a problem leading to gangrene and amputation: the result – a reduction of more than 60% in amputations. The whole focus is on early-stage treatment and diligent follow up.

A person with diabetes being cared for by CareMore initially has a comprehensive medical assessment. They are monitored across a range of areas each month with plan adjustments as necessary. They get nutrition and exercise support, wound care management and supplies, and routine foot care to avoid unnecessary amputations.

For the sickest 5% of patients who cause 70% of the costs, there is an identified lead carer and integrated care delivery. Each patient has someone responsible for overseeing all aspects of their health and coordinating the potentially many specialists caring for the patient. The primary care[136] doctor-led medical home model is augmented with a full-time community health worker and greater support from social workers. Patients undergo a comprehensive, multidisciplinary assessment of their medical and social needs, the results being used to create a tailored care plan. For patients with multiple social risks (e.g., housing instability, poverty, loneliness, food insecurity), this exercise helped clarify where to direct early attention and resources, allowing for rapid stabilisation in many of the most complex cases. CareMore have also partnered with community-based organisations and social-safety-net institutions, such as food banks and housing authorities to be able to more effectively address the non-medical issues patients face.

Patients get frequent, structured follow-ups. Weekly contact from the community health worker to check in, evaluate progress, and address barriers to them following the care plan (e.g., transportation or health literacy). The community health worker, social worker and GP review the care plan weekly, re-prioritising tasks and assigning new responsibilities. Patients visit CareMore care centres monthly to see the whole team. There are follow-ups as necessary with the community health worker accompanying some patients to specialist visits and social service appointments. The social worker provides counselling for behavioural health needs, helps navigate social services, and arranges for necessary referrals and medical equipment. The primary care physician sees patients in the office to address gaps in care and stabilise chronic conditions.

The impact was evaluated through a randomised controlled trial. The evaluation found that the programme led to a $7,732 (or 37%) reduction in total medical spending per patient per year. This was primarily savings in hospital use: patients were less likely to be admitted to hospital (50% decrease), and when they were admitted, their hospital stays were shorter (62% decrease). There was also a small decline in specialist visits, possibly due to more active management of chronic illnesses by the primary care doctor. Patients were highly satisfied with the programme: its net promoter score (measured three months after enrollment in the programme) was 100 out of 100. I find CareMore so impressive because it continues to refine what it offers by tracking its impact and continues to improve after thirty years.

In the way it has met unmet needs, CareMore is improving the quality of life for older people, reducing costs, making more profit and increasing the job satisfaction of the medical professionals involved. Zinberg had to convince the private medical community in the US and to prove what he said:

"If you put people before profit, you will profit."

Charles R. Swindoll

By apparently doing more, including things not traditionally done by doctors, it has saved money, with its costs being 18% below the industry average. It developed the Medicare Advantage programme as a strategy to get funding based on patient outcomes and has expanded beyond California and also now works with low-income people and those with mental illnesses.

Despite ownership changing several times, it has stayed true to its ethos as a primary care provider focusing on those with complex needs, providing more care and innovating.

Not only has the model worked for the patients, but the staff, particularly the doctors, are less stressed, as they have more time to do a good job.

They continue to innovate. CareMore's Togetherness Programme[137] launched in 2017 to address the loneliness epidemic, uses consistent personal interaction, particularly encouraging older people to participate in an exercise programme. As a result of the Togetherness Programme, outpatient emergency room use has declined by 5%; despite a higher disease burden, acute hospital admissions are 11% lower per thousand.

YOUR ROC© CHALLENGE

Is there an unmet need you could address in your market?

Unmet needs often are the problems that people have but don't think can be solved. CareMore is an example of meeting unmet needs by adding additional elements to existing services and focusing more on the customers' real issues, such as problems with transport or loneliness.

To find unmet needs that are opportunities, you can observe how people act or ask questions about their problems; you can also ask your staff what they have seen or about requests that they have received.

A Case Study: meeting unmet needs in an ethical way

In 1970, Malcolm Walker, who understood the type of customer who shopped at Woolworths, having worked there, identified an unmet need for these customers. They only had fridges with little ice boxes, so they couldn't buy the large packs of frozen food that were available without wastage, nor could they afford them, so he started selling loose frozen food so that they could buy what they needed.

This unmet need was the start of Iceland, recognising the need for poor people to access quality food cheaply. Frozen food retains nutrients because of its preparation method and is cost-effective due to less waste and because factories can produce large runs at one time, thus saving on downtime.

Iceland has remained true to its values of good food and good value while being successful. In 1986, it became the first UK supermarket to remove artificial colourings, flavourings and non-essential preservatives from its own-brand products, two decades before some of its major rivals. Also in 1986, it became the first UK supermarket to ban monosodium glutamate (MSG) from its own-brand products. In 1990, it banned mechanically recovered meat (MRM) from all Iceland brand products. By 1995, it had achieved national coverage in the UK, with 752 stores and twenty-five years of consistently growing profits.

It has continued to look for unmet needs in its market; for example, it has a uniquely free, national home delivery service, meeting the needs of people who are poor and can't afford cars.

In terms of doing *Good*, the company has also developed a partnership with the Cancer Research Campaign to promote the health benefits of eating more frozen vegetables.

Iceland is an example of a company that knows its market and is continually looking for how it can meet its needs and problems. From the original limited freezer space in the little fridge to the current desire to be healthy and the need for free home delivery of cheap food if you are poor with no transport. A classic example of creating a successful business by being and doing *Good*.

Its latest activities have been in response to the cost of living crisis. One of the initiatives is the Iceland Food Club,[138] which allows members to apply for microloans of £25-100 on a pre-loaded card, which can be used in any Iceland or The Food Warehouse store. The loans are repaid at the rate of £10 a week, on a day of the member's choice, and are available in six annual windows coinciding with school holidays, when family finances are usually most acutely stretched. The Food Club has been developed in partnership with Fair For You, an award-winning, charity-owned ethical lender that is backed by leading social investors and is dedicated to helping the staggering 20 million of our fellow citizens who struggle to access credit from mainstream institutions. During the trial, an independent social impact report showed that 95% of participants found the Food Club helpful; 92% were able to end or reduce their use of food banks; more than 80% were able to stop borrowing from high-cost loan sharks; 71% said they were less likely to fall behind on rent, council tax, or other bills; 65% said their diet had improved; and 57% reported a reduction in stress, anxiety and depression about their finances.

Iceland has also recognised the particular needs of older people and offers a 10% discount every Tuesday.

Promoting your niche

Many companies confuse marketing with promotion. Marketing is every element of the marketing mix: what is sold, at how much, to whom and how. Advertising is just a communication element.

Niches have an impact on every element and also provide strong themes for promotional campaigns, such as Dove's 'campaign for real beauty', targeting 'normal women'.

Identifying a marketing engine in your niche

In his blog 'Embracing the Power User', Seth Godin talks about the importance of heavy users in making markets work. So, for example, there are people who go to the theatre every other week, tweet every three minutes, or send 200 cards a year. As a company, the skill is to attract and keep power users, who will help you get more users, i.e., act as a marketing engine.

X (formerly Twitter) benefits from power users who have pushed its use. Wikipedia relies on the work of 5,000 power editors who generate the content that attracts millions, also a great example of the power of collaboration.

eBay originally grew because it attracted a few thousand home businesses that used it as a platform to bring in millions of buyers.

Generally, power users are attracted to you because you provide a win-win that helps them achieve their goals. It is a road to success if you can design your offering to achieve this more than your competitors. Make power users more successful if your product does well and they will spread the message and reduce your marketing spend. The opposite also applies: upset power users and they, in this networked world, will make sure that the bad news travels fast.

YOUR ROC© CHALLENGE

Can you clearly define your market niche, and would all your staff and customers say the same?

A niche needs to be easy to explain and understand, and it needs to make sense. It does not need to have profound or different components, it just needs to bring together things that people want and need differently. Amazon started by selling books (printing of books began in the fifteenth century) using the postal service launched for the UK public in 1635, so not exactly revolutionary. But what it added was its focus on making it simple, from one-click payment and ordering to identifying new books you might like. Its niche is still making buying easy with Prime, for example.

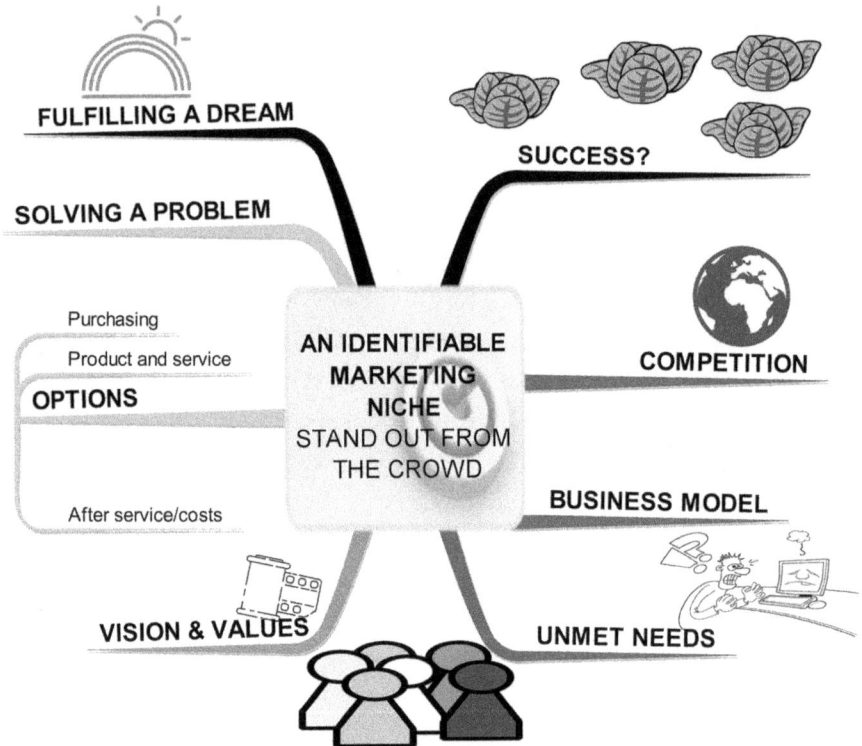

Figure 20: An Identifiable Marketing Niche – stand out from the crowd

Scoring yourself on the ROC©

Rate how you rank on having an identifiable market niche.

A score of ten would mean that everyone who needs to, from staff to prospects, knows your niche. A low rating would indicate you offer a 'me-too' product or service and there is a huge opportunity to improve. If you rate poorly here, this is an area of focus that will provide swift returns.

Chapter Twenty-six

Innovative Growth

Keeping up with change

The acceleration of innovation and the disruption it is causing is challenging for everyone, even the most innovative companies.

Across all industries, there is clear evidence that the technologies that underpin the fourth Industrial Revolution are having a significant impact on businesses. Not only are there new ways of doing things, but there are also different types of competition. Start-ups are bringing products and services to market using global digital platforms for research, development, marketing, sales and distribution. They threaten well-established businesses with their speed and how they improve the method, quality, or price at which they deliver. Part of this will be the impact of generative artificial intelligence (AI). The global AI market is expected to grow ten-fold by 2030 to $110 billion.

Innovation is no longer a choice, it is a necessity.

Like any business activity, clear criteria and measures of success must be established before you begin innovative growth activities.

However, unless you are operating in a very stable sector, you will need to regularly review the success criteria to ensure that you meet the current and future needs of the market. Thus, for example, in telecoms, opportunities used to be assessed by criteria such as voice minutes and text messages but now data and loyalty are critical.

The period 2020-23 illustrates how criteria for successful innovation can change rapidly:

- 2020: Example – innovate for products and services that can be used at home during lockdowns and don't require staff to work physically together.
- 2022: Example – innovate to reduce energy usage.

- 2023: Example – innovate to shorten supply chains and reduce reliance on Chinese suppliers as shipping costs quadruple, plus continued concern about China.

Innovation is not just about new products

Innovation is generally linked to new products, but it could be making an existing product differently or creating an innovative business model or marketing and distributing in a new way, for example, using mobile technology.

Innovative growth also includes updating how you do things to make improvements; whether it is investing in the latest equipment or software, investing in human capital by growing your people or adding in new skills.

Learning from innovative products can help update more traditional parts of your business. For example, Nestlé learned a lot about e-commerce and new business models from launching Nespresso.

A winning business is also a growing business. This does not just have to be about growing in financial terms; it can be building across other factors, be it knowledge, relationships, brand awareness, or growing staff as individuals.

> "It is not [price and output] competition which counts, but the competition from the new commodity, the new technology, the new source of supply, the new type of organisation-competition, which commands a decisive cost or quality advantage and which strikes not at the margins of the profits and the outputs of the existing firms but at their foundations and their very lives."
>
> Joseph Schumpeter[139]

Innovative growth is challenging. For example, how long will you bear losses if the innovative growth is about a new business model or service? Amazon, Google and Facebook all lost money for many years, though some argue this is partly to reduce taxes, but how far are you willing to go?

Most business models can be adapted to potentially move from loss to profit-making, so it can be counterproductive to accept or expect a long period to profit. In the eighties, in Advance, a commercial services company, as a new product development manager, I was only looking for break-even within three years for new products and services that we were bringing to market. In a reasonably stable market, this might still be OK, but in many markets, technology is having such an impact that in three years, the market may have moved on and you never get to profit.

Innovation is not always easy. James Dyson,[140] the inventor of the Dyson vacuum cleaner, 'failed' at more than 5,100 prototypes before getting it just right.

You need to decide as a business what and why you pursue ideas. The failure of the current technology prompted Dyson's innovation; the problem he had personally identified was the vacuum cleaner that clogged up and didn't effectively work.

Some ideas will pay off; some will fail. The key is to fail as quickly as possible. The speed of doing business has increased dramatically and every minute counts. The best companies try many different ideas and let the losers go speedily, with no remorse. But no one would say Dyson was wrong to take over 5000 attempts. Hence, the critical issue is to undertake your innovation within the broader context of your vision and how you want to change the world, so that you can use these parameters to decide what you continue to pursue. Dyson was driven by a definite problem that needed solving, not his ego.

A Case Study: How Eight19 developed a viable business model[141]

A story – an innovative business using ROC© principles

Clear Vision, Life Changing

1.6 billion people worldwide live without electricity. Without electricity, rural sub-Saharan African households are forced to use lighting alternatives, such as, candles, batteries and kerosene lamps, which can represent as much as a third of the net income for poorer households. Apart from being denied light at night, a lack of power also means simple things like recharging a mobile phone becomes a major logistical challenge, often necessitating a long journey to the nearest phone-charging kiosk. The price paid for mobile phone charging then becomes about 100 times the cost of equivalent power in the West.

The Azuri group, which started as Eight19, a printed plastic technology company originating from Cambridge University, had a vision for using the printed plastic technology to develop a low-cost solar product, so that poor people could get power. Azuri's long-term vision is to bridge the digital and services gap that exists between urban and rural communities through the power of solar.

In 2012, they pioneered pay-as-you-go solar in Africa. Since then, Azuri has delivered affordable solar home systems on a commercial basis to customers in twelve countries in sub-Saharan Africa. The company has sold more than 150,000 systems, having an impact on more than 750,000 lives.

The technology changes lives,[142] letting people charge mobile phones and light their houses safely instead of by oil, reducing both pollution harmful to health and increasing the money available for people to spend on good nutrition. It is 'go anywhere' technology for even the most remote locations. For every 10,000 units installed, 50,000 people get clean energy with an estimated saving of $1.99 million on energy-related spend over the solar product lifetime and 12,000 tonnes of annual greenhouse gas emissions offset.

Since then, they have launched a solar-powered TV and radio service, helping to raise awareness on health and social issues.

Financial inclusion is a major social issue in sub-Saharan Africa, leaving millions excluded from the formal economy. The mobile money and payment services that Azuri has pioneered has let their customers build a payment profile, so that they can access additional financial services. Azuri is also making it possible for off-grid consumers to access micro-insurance services through HospiCash, a unique, affordable income cover and life insurance exclusive to rural solar customers.

Shops no longer have to shut at sunset, solar irrigation systems improve outputs and, during Covid, children could watch educational channels on TV.

Azuri has created more than 5,000 new jobs across sub-Saharan Africa, many as local agents to support customers.

Sustainable Profit, Innovative Growth

Azuri could develop a product that they could sell for $70, but a moderately successful rural farmer earning $3 a day would struggle to pay it. The initial solution was to give the product away, but that was not a sustainable financial model. Relying on donations for funding was too risky.

The next idea was based on the UK model of leasing the solar installation and collecting regular subscription fees. In the UK, this is done through the banking system and with partnerships to finance the installation, but this model would not work for the very poor in developing countries as the banking systems are not in place.

The idea that worked and created sustainable profit involved product and service innovation, by combining mobile phone and solar technology with scratch cards used to access electricity over a time period. This is the Indigo, a pay-as-you-go lighting and charging system. The system is viable as the installation fees are gathered over time.

Initially, the customer paid $10 to buy the Indigo kit of a solar panel, lamps and charger. They then purchased scratch cards for $1 using SMS from a mobile phone, entering the resulting passcode into the Indigo unit and using the installation for a while (typically a week). After eighty scratch cards, the person owned the unit or could buy a more extensive system to access more energy and continue to purchase scratch cards.

The innovation has not stopped. Azuri identified that in Zambia, 60% of people rely on agriculture for their livelihood and they get most of their money between April and June. Azuri offers a harvest payment plan, which lets them overpay when they have the money during harvest and pay less in the dry season.

They offer a complete PayGo Solar TV package, which includes the solar panel, TV, four lights, a radio, phone charger and chargeable torch. AzuriTV delivers more than sixty channels of content on its thirty-two-inch and twenty-four-inch solar-powered televisions. Once the system is paid for, all the energy generated is free. Azuri has partnered with broadcasters Zuku and DSTV to deliver a mixture of local and international satellite content to off-grid households. Every product includes Azuri's HomeSmart technology to optimise runtime and Toughscreen technology to protect from accidental damage.

Choosing criteria for new product success

What criteria will you use to choose between new product opportunities? Here are some, but there are many others:
1. The potential size of the market.
2. High barriers to entry.
3. Profitability.
4. Ease.
5. Fit with vision and niche – how much it changes the world as you want.

6. Fit with your customer needs.
7. Speed to market.
8. Investment needed.

If you are thinking about innovating with new processes and systems that will save money, then how will you judge which to proceed with? Short-term gain, long-term savings, impact on overheads, etc.?

Having been involved in new product development for forty years, a key reason for failure I have seen is when the criteria for success are unclear before you start. The reason the criteria need to be in place at the start is that, once you have ideas, there is a temptation to make the criteria fit either to support the concept or to destroy it.

YOUR ROC© CHALLENGE

Do you have clear criteria for choosing the ideas for innovation that you pursue?
Do you use these to encourage people to come up with ideas?

Innovative growth within the context of the business

Innovation needs to occur within the context of a business's purpose. Just chasing market trends or responding to what customers say whether it fits with your mission leads to an incoherent product mix and a lack of trust, as customers and staff will get confused about what you stand for.

Surprisingly, the worst examples I have found of chasing money rather than being true to values and purpose have been in the charity sector.

Many charities who previously relied totally on public funding and donations have in the last decades started to think about earning income by setting up a social enterprise.

Initially, they want to understand if a social enterprise will work for them, so they approach us at inspire2aspire for advice. Early in the conversation, I ask them what they want to do to earn money and a frighteningly high number respond, "Anything." Anything is absurd, but they just want to earn money to support the charity and don't care how they do it. My role is then to help them understand that making money can only work if it fits with their values and passions – drug dealing is very profitable, for example, but is not to be recommended.

I encourage them to innovate and think of ideas within the context of their existing contacts, brand, resources or interests and their future strategy and vision. This approach is a surprise to many because they have assumed that being commercial means forgetting what they currently do.

For one charity, this exposed that they did not have a clear strategy for the future as a charity and they now no longer exist.

Innovation can often come from learning from other markets or learning from the past. For example, in developing countries, if you earn a dollar a day, it is not viable to use commercial products in constructing a building. Discussed for its environmental impact in chapter twenty-three, The Nubian Vault Association[143] in Africa addressed this by learning from the past. They are a non-profit association working through a social entrepreneurship approach. They train independent artisan-masons to create structures from mud bricks that are not only cheap and provide job opportunities, but also suit the environment, keeping cool in the heat and warm in the cool, saving money and greenhouse gases. 3000-year-old examples of these buildings survive in Luxor.

The idea of having a minimum viable product is generally accepted in the IT world, but testing products early in their development is applicable across all markets. One reason for this is that it means changes will feel less significant for a 'rough' product or service than if it is a highly finished prototype. It also means the testing can be quicker and cheaper.

It can be useful even to float some outrageous ideas, which will get a strong response and generate implementable ideas.

The importance of growth

I think the phrase, "If you are not growing, you're dying," is incomplete. I would add, "If you are not innovating, you will have no long-term future."

Growth is not just financial, it can be team, impact, reach, but it needs innovation.

To meet unmet needs, you do not have to be a great inventor and it can be challenging to bring inventions to market. You just need to identify how something can be done better or differently, how an existing product or service can be used in a new market or how as the market has changed an opportunity has developed.

If you can match the competition in product quality, you at least will be considered. Then you can start to think about addressing unmet needs.

Think about how you could innovate or collaborate with someone to create a package, for example, or:

- do it better;
- meet unmet needs.

Timing can be important, but it is not necessary to be first into a market. After all, as discussed, Amazon was neither the first bookseller nor the first online retailer! What they did differently was to do everything to make it very easy and cost-effective to buy from them.

What can you learn from your competitors in terms of best practice? If you think about what the customer wants, how do you fit in comparison?

Fostering Innovation

Ninety percent of job seekers look at company culture[144] when applying for jobs and in-demand employees tend to join organisations with great, innovative cultures. This, in turn, increases the productivity and drives long-term success.

Successful companies such as HubSpot, an online marketing company, encourage their staff to be innovative. They have been consistently innovative since they were founded in 2004 and consequently has grown to be worth over $10 billion.

HubSpot have had a three-step process since very early in their history by which employees introduce new ideas: Alpha, Beta and Version One. Staff initially develop ideas in their own time, then they present the project idea (the Alpha stage) to management, and if it looks like a good investment, it becomes Beta. HubSpot then provides resources in terms of people and development time for three months to attempt to gain traction. Anything that doesn't work is cut as soon as possible. What does work, graduates from Beta and becomes 'part of the way we do business', or Version One.

The majority of projects fail, but people keep on trying new ideas. HubSpot look for staff who have entrepreneurial zeal, want to start new things and are not afraid to fail. They also have a flat management structure and are particularly keen to empower people who are close to the customer and know what they need.

HubSpot is an example of fostering innovation but also being willing to move on quickly when it doesn't work out.

In my experience, the critical issue about innovation is the ability to support new ideas but not to fall in love with them. Too often, new product development is like the story of the Emperor's New Clothes because money has been invested in the development. Just like no one wanted to say the emperor had no clothes on, no one wants to be the person to suggest that what seemed like a good idea isn't and that, in cliché terms, the business should not throw good money after bad. The HS2 high-speed rail line, part scrapped in 2023, with its projected potential cost of over £100bn is just the latest high-profile example of this.

The skill is backing ideas and testing them as soon as possible, i.e., when a viable product is available taking it to market. Otherwise, giving staff time to develop ideas is a waste and, in the end, will act as a demotivator.

A Case Study: How 3M[145] encourages innovation

3M is committed to innovation. As well as giving staff 15% of their time to develop ideas that excite them, once a year, 3M hold an event where about 200 employees from dozens of divisions can make cardboard posters describing their projects and get feedback, suggestions and potential collaborators.

Wayne Maurer is an R&D manager in 3M's abrasives division and calls it a chance for people to unhinge their 'inner geek'. He elaborates: "For technical people, it's the most passionate and engaged event we have at 3M."

Past projects that are on the market now include clear bandages, optical films that reflect light and designing a way to make painter's tape stick to wall edges (to protect against paint bleed).

Not all ideas take off immediately. For example, one person thought that if he reshaped particles on sandpaper, they wouldn't go blunt so fast. Unfortunately, the technology was not ready to develop the product. However, thirteen years on, the same worker started looking at the problem again during his 15% time. He went to the event and, with the help of new employees and new technology, working together, they discovered they could retain a particle's sharp, pyramid-like shape just by changing the mixing order. The result: 3M created a winning product in Cubitron II, sandpaper that acts more like a cutting tool, which gave them a competitive edge in the market. If not for the 15% time, this worker's idea might never have taken off, but the real success happened because there were then the resources to develop it further.

Where to find new ideas

As well as looking at the potential parts of an offering that can create a niche, as discussed in the last chapter, you can look at different markets that may have been ignored and have specific needs. Sometimes they are ignored because it is assumed that they might not be profitable.

A classic example is the market for goods designed for people with disabilities, often referred to as the 'Purple Pound'. The Paralympics in 2012 showcased some designer prosthetic limbs, some even with diamonds inset. There are also a few designer walking sticks available. But, generally, disability and mobility aids are no more stylish than when they were invented. Yet with an ageing population, aids for people in terms of helping with reduced strength are becoming mainstream. Adding some design style so someone can feel good would have an impact on society, improve the quality of life and make money all at the same time.

The search for unmet needs is an endless task. It is a bit like a detective story, where you need to be looking for clues all the time. It is not easy, as often people can't imagine how a new product will meet their needs or how it will help them. You just need to think about all the products and services launched in the last two decades that we didn't know we needed but have met our unmet needs.

For example, ten years ago, when I was writing a book on a cruise, I didn't consciously know that I wanted to be able to research on the internet as we crossed the South Atlantic, and so I wrote a book with less research. Since then, I have had internet access every day by Wi-Fi across the ship and in cafés ashore, and I've used it and valued it. Now AI can speed up the research even more.

The first cafés to offer free Wi-Fi were meeting an unmet need; now we expect it, so it has moved from an opportunity to a necessity in most of the world.

Grasp unmet needs when you identify them as they don't stay unmet for long.

As with everything else, you need to think about unmet needs in terms of the Responsible Organisation Charter© – don't stray from your vision or values just because you find an unmet need. But if you do think it is an opportunity, maybe you could collaborate with someone else who does have a fit with it. There are lots of ways to win.

A Case Study: How even a traditional industry can be innovative

A story – a laundry using ROC© principles

I started work in the laundry industry by chance, with a wonderful company called Advance. Everyone in the company was on 'job and finish'; for example, when all the deliveries had been made, the drivers could go home; when the laundry staff had washed, pressed and prepared everything, they could go. People were trusted to do a good job and worked together to support each other, so everyone could finish as soon as possible. People were motivated to work hard and as a team, as everything had to be complete and perfect. Then, rather than finding things for people to do, they could go – genuinely motivational. Advance had a strong ethos and feel, so it attracted a particular sort of person.

When I worked for Advance Services, I ran the sales force as part of my role. We had a very loyal and successful set of people who generally had a long career with the company. We then merged with Initial, who worked in the same sector offering similar products, and their salesforce earned double what the Advance people did; however, few of their staff stayed more than twelve months. Higher pay did not motivate them or keep them loyal. The values and behaviour standards of the two companies were very different and Advance had a working style that kept people loyal.

I worked as a new product development manager for a time in Advance. It was very innovative, which led it to adopt and use computers much earlier than most, using PCs and networked mainframes across its depots in the early eighties. It also meant that in the eighties, long before required to by law, Advance realised that CFCs were harmful and, by 1985, we had banned their use in our air fresheners. We had plenty of time to cost-effectively develop a new product design to meet our needs – in this case, aerosols that would work differently. The new design was both environmentally friendly and made business sense. I was also investigating launching a range of reusable incontinence products for nursing homes when my role changed due to our merger. The products would have been an excellent service for the environment as well as an excellent profitable service for the business. Disposable incontinence products can contain up to 90% plastic and a single pad can take as long as 500 years to break down. Unfortunately, when I was researching for this book, I couldn't find a commercial laundry that is offering this service.

Crowdsourcing

> "The act of a company or institution taking a function once performed by employees and outsourcing it to an undefined (and generally large) network of people in the form of an open call. This can take the form of peer-production (when the job is performed collaboratively) but is also undertaken by sole individuals. The crucial prerequisite is the use of open call format and the large network of potential labourers."
>
> Jeff Howe[146]

Innovation doesn't have to happen solely within your company; many ideas are developed collaboratively or by putting calls out to communities of people who share an interest in the subject you want to innovate in.

Joint working engages and involves people in the innovation process. In large companies, this can be done internally, but even large companies like General Electric (GE) are now using external crowdsourcing in much of their innovation.

Case study: Crowdsource a new car

A story – getting innovation using ROC© principles

Fiat created the world's first crowdsourced car in 2009. Unveiled at the Sao Paulo car show in Brazil October 2010, the Fiat Mio was a futuristic concept car based on the ideas and solutions proposed by thousands of people around the world. More than 17,000 participants offered over 11,000 ideas and solutions, interacting with the company through the project website.

The car created was suitable for big cities with a pollutant-free engine, a compact design and innovative traffic solutions, plus the capacity to receive personalised updates and the ability to change in configuration.

At the other end of the scale, a new company Local Motors was founded in 2007, by Harvard Business School alumni Jay Rogers, based on open collaboration and co-creation. It offered low-volume vehicle manufacturing of open-source designs using multiple micro-factories and capitalising on 3D printing technology. By seamlessly connecting co-creation with micromanufacturing, their products had a better chance of product success by getting units into the hands of paying customers up to twenty-four times faster than traditional, expensive and time-intensive processes.

It produced the first co-created production car, the Rally Fighter, in 2009. Designed by a community member in a contest, community members also developed components for the vehicle and voted for the exterior design. The company estimated it spent only $3 million on the car's development, significantly less than the traditional development cost of a major automaker.

Local Motors created an innovative platform, which designers and hobbyists used to interact to bring to market low-volume 3D-printed cars at a fraction of the cost of a traditional original equipment manufacturer's (OEM) product development process. It had early success with crowdsourcing designs for the first 3D-printed car, the Strati, and developed the Olli, an electric self-driving shuttle, but shut in 2022 due to lack of funding.

YOUR ROC© CHALLENGE

What could you create with unlimited minds to help you?

The power of bringing together people who share an interest is also illustrated when people share data, which can help with innovation and new perspectives.

As early as 2011, Modernising Medicine[147] launched, as an iPad-based speciality; a specific electronic medical records platform with a crowdsourcing addition. For example, all the dermatologists who sign up with Modernising Medicine (25% of all in the US) have their outcome data, i.e. the problem and the treatment prescribed, aggregated. Also, they have now linked with Watson, which has millions of journal articles, textbooks, patient outcomes and scientific papers, etc. All this information is now available to the dermatologists as they work with their patients. They can instantly get answers to questions based both on what their colleagues are doing and also on millions of individual documents, with the source and confidence level included. A massive step forward from the doctor pulling a textbook off the shelf!

Data can be a source of innovation in many areas. Currently, a large amount of learning and data, which could spark change, is being lost, particularly in the NHS.

When my husband's Type 2 diabetes improved radically, so he didn't need hospital support any more, no one sought to understand why it had happened; they just changed his appointment. We tried to tell them about the exclusion diet, but there was no interest or maybe no methodology to collect data. Innovation needs to happen in the public sector, particularly the NHS, to not only improve services but also to save money.

YOUR ROC© CHALLENGE

How are you capturing innovation opportunities? When did you last consider one?

Innovation for Growth

Innovation for growth might include developing a new product or even looking for a new market for an existing product. Whoever you are, there are always more non-customers than customers, so finding ways to take a current product or service to them can result in enormous scope for growth.

For example, some years ago, Nintendo undertook a review of its position in the mainstream gaming market. It realised that for 'hardcore' gamers, their handsets and graphic quality were worse than the competition's and that it would take a large amount of investment to get to be as good. So, instead of looking to upgrade their product, they sought to identify if what they offered might meet an unmet need in another market.

They found that non-gamers would like a simple offering that provided games such as golf and tennis to play alone and as a family, and the Nintendo Wii was born. What were the disadvantages for the experienced gamers were benefits for people who would not call themselves gamers but were just looking for simple leisure time activities. From this, they also identified new product opportunities and developed Wii Fit as a fun way to get fit.

Many businesses think of growth in terms of increased sales of existing products, but it's also essential to focus on how to maintain or improve your profitability. Can innovation in production or service methods reduce costs, or can specification changes improve margins?

Learning from your customers

The most powerful innovations are driven by your customers' issues as summarised in Figure 21.

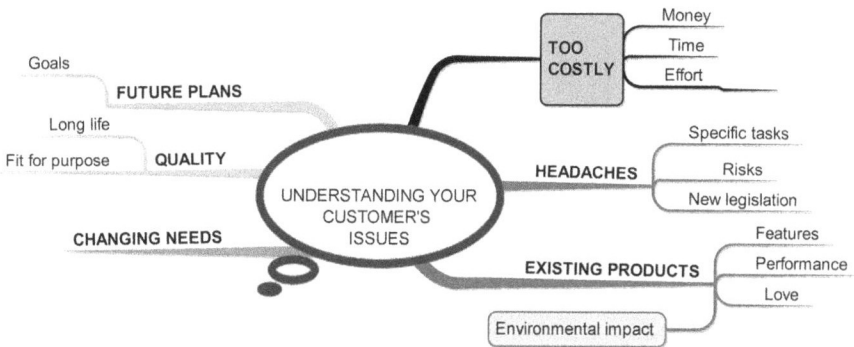

Figure 21: Understanding your customer's issues as a basis for innovation

The original subscription models, before it became fashionable, were when people rented washing machines or TVs. The unfulfilled need was customers not being able to afford the initial investment.

Other people are time poor, which has driven innovations like the meal recipe packs that get delivered to save time on thinking about what to eat, finding recipes and shopping, plus they meet dietary needs. The demand for instant fixes and immediate gratification/results depresses me when people want it for their organisations, but it is widespread. For us, it translates into checklists people can consult and we have developed digital tools and business skills sessions so people can access advice whenever they need it.

YOUR ROC© CHALLENGE

What innovations in your organisation have been driven by customer needs?

How to successfully innovate

You must consider new methods and ideas as seriously as the existing ways you work and services and products you offer if you are to create a culture of innovation.

The idea of the 'big idea' is hazardous, like making a single large bet on the roulette table. More successful is continuous innovation and testing of new ideas and incremental changes.

Market testing is essential, whatever the market research or experts say, and the more ideas you have in play, the less likely it is that people will fall in love with the single big bet, which can be dangerous.

Innovation needs to be a priority, even when the business is very successful, as the world is changing so fast. Successful innovation requires a pioneer learning attitude rather than a fear of risks and change, so that staff and customers are excited rather than scared.

You also need to consider how you can minimise risk by testing as fast as possible to check viability; can you provide it consistently and will it sell?

Even to stand still, you now need to innovate.

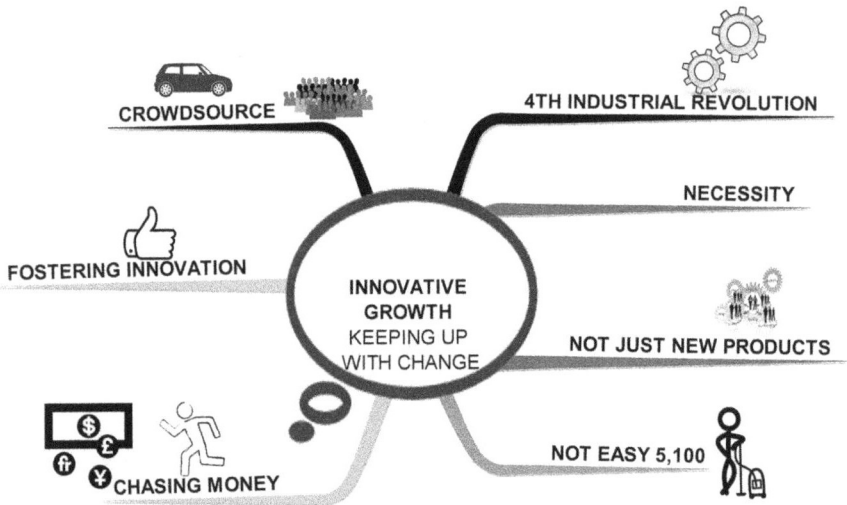

Figure 22: Innovative Growth – keeping up with change

Scoring yourself on the ROC©

Rate how innovative you are.

A score of ten would mean that you encourage innovation, have failures and move on. A low rating would indicate risk aversion or a need to bring in some creative thinking to promote change.

Chapter Twenty-seven

Sustainable Profit

Guaranteeing the future

"You make money when you work out what you do well."
Robin Rowland, YO! Sushi[148]

Winning by Being Good means being financially successful. You do no *Good*, only harm, if you are a financial failure and people lose their jobs, suppliers are unpaid and there is no money to support worthwhile activities.

"Turnover is vanity, profit is sanity."
Anon

There is no right or wrong level of profit and none that makes you *Good*. Profit levels vary radically by industry, but what is essential is that you understand your financial figures, know where your profit is coming from and think about how much profit you want to make.

Scarily, we come across too many organisations of all types that do not know which of their products or customers make them a profit. Even more scarily, many cannot explain their pricing strategy.

YOUR ROC© CHALLENGE

What is a sustainable profit for your organisation?

A sustainable profit has various elements, some of which you can control and others depend more on outside factors. The things to consider include:
- revenue model,
- cost structure,
- margin,
- use of resources.

New models of sustainable profit are now being made possible by the internet and cheap technology: the fourth Industrial Revolution.

The film industry illustrates the extremes of revenue models in a single sector and how both can create profit. At one end you have the making and launch of blockbuster films, relying on large volumes of people going to see them. At the other end, there is Netflix, the online video rental company, which licenses large numbers of niche films. Each film may be seen relatively rarely but aggregated together it makes a sustainable and profitable business.

The impact of technology

Change is happening so fast that anything written is going to be out of date before it is published. Technological advances are reported daily, from self-driving cars and drones to virtual assistants or exciting new software.

You can enhance all sorts of physical products and services with digital capabilities that increase their value and potential for sustainable profit. New technologies can make things more durable and resilient, while data and analytics can transform how they are maintained. The internet can enable online learning, instant communication and the opportunity for sharing knowledge and best practices.

It is difficult to predict the future as the 2020 pandemic proved. Even Steve Jobs could make mistakes as he showed when he predicted that Segways would be the future. However, outlined below are some of the important trends that are likely to have an impact on sustainable profitability.

Paper to electronic
Everywhere, paper is being overtaken by digital devices, from money to tickets to clipboards.

In business, reduced use of paper saves money in multiple ways, from printing costs and paper purchases to space and time to file it or costs of disposal. Yale reported saving $100,000 by merely replacing paper timesheets in their student employment office with an electronic system.

However, the consequences of moving to electronic processes are a reliance on the technology working.

A while ago, I was in a small restaurant, which had a broken cash register. The till not only calculated the bill, it told the kitchen what to cook, placed orders with suppliers and monitored how much money each member of the waiting staff needed to put in the till. The cost to replace this critical bit of software and hardware was £7,000, but without it, the manager felt totally out of control. Even worse, the cost was so high because he had lost past information. He had relied on a staff member who had since left to manage back-ups and it had not happened, so all the data had to be rebuilt. (In fact, this business went under within six months.)

The cloud

With cloud storage, software in the cloud and the ability to communicate wherever you are, you can run a business anywhere and with anyone, wherever they are. Storing and sharing documents through Dropbox, Google Docs and other cloud storage sites means you can work with freelancers across the world as efficiently as you would in an office.

As well as saving the costs of renting a space and providing equipment, it can also allow you to access skilled people who may not be available locally and frequently it is at a lower rate.

However, to build a long-term sustainable profit, you will still need to act ethically and build a team that shares your values and this is more complex if you are not in the same physical location. Processes need to be adjusted to allow for the different needs of developing a virtual company.

Linked to this is the ability to undertake most financial actions, from banking to invoicing and paying taxes, through the internet, which again means that physical location is not relevant.

The growth of information

Big data is a massive opportunity for those who can use it effectively. It should be an opportunity to increase profitability, as knowledge is money. Simple examples are the use of data to predict what customers need and to identify who are likely customers. Data may be sold, in accordance with data protection laws. For example, I am collaborating with a sports client who will collect data on the impact of participating in the sport, which will have value and improve targeting reducing marketing costs.

Crowdsourcing big data can also have significant benefits, for example improving efficiency and reducing costs, when environmental disasters like earthquakes strike. In these circumstances, it gathers data on where problems are and creates up-to-date maps using sites like OpenStreetMap.

Social media

Social media is one of the most popular online activities. In 2022, over 4.59 billion people were using social media worldwide, a number projected to increase to almost six billion in 2027.

Social media is both an opportunity and a threat in terms of sustainable profit. Creative use of it can make it a powerful, cost-effective marketing tool, particularly if you can create a campaign that goes viral. It is rapidly evolving and, like any marketing, is only as good as the underlying strategy and clarity of whom you are targeting and what your messages are.

While many tools make it possible to set up automated campaigns, the real power of social media comes from interaction, so it is not necessarily as easy as it appears to use well.

It can be particularly useful in terms of promoting a more general social purpose. Unilever, for example, ran a campaign to encourage kids to get outside and get dirty, using social media, highlighting statistics such as the fact that prisoners in the States spend more time outside each day than children. As well as promoting their washing powders, it was also an effective way of building long-term relationships with millennials and critical target markets, thus ensuring sustainable profit.

However, social media can also threaten profits if people attack your company or spread negative messages, which might not even be accurate.

Also, estimates are that a third of web advertising is wasted, as 40% of internet traffic is criminal bots. There is a need to protect against this and other frauds.

The internet of things

Forecasts are that there will soon be 17 billion connected devices, doing everything from feeding the dog to remotely opening your car with your mobile phone. NB: it made the news when a remote dog feeding solution failed! Linked to the internet of things are wearables that can connect to things and data.

As well as opportunities to create new products and services, the internet of things also provides marketing opportunities; for example, helping people lead simpler lives by reminding them when they need to reorder consumable products. Keeping up with this technology is essential for all sizes and types of organisation.

3D printing

3D printing has existed for over forty years, but is now really beginning to have an impact. There are infinite ways the technology can be used to change lives.

3D printing is changing the world, as did printing on paper 600 years ago. It is transforming business processes and making it possible for people to set up businesses and services, which would previously have been uneconomic. A simple prosthetic arm can be made for a child for as little as £30 as a guy working in his garden shed has shown.

It is one of the most inspirational uses of 3D printing I have found. Stephen Davies was so unhappy by the look of the prosthetic hand the NHS gave him that he decided to start designing and building them himself. He has now set up Team UnLimbited to make colourful prosthetic limbs for children. Using a 3D printer in his garden shed to make them at the cost of just £20 an arm, he has made the design freely available so that anyone can do it across the world and the design has already been downloaded over 140,000 times. With children growing so fast that they need new arms as often as they need new shoes, this is changing lives.

3D printing has already been used to build a set of houses and could revolutionise how buildings look in the long term.

Some of its attractiveness is because it is environmentally friendly; instead of building a significant manufacturing piece of equipment taking resources and time, a 3D printer can be multifunctional.

Any business needs to consider how it might use 3D printing in its future strategy as part of maintaining sustainable profitability.

Virtual meetings and activities

I was helping BT promote virtual meetings in the late 1980s, but they took off in 2020 with Covid-19, and they have expanded to include everything from yoga classes to full virtual exhibitions and conferences. They change how businesses can work and who you can support and target as customers.

Virtual reality

Virtual reality to date has been mainly used in entertainment and gaming. But recently, I was inspired by a nursing home in the UK that is using virtual reality for people with dementia to enhance their quality of life. It means that they can safely experience going to the seaside or outside. 360-degree cameras have radically dropped in price, so the opportunities for any business to offer virtual reality experiences are already available.

Robotics

Manufacturing has used simple robots for decades. They have increased productivity, changed the roles needed and are part of the reason that manufacturing jobs in the USA have reduced by over 60% since 1970.

> "The factory of the future will have only two employees: a man and a dog. The man will be there to feed the dog. The dog will be there to keep the man from touching the equipment."
>
> Carl Bass, Autodesk CEO[149]

But robots are also beginning to have a broader role, used in healthcare and the service sector. Rather than just being a means of replacing humans, robots are now being designed to assist humans. For example, fire fighting robots can deploy about 2,500 gallons of water per minute and plough through doors/walls to put out fires in dangerous and inaccessible places. The fire-resistant Walk-Man, controlled by remote control, can carry heavy objects long distances and can be used to assess fires. It has onboard cameras, a 3D laser scanner, and microphone sensors to help it navigate and access the emergency situation. It can also be equipped with chemical sensors if needed.

Nanotechnology, biotechnology, materials science and energy storage

What makes the fourth Industrial Revolution different is the interaction across sectors, such as digital fabrication technologies[150] interacting with the biological world. Engineers, designers and architects are combining computational design, additive manufacturing, materials engineering and synthetic biology to pioneer a symbiosis between microorganisms, our bodies, the products we consume and even the buildings we inhabit. Technologies are merging, such as 3D printing and genetic engineering.

Using nanotechnology, researchers are investigating how to 'scavenge' invisible power from low-frequency vibrations in the surrounding environment, including wind, air or even contact-separation energy (static electricity). This could be used to charge your mobile, and a pacemaker might be powered by the inbuilt organic energy sources within the human body.

Pricing and revenue models

Pricing and how you charge, i.e. your revenue model, are inextricably linked and are a fundamental part of a sustainable profit.

The pricing strategy for a business should reflect its values and is also critical in managing demand and profitability.

No specific pricing strategy is more ethical than another. A successful business targeting luxury markets making high margins that it uses to pay staff well and help the wider community can be as worthwhile as a company selling cheap products to less well-off markets.

The price structure needs to ensure sustainable profits – that is, it needs to cover not only direct costs but also overheads and also ensure that the profitability gets better as the revenues increase. The revenue received by any business obviously also depends on the channels to market and the supplier costs. The more volatile these are, the less sustainable is the profit.

In the twenty-first century, established revenue models have come under pressure as more and more things are offered free and what were separate products have become available digitally, e.g. in your mobile phone. The way we do things has changed, from ordering a taxi or takeaway meal to booking a flight, buying a product, making a payment, listening to music, watching a film, or playing a game – any of these can now be done remotely.

One industry that has been radically affected by this is music. Where once people bought records, then tapes, then CDs, now they stream music and often don't pay. Musicians who had retired are currently reforming their groups as their royalty payments tumble and they need to earn some money. NB: vinyl and CDs have been making a comeback – markets change!

Any business must, however, consider revenue models and the full business model.

Global competition can mean that to continue to achieve a sustainable profit means changing your model, as the Hilti case study in chapter three on being adaptable illustrates.

Lifetime value

Part of sustainable profit is finding ways to increase the lifetime value of a customer. Many companies may loss-lead the initial purchase to get the ongoing income. A classic example of this is the printer sector, where the initial hardware purchase can be very cheap because the ongoing consumables are so profitable, provided you can prevent the customer from using other brands to replace yours. This has prompted some firms to offer a subscription model claiming it saves up to 90% on costs and means you never run out!

A very profitable business model is to start the relationship by giving away useful information – this is possible in the digital age when downloads cost nothing once created. HubSpot has built a very successful business based on this model.

A Case Study: A company with a different way of building lifetime value

HubSpot is the company that invented the phrase 'inbound marketing'. which they explain as a methodology to attract loyal customers to your business by aligning with your target audience's needs.

They practise what they preach, using free eBooks and tools, mainly focusing on content marketing. One example is their Website Grader, which was launched in 2006 and is still used to review websites for free and has been used by millions. It gives useful information on what is working on sites and what isn't. As an automated tool, it does not take many resources from HubSpot and promotes the need for inbound marketing.

HubSpot used another powerful tool to supercharge their social media campaign in 2008, being the first company to hold a webinar on the subject of 'Using Twitter for Marketing and PR'. The webinar had over 3000 registrations and lots of new followers and broke new ground using X (formerly Twitter) for discussion during the webinar. HubSpot's hashtags for their webinars have become trending topics on X (formerly Twitter) – with more than five of their webinars reaching the global top ten trending topics.

HubSpot has been particularly good at using tailored calls to action in its blogs, which all contain useful and shareable content; 20% of

HubSpot's organic leads come from this source. Overall, by 2012, 70-80% of their leads – with a volume of 40 to 50,000 per month – came from their inbound marketing efforts. In comparison, the industry average is 20%.

Since people come upon HubSpot because they want information and build the relationship under their own terms, there is none of the feel you get from spam marketing – outbound marketing – it builds better quality relationships and is less costly, since there are no lists to buy.

HubSpot is an example of a company that is applying many of the principles of *Winning by Being Good*. It has a HubSpot Culture Code, which has been updated more than twenty-five times since its inception, reflecting its commitment to constant learning and innovation. It is obsessive about return on investment based on the numbers it achieves, since this is its core business. It takes recruitment seriously, hiring less than 3% of applicants and preferring to leave a post unfilled than hire inappropriately. It is a learning company, evolving as the market changes. It also seeks to foster innovation and encourages all its employees to be entrepreneurial.

YOUR ROC© CHALLENGE

What do you do to increase the lifetime value of your customers?

The Responsible Organisation Charter© is designed to help build the lifetime value of customers. It creates an organisation that people will want to keep on using because it is consistent; the staff are motivated; it cares about the environment, provides life-changing products and services and is a good citizen. Hopefully, as 'enthusiastic supporters', they should also take pride in being your customers and advocate for you to others.

As a company, it is critical to review every stage of a customer's relationship with you to check you are doing nothing to put the long-term relationship at risk. Customer service and after sales support should not, for example, be seen as a cost but as a profit centre, which is retaining clients to maximise their lifetime value.

A Case Study: How a charity shows that sustainability can be built into your operating model

A story – a charity using ROC© principles

ONE ACRE FUND[151]

Clear Vision

The One Acre Fund exists to serve poor, rural farmers in Africa.

Its vision on its website is:

> "When farmers improve their harvests, they pull themselves out of poverty. They also start producing surplus food for their neighbours. When farmers prosper, they eradicate poverty and hunger in their communities."

One Acre Fund is a social venture that teaches and promotes best practices in agriculture in Africa, specifically Kenya, Rwanda, Burundi and Tanzania. Its original goal was to have a positive impact on more than 20 million children by 2025 and serve 1 million farm families, which translates to more than 5 million people, by 2020. They revised this as they smashed that goal. Now they state:

> "By 2030, we aim to serve 10 million farmers – fully 10% of the families in the world living on $1 a day. In 2022, we served 4 million farmers, both directly with a bundle of farm services and indirectly by improving access to farm services in an entire region."[152]

It was launched in 2006 as a pilot project with forty farmers and, by the end of 2014, it was serving 200,000 farm families, touching more than a million people in Kenya and Rwanda and expanding in Tanzania and several other countries. Its impact has been to double and triple crop yields for farmers who have traditionally had to live on $1 a day. It illustrates how blurred the lines are between charity and business because it charges all the people it helps.

Good Citizen

One Acre is all about changing the world. It started because subsistence farmers without access to seeds and fertilisers were going hungry despite working hard.

The impact of One Acre Fund on a single farmer illustrates this; her one-acre plot now produces five times the yield she got previously. She produces more than enough to feed her family and by selling the surplus has purchased a cow and a goat, bought clothing for her family and constructed a modest home. Farmers One Acre work with are more likely to have a steady supply of food all year.

Environmentally, farmers they serve directly are more likely to enrich their soils with compost and to plant trees alongside their crops, which both capture carbon and build farmers' assets. One Acre Fund farmers have planted 100 million trees to date, and are positioned to plant 1 billion trees total by 2030.

Beyond this, the One Acre Fund has an impact on communities, as farmers expand, becoming business people, employing others and becoming community leaders. Additionally, as the children get education and can fulfil their potential, they also can create businesses or become teachers or doctors having an impact on the success of their country and the wider world.

As a good citizen, One Acre Fund has also grown to employ over 8000 people, mostly locals and many previously subsistence farmers It measures its social impact as $316 million in new farm profits and assets. For every $1 of donor investment, it creates $3.20 new farm profits.

Pioneer Learning

The success of One Acre is based fundamentally on learning. The model has four steps:

1. Truck distribution of thousands of tonnes of seed and fertiliser to distribution points in rural areas where 100-200 farmers pick up supplies on foot. Initially, One Acre tried more exotic crops but learnt from the farmers what was working and what wasn't and refocused on basic staples.
2. Providing finance, typically $80, so farmers can purchase the seed and fertiliser. The funding comes with training for the farmers about how the loan works and how they have to pay it back. The loans are paid back piecemeal in small payments that are recorded using a paper-based system. 99% of the farmers pay on time.

3. Maximising crop yields. As well as learning what crops will work in a particular area, One Acre teaches the farmers simple techniques to improve their crops. Examples include a planting string marked at intervals so that the seed spacing allows each plant to get enough water and light and how to use a thimbleful of fertiliser in each planting hole so it goes to the plant and doesn't just run off into the environment. Farmers gather weekly in groups of thirty to attend training sessions where they have a short explanation and then go into the fields to practise.

4. One Acre practises what it calls 'market facilitation' to ensure farmers maximise their profits. Individual farmers have limited negotiating power with the middlemen who buy their crops, so One Acre negotiates on behalf of about 100 farmers to increase efficiency and the price achieved. This last step is critical to make the others work.

As they have developed this model, there have been many learnings and failures. Andrew Youn, the co-founder, says, "Establishing a culture that tolerates failure is very important."

Among the early failures was the attempt to get farmers to grow high-value exotic crops, "without listening to my customers (the farmers). It was my 'idea driven' failure," says Andrew. He learnt: "To fail small and quickly (and), since that experience, we have learnt to listen to our customers much better, and to elevate them, so that we see them as our bosses."

Collaborative

One Acre is an excellent example of collaborative growth, going from a small pilot to an internationally acclaimed organisation in less than a decade.

The Bill and Melinda Gates Foundation in November 2013 launched a three-year $11.6 million partnership to leverage the One Acre Fund operating model to bring innovative agriculture technologies to more rural farming families. This was renewed in 2016 with a three-year $6.3 million partnership to create more agronomic recommendations to boost crop yields and to test new types of financial services for farmers.

Mastercard Foundation in October 2013 announced a $10 million partnership to expand access to financial services and training for smallholder farmers. The partnership links to Kenya's microfinance sector with the aim of increasing lending in rural Africa. It also allows One Acre Fund to employ more than 770 additional staff.

One Acre Fund has been successful because it has attracted other foundations who recognise that working with the fund will help them achieve their goals as foundations – the perfect collaboration. Consequently, The Barr Foundation has given $3.7 million to support crop insurance, tree planting, solar lights and staple crop diversification. The donation follows an initial smaller gift of $1 million, which showed the collaboration would work. USAID has given $3.5 million.

One Acre Fund views its work with farmers as a partnership, as it will only work if they do their part. Similarly, it seeks to collaborate and partner with the other areas in the supply chain, from the distribution of supplies to marketing the end products.

Often when I talk about One Acre Fund, people assume it must be a business because it doesn't give things away, but that is what I find so inspirational. It has found a structure that is life changing and, because it is financially sustainable, it can have an impact on millions, keep growing and not be reliant on gifts.

Cost structures

Control of costs will not help you grow, but it is essential for sustainable profit.

In 2008, Starbucks identified that they had been quite inefficient during the boom years:

> "We took out $580 million of costs in 2008. Some 90% of it has been permanent. None of it is customer facing. That was there for many years. Why did it take a crisis to allow us to have the courage to do that?"
>
> Howard Schultz, Starbucks CEO[153]

Some businesses are more cost-driven than others, and this is likely to depend on how you change lives and your market niche.

In businesses where fixed costs are high, such as manufacturing, utilisation is critical and will be a metric for sustainable profit. Production is a classic sector where collaboration and 3D printing can have a radical impact on processes and cost structures and times to market.

How a business changes lives may change as it grows. Larger companies can take advantage of economies of scale to reduce costs and hence potentially reduce prices and change lives of more or different people. Similarly, there can be economies of scope as a business grows and it can use the same distribution channels and marketing activities for multiple products. Both these effects can also be achieved by collaboration as the One Acre Fund case study illustrates.

Many charities don't like the word profit, but whatever your organisation, you need enough money to keep doing good.

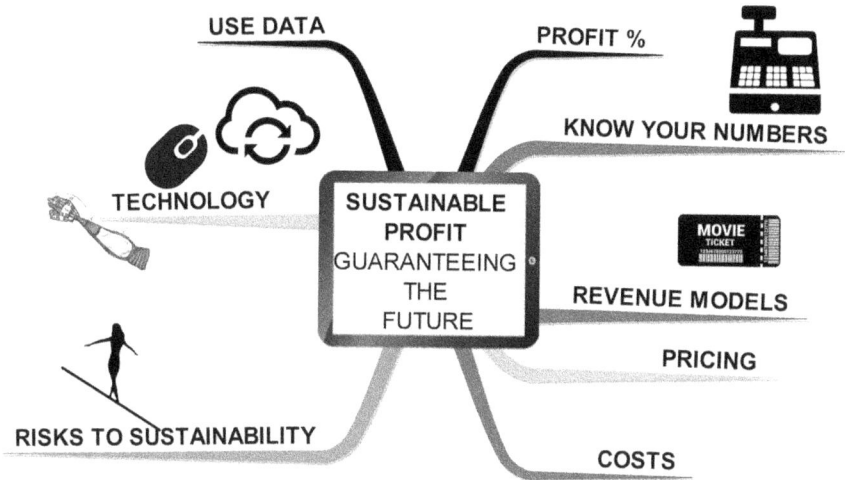

Figure 23: Sustainable Profit – guaranteeing the future

Scoring yourself on the ROC©

Rate how sustainable your profit is.

A score of ten means considering all elements and opportunities for sustainable profit mentioned in this chapter and having strategies for relevant ones. A low ranking would indicate you are vulnerable because you haven't, and this needs to be an area of focus.

Chapter Twenty-eight

Using the
Responsible Organisation Charter©

It is useful to understand what management and staff think about each principle and how they would score your company. Involving everyone will maximise the benefits of the Responsible Organisation Charter© as a practical management tool.

To be effective, everyone must understand the ROC© and both what it means within the company and their role in improving the scores. Suppose your structure is less about the staff and more about suppliers, subcontractors, associates and collaborators. In that case, they need to understand and sign up to your ROC© as how they behave will be a reflection of your company.

The Responsible Organisation Charter© is suitable for any size or type of organisation, from the major corporate at board level to a sole trader business or small community group.

Compiling your score

The best way to start is for everyone to decide how they would score your company for each principle as individuals and then compare your scores. If you work on your own, then customers' and suppliers' perspectives are a valuable addition. As well as doing it for the whole organisation, it is compelling when different divisions and departments do it for their part of the business.

Where you have discrepancies in the scoring, this allows you to discuss the differences in perspective that different people have. The goal is to come to agreed scores across the group and to use these to decide on priorities for the next quarter. At the end of the quarter, you will score again and identify more issues. So start now with your gut feel and summarise your results here.

	Poor			Average				Excellent		
	1	2	3	4	5	6	7	8	9	10
Leadership										
Behaviour driven by Shared Values										
Clear Vision										
Action-focused										
Culture										
Adaptable										
Pioneer Learning										
Collaborative										
Relationships										
Treat Staff Well										
Treat Suppliers Fairly										
Good Citizen										
Product Offering										
Life Changing										
Reliably Consistent										
Minimising Environmental Impact										
Financial Success										
An Identifiable Market Niche										
Innovative Growth										
Sustainable Profit										

Creating a more considered score

It is useful to write notes as you develop the score, so that you remember what prompted you to score as you did. To produce a more in-depth score, you can use the questions listed for each principle in the template for assessing your ROC© score, which you can download from inspire2aspire.co.uk.

Does everyone agree and understand the fundamentals?

I would recommend starting scoring in the leadership section. It is crucial to understand any differing perspectives, particularly on your values and vision as these are fundamental to any organisation.

How do you behave as a company, i.e., are there values that everyone shares and that translate into the way people act across the organisation? Is there is a clear vision that people agree on and then if there is, is there clarity about how you are getting to your vision? Lastly, is the company going places, or is it stuck, is there a sense of urgency, a focus on action?

These are the fundamentals for a business in terms of its journey: **a definite destination, shared agreement on how you want to get there, what is acceptable and actual movement towards the goal, rather than stagnation.**

Scoring behaviour driven by shared values

To score well on 'behaviours driven by shared values' means that everyone knows how we do things around here and that this is guided by following ethical values. Bear in mind this is not a score of the values you have, but rather a rating of whether they have any impact. Values also need to be ranked in order of importance. However, if you have no specified values or have to look them up before you complete this section, then you cannot score anything but poorly until you have clarified your values. A good indicator is if your staff feel empowered and show initiative as this means they understand what will be appropriate behaviour, even if something unexpected happens. If you have brought your company values to life, so they are a reality, then score yourself highly; if not, or not consistently for every value, then your audit score needs to be lower.

Test this score by asking people to list what they think the values are as a starting point. Doing this will often lead you to adjust your score. Also check which people think is the most important.

Record or take notes of the discussion, as this will provide useful input as you develop your ROC© Plan of Action.

Behaviour driven by shared values	Score
Comments	
Key actions required	

Scoring your clear vision

You can only score highly for a clear vision if you and your staff can write/describe the vision in a way that captures its essence. Just because people have learnt it by heart, you should not score a ten unless they understand how it translates into what the business is and how they as an individual behave.

Score highly if your vision inspires action and encourages people to take the initiative to achieve it. Are the stories you tell in your company about how you are making progress towards the vision?

Clear vision	Score
Comments	
Key actions required	

Scoring being action-focused

This area is carefully named – it is not active but action-focused, i.e., purposeful action, not the 'headless chicken' version of activity.

Experience shows this is the score that will often vary radically across an organisation depending on an individual's management style and how they work. Being action-focused does not mean working in a specific way; instead, it is an attitude. Score highly if you have systems that encourage and reward useful actions, not an activity for its own sake.

A high score on being action-focused will indicate that everyone in the organisation has similar clarity about how to act, even if there are not written-down rules.

Action-focused	Score
Comments	
Key actions required	

Have you got the right culture?

Scoring this section of the ROC© helps you identify if you have the culture in the organisation to be effective in achieving your vision in the way you want. Do you learn and adapt as you go along and do you recognise the ever-increasing importance of collaboration?

Scoring being adaptable

By nature, as humans, we are adaptable, and this has been a critical reason for our success. We adapt to circumstances all the time but being flexible in an organisation is about identifying which adaptations should be embedded and which are temporary. A high score on being adaptable will reflect that you are willing to revert to the norm if the adaptation is not what you need to achieve your long-term vision.

A good test is to think back for three years and consider how much of what you do today has changed/been adapted. As Google and Dave Brailsford show, small adaptations can have a tremendous impact or just slightly improve what you do. If you can think of very little that has changed, then it is very likely that you need to give your organisation quite a low score on being adaptable.

Adaptable	Score
Comments	
Key actions required	

Scoring being a pioneer learning organisation

Pioneer learning is so much more than having a training budget. To score highly on the ROC© audit on this principle, you need a culture where people are excited about learning new things and share their learning.

Overall, the score for pioneer learning will be high if you have clear examples of learning, which probably have excited you and had an impact on how you operate or think as an organisation. Whatever systems for learning you have in place, if you can't think of examples of where what you have learnt has had an impact on your business, then you need to reduce your score. As with all the parts of the ROC©, they work together, learn and then act.

Pioneer learning	Score
Comments	
Key actions required	

Scoring yourself on collaboration

Successful collaboration only happens if you have a sharing culture. If different departments within your organisation don't work together then, even if you collaborate externally, you will have a low score on the ROC©.

A good score on a collaborative culture will feel right if you have an organisation where there is lots of joint working in the organisation, as well as external relationships.

If your organisation is highly individualistic – for example, it is an individual's success that is praised and rewarded – then it is doubtful that you will score highly on a collaborative culture.

Collaboration	Score
Comments	
Key actions required	

Do you have good relationships?

The focus of the ROC© in terms of relationships is on the three key ones for most organisations: staff, suppliers and the wider community as a good citizen, with customer relationships picked up under what products or services you offer. When you map your stakeholders, you may identify that investors or funders are a critical relationship for you and you may want to consider them as well.

Scoring whether you treat your staff well

Treating staff well has little to do with how much you pay and much more to do with your values and culture. Identifying how good your staff relationships are and if they need improving will have a radical impact on your organisation, as disengaged and demotivated staff fundamentally affect what you can achieve and reduce productivity.

The fundamental indicator of how good staff relationships are is: do your staff care? If they care about the organisation and what happens, then this is generally an indicator that the relationship is good. If you wouldn't recommend to someone you are close to that they work for your company, then the score should be low for this principle.

Treat your staff well	Score
Comments	
Key actions required	

Scoring your supplier relationships

Considering that supplier relationships can be so critical to being successful, it is remarkable how little time senior management spend considering the health of these relationships until something goes wrong.

A high score on your supplier relationships is likely to put you ahead of most of your competition and should mean that you feel that you are getting a lot more than a basic service from your suppliers. All parties think that they benefit from the relationships; it's genuinely win-win.

Supplier relationships	Score
Comments	
Key actions required	

How do you rate as good citizen?

Being a good citizen does include how much and what you donate to charity, but it is a lot more. Your score as a good corporate citizen on the ROC© will not be based on the amount of money you donate but on how you behave and focus what you do across all the areas you work in and touch. It is potentially the hardest area to score because it can have so many elements, which is why there are so many questions listed in the template to help you with the judgement. How involved you feel with your sector and the community will be an indicator, as will how much staff volunteer or have community roles.

Good citizen	Score
Comments	
Key actions required	

Is your product offering good?

A good organisation must change lives for its customers. It is pointless fulfilling every other element of the ROC© but not offering a life-changing, consistent service, which is friendly to the environment.

How do you rate as life changing?
When assessing your score on how life changing you are, you will have a high score on the ROC© Audit if you have a clear theory of change as mapped below:

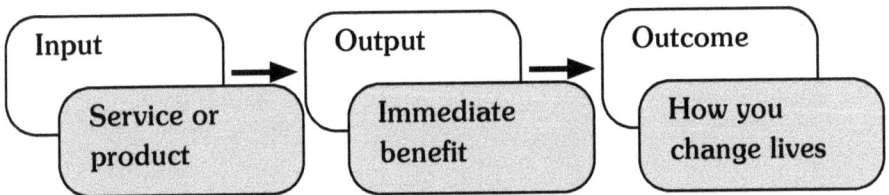

Input	Output	Outcome
Service or product	Immediate benefit	How you change lives

Many companies have never thought that they change lives, they just give excellent service, but asking 'so what' generally identifies what impact you have. If you score high on this area of the ROC©, you have a strong business foundation and any lack of demand is likely to be because you have not effectively promoted how you change lives.

Life changing	Score
Comments	
Key actions required	

How do you rate on being reliably consistent?

If you are not consistent, then every score on the ROC© is undermined.

The first test for consistency is whether your customers trust you to deliver. If they do, then you are providing reliable consistency and can give yourself a high score. If you don't know if your customers trust you, then you immediately have to reduce your score – to get an accurate score, ask them.

Reliably consistent	Score
Comments	
Key actions required	

How do you rate on your environmental impact?

Just having an environmental policy or complying with legal requirements is not enough to score highly. Your impact on the environment needs to be integral to how you work in every aspect of the organisation. You can score highly on the Responsible Organisation Charter© in terms of environmental impact if you have taken active steps to improve and are continually reviewing what you can do. You will also be maximising the competitive advantage you can gain from a focus on being more environmentally aware.

Your score is likely to be relative to what is possible in your business. It should also be influenced by whether you can see that you are improving. A high score will indicate that environmental thinking is core to your business, not just an add on or a response to legislation.

Environmental impact	Score
Comments	
Key actions required	

Are you achieving financial success?

Your ROC© scores in this area will depend on what you define as success in terms of money.

But also, financial success in ROC© terms is about being sustainable in terms of being around for the long term. Consequently, it is built on having a definite niche, keeping on innovating and achieving a sustainable profit.

How do you rate in terms of a strong niche?

Having a niche increases your potential margins and reduces your vulnerability to the competition. The first test for a niche is whether your staff, customers and the broader market know what is unique about you and refer you to others because of it. If they do, then you have a clear niche and can give yourself a high score, if you don't know, then you immediately have to reduce your score, and to get an accurate rating go and ask them. It's not enough to think you have a niche; others need to understand it and know about it.

Strong niche	Score
Comments	
Key actions required	

How do you rate in terms of innovation?

Innovative growth is under financial success because in a world that is changing so fast if you don't innovate you can't maintain sustainable profits. While some companies have a target for the percentage of turnover from new products, this can limit your horizons on innovation. Innovation needs to be part of every element of the organisation if you are to score yourself highly on this principle. This section also means you need to score yourself on growth – are you growing? If you're not, then you can't score highly.

Your score on innovative growth needs to reflect both innovation and growth in a way that over time you will be able to track, it should be objective. If you don't monitor it, then you should probably give yourself a low score and start tracking now, so in the future, you can provide an objective rating.

Innovation	Score
Comments	
Key actions required	

How do you rate in terms of sustainable profit?

Profit is significant, but it needs to be sustainable and built on the ROC©. It will only be sustainable if you can keep your staff, provide a consistent service, have a niche, grow and innovate and know where you are going. So, looking at the numbers is not enough. Considering everything, is it sustainable or will you lose all your best staff if they get a better offer? If you have low scores elsewhere, you might be making a profit and scoring on that, but the 'sustainable' bit is likely to be suspect. If everything else is excellent, but you aren't making a profit, then maybe you need to consider your other scores, particularly on niche and reliable consistency, as both of these drive new customers and customer retention.

Your score on sustainable profit needs to be based both on your financial results and also the broader management issues that will ensure that you sustain your profit over time. If you focus on short-term profit, then you should probably give yourself a lower score and consider how you are doing in terms of creating a business that will have profits over the long run.

Sustainable profit	Score
Comments	
Key actions required	

Appendices

Download the FREE companion worksheet for THIS book at:
https://inspire2aspire.co.uk/winning-by-being-good

inspire2aspire Consulting Website
If you are interested in working directly with Sarah to help you to be *Good*, simply go to inspire2aspire.co.uk for contact details.

Webinar on Responsible Organisation Charter©

Winning by Being Good **training**

Winning by Being Good **Seminar**
For in-depth and personalised training on how to create a winning company, attend Sarah's next *Winning by Being Good* leadership seminar.

Winning by Being Good **Keynote Speaking**

Recommendations for additional reading

A multitude of books, articles and radio programmes have influenced my thinking and this book. The book has taken a long time to write and I am grateful for everyone who has shared their story and given me feedback. If you want a book that goes into why being ethical makes sense in the current world context, then a good place to start is *We First* by Simon Mainwaring. It explains the issues facing the world, the role of business and the context of social media.

Here are some other books that I would highly recommend:
- *Images of Organization* by Gareth Morgan (SAGE Publications, Inc., 2006)
- *Becoming the Best* by Harry M Jansen Kraemer (John Wiley & Sons, 2015)

- *Bold* by Peter Diamandis and Steven Kotler (Simon & Schuster, 2015)
- *Beyond Measure, The big impact of small changes* by Margaret Heffernan (Simon & Schuster, 2015)
- *Growing Wings on the Way* by Rosalind Armson (Triarchy Press Ltd, 2011)
- *Values-Driven Organisation* by Richard Barrett (Routledge, 2017)
- *Black Box Thinking* by Matthew Syed (John Murray, 2016)
- *Switch* by Chip and Dan Heath (Random House Business, 2011)

Index

F

Facebook 12, 107, 108, 193, 230
failure 23, 33, 54, 66, 80, 85, 89, 92,
   95, 106, 107, 112, 114, 152, 160, 161,
   182, 223, 231, 234, 246, 257
fair trade 21, 54, 183
Federal Express 58, 59, 158, 159
feedback 25, 26, 37, 79, 81, 99, 101,
   102, 106, 107, 114, 139, 173, 194,
   200, 237, 273
financial results 6, 215, 272
Ford 17, 112
fourth industrial revolution 285
Fourth Sector 175, 285

G

General Electric 240
Georgia Pacific 156
Germany 142, 208
goals 9, 10, 67, 75, 77, 78, 79, 83, 84,
   85, 99, 101, 103, 110, 120, 144, 162,
   182, 227, 258
good citizen 22, 23, 28, 85, 135, 164,
   167, 168, 169, 170, 171, 174, 175,
   180, 254, 256, 266, 267
Google 12, 53, 67, 102, 128, 147, 209,
   230, 248, 264, 284
Green & Black's 161
Gripple 97, 98, 142, 146, 284
grow 6, 18, 32, 37, 44, 56, 61, 70, 72,
   73, 105, 123, 138, 147, 154, 156, 163,
   174, 209, 216, 221, 229, 257, 258, 271

H

habits 89, 103, 147, 183
healthcare 11, 25, 106, 110, 144, 222,
   251
Hewlett Packard 71, 128,147, 206
hierarchical 90, 106
HubSpot 236, 253, 254

I

Iceland 54, 148, 149, 159, 225, 226, 286
Iceland Foods 149

India 177
Industrial Revolution 96, 176, 177,
   229, 247, 251
initiative 20, 80, 99, 105, 129, 141, 147,
   154, 205, 262, 263
innovation(s) 3, 5, 17, 18, 30, 32, 33,
   52, 53, 57, 65, 66, 85, 90, 96, 103,
   108, 113, 117, 119, 121, 122, 123,
   126, 127, 141, 142, 147, 150, 162,
   174, 204, 215, 229, 230, 231, 233,
   234, 235, 236, 237, 240, 241, 242,
   243, 244, 245, 254, 271, 282, 285, 286
innovative 30, 31, 32, 33, 36, 85, 100,
   104, 108, 111, 115, 121, 126,128, 147,
   162, 164, 171, 172, 174, 175, 205,
   210, 214, 220, 229, 230, 231, 232,
   233, 234, 235, 236, 237, 239, 240,
   241, 243, 245, 257, 261, 271, 284
integrity 8, 50, 52, 140, 155, 164, 204
internet 19, 30, 33, 120, 184, 195, 197,
   199, 208, 209, 218, 238, 247, 248, 249

J

Japan 109, 210, 212
JCI UK 147
John Lewis 142, 219

K

Kodak 65, 66, 219
Kolbe 150, 151, 152

L

leadership 3, 6, 7, 8, 9, 13, 17, 41, 42,
   43, 44, 45, 46, 47, 55, 73, 123, 139,
   140, 147, 173, 202, 262, 273
learning 15, 17, 18, 32, 35, 42, 46, 61,
   79, 80, 83, 85, 89, 90, 96, 98, 99, 101,
   105, 106, 107, 108, 109, 110, 111,
   112, 113, 114, 115, 116, 117, 118,
   123, 129, 130, 134,195, 215, 230, 235,
   242, 243,244, 247, 254, 256, 257, 261,
   265, 273
Legacy Sport 150
LensCrafters 74, 75, 180
Life Changing 117, 184, 185, 187, 189,

Endnotes

1   *The Economist*, January 2005, The Good Company
2   Quoted in *Becoming the Best* by Harry Kraemer p174 (John Wiley and Sons 2015)
3   A New Approach to Capitalism in the 21st Century – speech delivered at World Economic Forum Davos 2008
4   Source: https://econ.st/2FzGZmC
5   Source: https://www.forbes.com/lists/global2000/
6   Source: World Economic Forum
7   Source: AI revolution spurs transformation in the European boardroom – IBM UK & Ireland – Blog (https://www.ibm.com/blogs/think/uk-en/ai-revolution-spurs-transformation-in-the-european-boardroom/)
8   Source: *Good Profit*, Charles Koch p99 (Piatkus 2017)
9   Source: http://www.conecomm.com/global-csr-study 2013 Global CSR Study
10 Source: https://yougov.co.uk/news/2017/04/07/one-five-consumers-have-boycotted-brand/ One in five consumers have boycotted a brand | YouGov
11 Source: IPA President Tom Knox's Inaugural Address, Wednesday 29th April 2015, The Rosewood Hotel
12 Source: 17 CSR Facts You Need To Know – Learn – GlobalGiving (https://www.globalgiving.org/learn/listicle/csr-facts-you-need-to-know)
13 Source: How To Achieve Your Goals in College (freshessays.com)
14 According to The Millennial Impact Report, a study by Achieve for the Case Foundation (https://blog.freshessays.com/how-to-achieve-your-goals-in-college/)
15 Source: The 2013 Global CSR Study by Cone Communications
16 In *Conscious Capitalism* John Mackey, the CEO of Wholefoods, makes the higher purpose argument and quotes research by his co-author, Professor Raj Sisodia from his book *Firms of Endearment: How World-Class Companies Profit from Passion and Purpose.*

17   Source: *Conscious Capitalism*, John Mackey and Raj Sisodia (Harvard Business Review Press 2018)

18   Reference 2012 Edelman good purpose study

19   'The Social Economy: The dispute over doing well while doing good', Third Sector (Stephen Cook) 18.12.14

20   Source: Study finds hints of social responsibility in top companies' mission statements | Temple Now (https://news.temple.edu/news/2014-04-11/study-finds-hints-social-responsibility-top-companies-mission-statements)

21   Source: CAF Corporate Giving | Using the power of brands to connect consumers with causes (cafonline.org)

22   Source: https://inspire2aspire.co.uk/blog/three-reasons-to-do-good-in-a-business

23   Source: *We First*, Simon Mainwaring, p43 (St. Martin's Press 2011)

24   Source: *The Values-Driven Organization*, Richard Barrett, p 22 (Routledge 2017)

25   Global Indicator: Employee Engagement – Gallup (https://www.gallup.com/394373/indicator-employee-engagement.aspx)

26   Source: Gallup State of the Global Workplace: 2023 Report

27   Source: Ivey Business School research at Western University

28   Source: *Switch*, Chip and Dan Heath, p82 (Random House Business 2011)

29   Source: *Start with Why*, Simon Sinek, p140 (Penguin 2011)

30   Source: Gallup Releases New Findings on the State of the American Workplace (https://news.gallup.com/opinion/gallup/170570/gallup-releases-new-findings-state-american-workplace.aspx)

31   Source: 2010 survey by PricewaterhouseCoopers (PwC)

32   Source: *Metro*, 16th November 2015

33   BIS Department for Business innovation and Skills

34   Source: Global Customer Experience (CX) Trends Report by Zendesk, Inc.

35   Source: Forrester's: The State of Customer Experience 2010

36   Source: Research by Robb Willer at University of California, Berkeley in *We First* by Simon Mainwaring, p88 (St Martin's Press, 2011)

37   Source: 2008 Growing Global Executive Talent; study conducted by the Economist Intelligence Unit

38   Koch p132

39   Study by The Great Place to Work Institute 2007-11

40   Source: Heard in a speech at Made in Sheffield

41   Koch Good Profit p238

42   See more: https://www.southwest.com/about-southwest/

43   Source: www.Southwest.com

44   Source: *The Values-Driven Organisation*, Richard Barrett p157-8 (Routledge 2017)

45   Source: https://www.capitalone.com/about/corporate-information/our-company/

46   Source: https://www.fedex.com/en-gb/about.html

47   *The Values-Driven Organisation*, Barrett, p175

48   Source: Our values & whistleblowing (volvogroup.com)

49   Source: https://www.bbc.com/aboutthebbc/governance/mission

50   Speaking at Made in Sheffield conference.

51   Source: *Bold*, Peter Diamandis and Steven Kotler (Simon and Schuster 2015)

52   Source: https://www.kiva.org/impact

53   Source: (Barrett, 1998, p. 108)

54   Source: (Calloway, 2009, p. 34)

55   Source: (*Switch*, 2011, Chip and Dan Heath, p62)

56   ibid p48

57   ibid p12

58   Koch p76

59   Koch p157

60   ibid p157

61   Source: (*Switch*, 2011, Chip and Dan Heath, p54-57)

62   Source: *Value Proposition Design*, Alex Osterwalder, Yves Pigneur, Greg Bernarda, Alan Smith, p164 (John Wiley and Sons 2014)

63   *Black Box Thinking*, Matthew Syed, p198 (John Murray 2016)

64   *Black Box Thinking*, Matthew Syed, p196

65   750 avoidable deaths a month in NHS hospitals, study finds | Hospitals | The Guardian

66   *Black Box Thinking*, Matthew Syed, p27

67   Source: *Switch*, Chip and Dan Heath, p164-5

68   Source: World Economic Forum – 10 jobs that didn't exist 10 years ago, 2016

69   Source: Harvard Business Review, How ByteDance became the world's most valuable startup 2022

70   Source: *Switch*, Chip and Dan Heath, p156

71   Source: *Black Box Thinking*, Matthew Syed, p52

72   Source: Virginia Mason Institute

73   Source: *Switch*, Chip and Dan Heath, p173

74   Source: March 2009 issue of *The Systems Thinker*, an electronic newsletter published by Pegasus Communications

75   *Good Profit*, Koch, p149

76   Source: The Collaboration Imperative – Ivey Business Journal

77   Source: P&G Partners with Durham University and Imperial College (pg.com)

78   Source: *Becoming the Best*, Harry Kraemer, p125

79   Source: *The Speed of Trust*, Stephen Covey, p13 (Simon & Schuster UK; Export edition 2008)

80   Source: *Bold*, Diamandis and Kotler p226

81   Source: Smart companies see the importance of collaboration | Guardian sustainable business | The Guardian

82   Source: *The Values Driven Organisation*. Richard Barrett, p26

83   Source: Workforce burnout and resilience in the NHS and social care – Health and Social Care Committee – House of Commons (parliament. uk)

84   Source: 2012 UK Engage for Success Task Force report

85   Source: *Conscious Capitalism*, John Mackey and Raj Sisodia, p240

86   Source: How to prepare your organization for AI | McKinsey

87   Source: How Artificial Intelligence Can Improve Organizational Decision Making (forbes.com)

88   Source: The global impact of AI across industries | Transform (microsoft.com)

89   Source: GLIDE – Our Employee Ownership Model | Gripple

90   Source: *Conscious Capitalism*, John Mackey and Raj Sisodia, p241

91   Code available here 952f5e64-473c-47c2-a396-3ddb81b303db (nordstrom.com)

92   Source: 3M's 15% Culture | Cultivate & Pursue Your Innovative Ideas | 3M United Kingdom

93   Source: Google Took Its 20% Back, But Other Companies Are Making Employee Side (fastcompany.com)

94   Source: Google Took Its 20% Back, But Other Companies Are Making Employee Side (fastcompany.com)

95 Source: https://icelandcareers.co.uk/

96 *Good Profit*, Koch, p224-5

97 Source: *Retail Gazette* Industry watchdog finds Morrisons treats suppliers the worst – *Retail Gazette* and 2017 research results.

98 Source: *The Telegraph* article 2010

99 Source: http://www.bbc.com/news/business-35408064 Treat-suppliers-as-you-would-treat-yourself

100 Source: bcorp_annual_report_2014.pdf (patagonia.com)

101 Source: What is the PPC – Small Business Commissioner

102 https://www.clintonfoundation.org/press-and-news/general/press-release-president-clinton-and-leading-ceos-call-on-private-sector-to-devel/

103 More information: https://inspire2aspire.co.uk/blog/being-human-not-corporate-the-road-to-success

104 Source: LM3online | Calculate local economic impact and sustainability

105 Source: *Becoming the Best*, Harry M Jansen Kraemer, p178 onwards (John Wiley and Sons, 2015)

106 Source: *Switch*, Chip and Dan Heath, p101 -107

107 Discussed in Accenture Development Partnerships' report, "The Convergence Continuum towards a Fourth Sector in Global Development."

108 Source: What does the fourth industrial revolution mean for civil society? | World Economic Forum (weforum.org)

109 Source: Impact Overview | TOMS

110 Source: *Conscious Capitalism*, John Mackey and Raj Sisodia, p76

111 Source: Donate To Beat Cancer | Cancer Research UK

112 Source: *Switch*, Chip and Dan Heath, p76-81

113 Source: Accenture global customer satisfaction report 2008.

114 Source: The three Cs of customer satisfaction: Consistency, consistency, consistency | McKinsey

115 Source: https://www.theguardian.com/business/2022/jul/05/uk-customer-service-complaints-at-highest-level-on-record-research-finds

116 Source: 11 Customer Acquisition vs Retention Statistics (2024) (markinblog.com)

117 Source: 20 Customer Service Statistics for 2011 | CustomerThink

118 Source: *Switch*, Chip and Dan Heath, p199

119 Source: How Many Orders Does Amazon Receive Per Day? (shipscience.com)

120 Source: World population projected to reach 9.8 billion in 2050, and 11.2 billion in 2100 | United Nations

121 Source: https://www.un.org/en/development/desa/publications/world-population-prospects-2015-revision.html

122 Source: The People and Nature Survey for England: Data and publications from Adults survey year 1 (April 2020 – March 2021) (Official Statistics) main findings – GOV.UK (www.gov.uk)

123 Source: What is ESG and five reasons it matters even if you are a charity | Inspire2Aspire

124 Source: Why Sustainability Is Now the Key Driver of Innovation (hbr. org)

125 Source: AIM2Flourish | Patagonia: Upscale, Sustainable, and Environmentally…

126 Source: Patagonia – Turning Social Responsibility into Company Business. – Technology and Operations Management (harvard.edu)

127 Source: Inside Patagonia's Corporate Culture That Prioritizes Flexibility and Work-Life Balance – Business and Tech (futureofbusinessandtech. com)

128 Source: Patagonia and Corporate Responsibility (scu.edu)

129 Source: https://www.bbc.co.uk/news/uk-england-london-63846028

130 Source: *We First*, Simon Mainwaring, 2011 p78

131 Source: https://hbr.org/2009/09/why-sustainability-is-now-the-key-driver-of-innovationRam Nidumolu, C.K. Prahalad, and M.R. Rangaswami

132 More information: Opinion: Why It Is Time For The Blended Wing Body | Aviation Week Network

133 Source: Video: Nubian vault building technique could "transform housing in Africa" (dezeen.com)

134 Source: https://bit.ly/3HmqI0R

135 Source: *Value Proposition Design*, Alex Osterwalder, Yves Pineur, Greg Bernarda, Alan Smith. 2014 p 266

136 Source: How to Improve Care for High-Need, High-Cost Medicaid Patients (hbr.org)

137 Source: CareMore's Togetherness Program Addresses a Symptom of Living With Chronic Illness: Loneliness (ajmc.com)

138 Source: The cost of living is now such an emergency we're offering Iceland supermarket customers interest free loans – About Iceland

139 Source: *Good Profit*, Koch, p66

140 Source: https://bit.ly/31n2CO7

141 Source: *Value Proposition Design*, Alex Osterwalder, Yves Pineur, Greg Bernarda, Alan Smith. 2014 p146

142 Source: Azuri Technologies (azuri-group.com)

143 More information: Our actions – The Nubian Vault (lavoutenubienne. org)

144 Source: Workplace Culture: What Is It and Why Is It Important in 2023? | Workhuman

145 Source: http://www.fastcodesign.com/1663137/how-3m-gave-everyone-days-off-and-created-an-innovation-dynamo

146 Source: Bold Diamandis and Kotler, p144

147 Ibid, p57

148 Source: Robin Rowland, YO! Sushi, heard speaking at Made in Sheffield

149 Source: What happens when robots take our jobs? | World Economic Forum (weforum.org)

150 Source: What happens when robots take our jobs? | World Economic Forum (weforum.org)

151 Source: *Becoming the Best*, Harry M Jansen Kraemer, various and p186 onwards

152 Source: Our model | One Acre Fund

153 Source: *Conscious Capitalism*, John Mackey and Raj Sisodia, p121